New Light on
JOYCE
from the Dublin Symposium

Edited by Fritz Senn

New Light on

JOYCE

from the Dublin Symposium

INDIANA UNIVERSITY PRESS
Bloomington & London

72-857

Published in Canada by Fitzhenry & Whiteside Limited,
Don Mills, Ontario
Library of Congress catalog card number: 72-75638
ISBN: 0-253-34015-2
Manufactured in the United States of America

CONTENTS

PREFACE

The Second International James Joyce Symposium lured between two and three hundred people to Dublin for a series of events that lasted, officially, from June 10 to 16, 1969. Their locations were, mainly, the hospitable halls of Trinity College Dublin and some hotels and licensed premises that had long become literary allusions, as well as the streets and lawns and quays of Dublin the city, with incursions to the Joyce Museum in Sandycove, St. James's Gate, Glasnevin cemetery, Chapelizod, and back to Howth Castle and Environs. Enumerations and statistics of this kind, or even the professed enthusiasm of individual participants, can do no more than hint at the possible success of the Symposium, just as its flaws cannot be reliably deduced from the incisive remarks of amused Dublin bystanders alone. A few of the attainments can be fixed in records, such as this volume: other results of the discourses, public and *ad hoc,* and the exchange of ideas are less tangible and may consist in such vague entities as the stimulation and the impulses, the challenges and contacts and friendships among those who availed themselves of the amplest opportunity accorded so far to share a few tastes and compare a few prejudices about one single modern writer.

The Symposium was attended by scholars, teachers, translators, and others with a stake in the world of letters, but they all mingled easily with, in fact most of the time became themselves, innocent readers, amateurs, even tourists, who had come just to listen and to have a good time. On the whole, most of them did; there was much to choose from. Symposing on Joyce was not limited to academic practices. Audio-visual aids and entertainment included a few films, the staging of Joyce's more lively correspondence in the Abbey Theatre, an impersonation of Molly's monologue, and an evening that provided good examples of Joyce's incidental musical background in an appropriate, even reminiscent, atmosphere. In view of so many adaptations for the stage of words never intended for it, Joyce's one play *Exiles* ironically failed to make its bow to the public because of last minute copyright difficulties. An exhibition of Joyce illustrations and art work was held in a Georgian house in Mountjoy Square. Mountjoy Square, sadly marred by gaps and dilapidation, was more impressive for its literary overtones than its architectonic presence in 1969, and number seven Eccles street had been reduced to part of its front wall and all of its railing. Even so there was enough left still for us to browse in the catalogue of Dublin's street furniture. And so perambulations were undertaken either individually or, at scheduled times, in guided groups (with slightly embarrassed guides), "touring the no placelike no timelike absolent." There is something intriguing about readers thinking it worth their while (and going to the physical effort to prove it) to travel far and look intently at buildings or streetcorners or greenhouses simply because these are mentioned, and briefly at that, in the fictional chronicles of characters that never "really" existed—due to some strange and fascinating power of words in a few books.

The words in Joyce's books, and the man who wrote them, and the backgrounds that helped to shape him and them, naturally came in for a good deal of scrutiny and speculation during the Symposium. Seven panels were devoted to general questions like symbolism, the function of biographical evidence, translation, or else to specific problems like the establishment of dependable texts or, in some detail, the meaning of chosen passages. Together with about three dozen papers that were read during one strenuous week, the topics presented in Dublin amount to a cross section that is fairly indicative of the pursuits that Joyce scholars in the late sixties were engaged in.

The order that has been imposed on the essays collected here is frankly artificial and does not represent the format of the Symposium; nevertheless, the critics do fall into recognizable groups. The collection begins with three discussions of Joyce the man: Phillip Herring's contemplation of Joyce's politics, Darcy O'Brien's psychoanalytic interpretations, and James Carens' account of Joyce and Gogarty. These biographical explorations give way to a series of papers that complement one another. We have first two essays on problems of language: Strother Purdy's notes on the grammar of the *Wake*, and Erwin Steinberg's analysis of sentences from *Ulysses*. Then come two studies in textual scholarship by Jack Dalton and Fred Higginson, who consider the elemental question of what Joyce actually wrote. Father Robert Boyle's paper, which is partly about the priestliness of Stephen, has a sort of companion in Morton Levitt's discussion of the Jewishness of Bloom. These are followed by Zack Bowen and Mabel Worthington, who address themselves to Joyce's interest in songs. Finally, a pair of critics as artists: Ihab Hassan's quasi-poetic little scenario about Joyce and Becketr, and Leslie Fiedler's confessions of a middle-aged academic.

The selection from this variety has a number of determinants; among those within the jurisdiction of the editor a certain bias toward useful factual information and close study of the text may be discerned. Some of the papers were omitted from this collection because they are more suitable for publication in periodicals, such as *The James Joyce Quarterly*. Of those included, only Leslie Fiedler's and Ihab Hassan's have been published already, in the maiden issue of the *Journal of Modern Literature*. While the exigencies of a tight schedule in Dublin imposed a rigid time limit on the speakers, in the printed versions the arguments could in some cases be more fully developed. So a few of the papers have been expanded and revised, others appear in their pristine form. Editorial interference involves mainly references and the necessary notes. The editions uniformly referred to and quoted from (unless stated otherwise) and the abbreviations adopted in this volume are:

CW	*Critical Writings,* ed. Richard Ellmann and Ellsworth Mason, New York, Viking Press, 1959.
D	*Dubliners,* ed. Robert Scholes, New York, Viking Press, 1967.
Ellmann	Richard Ellmann, *James Joyce,* New York, Oxford University Press, 1959.
FW	*Finnegans Wake,* New York, Viking Press, and London, Faber & Faber, 1964.
Letters I	*Letters of James Joyce: Volume I,* ed. Stuart Gilbert, New York, Viking Press, new edition with corrections, 1966.
Letters II, III	*Letters of James Joyce: Volumes II* and *III,* ed. Richard Ellmann, New York, Viking Press, 1966.
P	*A Portrait of the Artist as a Young Man,* the definitive text, corrected from the Dublin Holograph by Chester G. Anderson and edited by Richard Ellmann, New York, Viking Press, 1964.
SH	*Stephen Hero,* ed. Theodore Spencer, new edition incorporating additional manuscript pages, ed. John J. Slocum and Herbert Cahoon, New York, New Directions, 1963.
U	*Ulysses,* new edition, corrected and reset, New York, Random House, 1961.

The page references follow the quotations within parentheses (e.g. p. 215). Some authors who analyze specific passages prefer to indicate the lines as well; this has been done in the accustomed manner, with a period separating page from line reference (e.g. U 166.19, FW 211.24).

For help and advice in the gathering, the selection, and the editing of the following papers I am pleased to thank, first of all, the contributors themselves for their cooperation and patience, and the two co-organizers of the Second International James Joyce Symposium, Thomas F. Staley and Bernard Benstock, as well as all who made the Symposium possible. In particular I would like to thank my friends Mrs. Alice H. Goodwin, Clive Hart, Gerry O'Flaherty, James Naremore, and Breon Mitchell and, for assistance in the preparation of the typescript, Miss Emily Foster of Columbus, Ohio.

FRITZ SENN

New Light on
JOYCE
from the Dublin Symposium

Joyce's Politics

Phillip F. Herring

UNIVERSITY OF WISCONSIN

T HAT THE CYCLOPS in Homer's *Odyssey* exemplified the un-
civilized "caveman," a creature so primitive as to be ignorant of the laws of hospitality and social behavior (one does not
dine *on* one's visitors, but *with* them) was presumably well understood by Homer's contemporaries and by Joyce himself. His
single eye was for the Greeks a sign of social retardation; it was
clear that unifocal vision prevented a man from seeing more than
one side to any question.[1] Joyce's Fenian counterpart, the Citizen,
is cut from the same cloth: he is a bigot, a petty Irish chauvinist
who cares little whom he strikes with the boulders he hurls.
Since the art of the Cyclops episode of *Ulysses*, as Joyce described it to Stuart Gilbert, is politics, the Joycean is tempted
here, perhaps more than in his other works, to question Joyce's
own political beliefs. It ought to be safe to infer that his position was diametrically opposed to the one he satirized; in other
words, if the Citizen's political view was stupid and provincial,
Joyce's might presumably be liberal and enlightened. Unfortunately it was not. Ironically enough, his view was much closer
to that of Homer's Cyclops than was the Citizen's, because Joyce
too was politically nearsighted: he believed that those things
closest to him were most important.

In the *Odyssey* the Cyclopes are repeatedly disparaged as creatures who respected neither the laws of the gods nor those of
men. Odysseus says that they "have no assemblies for the making

of laws, nor any settled customs, but live in hollow caverns in the mountain heights, where each man is lawgiver to his children and his wives, and nobody cares a jot for his neighbors." [2] Being travelers, Odysseus and his men plead that they are under the patronage of Zeus and that their host is bound by law to grant them hospitality. The Cyclops sneers at this, saying "We Cyclopes care not a jot for Zeus and his aegis, nor for the rest of the blessed gods, since we are much stronger than they," [3] and he proceeds to devour several of the crew. Yet, when blinded, he prays to his father Poseidon, god of the oceans, to avenge him against the invaders. A state unto himself, he spurns all higher authority, but invokes it when it suits his purpose.

Joyce's Citizen, for all his ignorance and blind patriotism, is politically far more advanced than Homer's Cyclops. He may be a bigot, wishing to purify Ireland of all foreign influence; he may have an absurdly exaggerated view of Ireland's wealth and of her destined role among the nations of the world; perhaps he is even a more dangerous threat to other men than Homer's Cyclops. *But he does not put himself before all others.* Though he denies hospitality to strangers, he sees himself as a functioning element in a political state. The name he answers to, once more, is "The Citizen," and his cause is Irish nationalism.

Like the one-eyed giant of Homer, Joyce the artist was also a semi-independent state. Asked to define the word "nation" in the Cyclops episode, Leopold Bloom says "A nation is the same people living in the same place. —By God, then, says Ned, laughing, if that's so I'm a nation for I'm living in the same place for the past five years" (U 331). So it was with Joyce. He could never quite bring himself to give up the convenience of a British passport, but he was for all impractical purposes a small Albania in the world of letters. He considered it his duty as an artist to wage war against the institutions of State and Church from the sanctuary of his vocation and his foreign residence. Institutions were important only because his personal reaction against them helped to define his artistic consciousness. In *Stephen Hero* Joyce has Stephen say that his own mind is more interesting and ultimately more important to him than the entire country (SH 248). And in *Ulysses* (p. 645) Stephen says ". . . I suspect . . . that Ireland must be important because it belongs to me." It is in statements such as these that Stephen's pose eclipses Joyce's carefully prescribed egocentricity.

But there is one important distinction between the political position of Joyce and that of Homer's Cyclops. All the Cyclops wishes for is to be left alone to tend his sheep and goats. He is a self-sufficient entity who only becomes violent when his cave is invaded. Joyce saw himself as an outcast (not a hermit), alienated from the society that produced him, yet bound as closely to it abroad as he ever was in the homeland. From the point of view of society (if one can say that) each would be a cave dweller, but one demands support and protection so that he may create art out of the bitterness of self-imposed exile.

Richard Ellmann says of Joyce that

> . . . like other revolutionaries, he fattened on opposition and grew thin and pale when treated with indulgence. Whenever his relations with his native land were in danger of improving, he was to find a new incident to solidify his intransigence and to reaffirm the rightness of his voluntary absence. In later life he even showed some grand resentment at the possibility of Irish independence on the grounds that it would change the relationship he had so carefully established between himself and his country.[4]

Though Ellmann calls Joyce a revolutionary, I do not believe he was one. Dictionaries tell us that the revolutionary seeks *change*. He is passionately committed to the fundamental *alteration* of an institution. Joyce did not advocate change because he had abandoned as hopeless both Ireland and her rulers, and for all his disgruntlement was surprised and rather hurt that improving conditions there could force him to reassess his image of her. At this point one might well call Joyce's politics reactionary. Ireland's continued progress was a direct threat to him because it undercut the legitimacy of his prolonged exile, made it more difficult to defend, and, further, threatened to obscure his gallery of paralytic portraits, to date them as the product of a particular era of Ireland's past.

Joyce was explicit about the hopeless condition of Ireland when in 1907 he delivered his lecture entitled "Ireland, Island of Saints and Sages" to a Triestine audience. He said:

> The soul of the country is weakened by centuries of useless struggle and broken treaties, and individual initiative is paralysed by the influence and admonitions of the church, while its body is manacled by the police, the tax office, and the garrison. No one who has any self-respect stays in Ireland, but flees afar as though from a country that has undergone the visitation of an angered Jove. (CW 171)

His attitude toward British rule was essentially one of indifference at this time. As an Irish Catholic he had never developed any real sense of loyalty to the Crown, but like many of his compatriots was wary of exchanging the known evil of British authority for the unknown evil of Home Rule and possible fratricide. In this same lecture he said:

> I find it rather naïve to heap insults on England for her misdeeds in Ireland. A conqueror cannot be casual, and for so many centuries the Englishman has done in Ireland only what the Belgian is doing today in the Congo Free State, and what the Nipponese dwarf will do tomorrow in other lands. (CW 166)

The near extinction of Irish culture and language and the systematic persecution of Catholics were effectively counterbalanced by Ireland's history of self-betrayal. Though he was briefly interested in the policies of Arthur Griffith and Sinn Fein,[5] the plight of Ireland left him cold and somewhat bored. Joyce did not become definitely anti-British until 1918, when his personal sovereignty was threatened by a British consular official in Zurich.

Then the English become mad colonialists who build water-closets wherever they go, "a race of mighty valorous heroes, rulers of the waves, who sit on thrones of alabaster silent as the deathless gods" (U 325). They lived in accordance with the eight British beatitudes: "Beer, beef, business, bibles, bulldogs, battleships, buggery and bishops" (U 424). Another sovereign state had entered the war.

If it required a menace to his person, both physical and legal in this case, to enkindle his resentment against the British, it took a definite affinity to awaken in Joyce an enthusiasm for a fellow Irishman. When *Finnegans Wake* seemed an impossible task he thought of turning it over to James Stephens for completion. In 1926 Stephens revealed the basis of Joyce's interest in him:

> . . . he revealed to me that his name was James and mine was James, that my name was Stephens, and the name he had taken for himself in his best book was Stephen: that he and I were born in the same country, in the same city, in the same year, in the same month, on the same day, at the same hour, six o'clock in the morning of the second of February.[6]

Similarly, his championing of the tenor John Sullivan was less due to the quality of his voice than to the secret belief that Sullivan was the great tenor Joyce might have become had he chosen a singing career. Joyce was, in a sense, listening to himself at the opera in Paris. So, too, with other affinities. My point is that such preoccupations reveal the anxiety and loneliness of a man completely at ease only with his family, the second circle round the family hearth consisting of those made presentable for adoption.

On the political level the most important affinity was, of course, Charles Stewart Parnell. Parnell was a sort of political projection of his own role as persecuted artist victimized by the traitorous people he sought to serve. In Joyce's work the figures of Christ, Stephen Dedalus, and Parnell are throughout shadows of each other and of himself. In 1912 he wrote an article on Parnell for *Il Piccolo della Sera* that ends as follows:

> The melancholy which invaded his mind was perhaps the profound conviction that, in his hour of need, one of the disciples who dipped his hand in the same bowl with him would betray him. That he fought to the very end with this desolate certainty in mind is his greatest claim to nobility.
>
> In his final desperate appeal to his countrymen, he begged them not to throw him as a sop to the English wolves howling around them. It redounds to their honour that they did not fail this appeal. They did not throw him to the English wolves; they tore him to pieces themselves. (CW 228)

His bitterness at the fall of Parnell did not apparently result from any sympathy for the man personally or the cause he championed, but from the conviction that great Irish leaders, whether in politics or art, must be prepared to play the messianic role, contend with traitors at every turn, and ascend the cross when the tide of popular opinion turns against them. Throughout his life Joyce held himself aloof, carefully preparing for the inevitable betrayal of his friends, even his wife, secretly desiring it as confirmation of his high destiny.[7] At the same time, like Christ in Gethsemane, he prayed that this cup might pass from his lips. He wasn't going to make it too easy for the Irish wolves yapping round his doorstep.

Exile was the only possible course consistent with his artistic integrity, but it is naive to think that Joyce bore the cross of loneliness and isolation so that modern literature could be free of narrow-minded censorship, or that other writers might escape persecution. He may have been a martyr to his own cause, but he would never have jeopardized his career for another writer's integrity. With few exceptions he regarded contemporary writers as potential rivals; he rarely read their works and was mostly contemptuous of them. His friends he often used as lackeys and sounding boards for his own ideas. It is all the more ironic that the Random House edition of *Ulysses*, containing the laudatory foreword by Morris Ernst along with the decision of Judge Woolsey lifting the ban on *Ulysses*, encourages readers to revere Joyce as a new Prometheus bringing freedom of expression to the world of letters. It is an honor he might well have traded for an annual government subsidy and guaranteed distribution of his books.

A second beautful irony is that as early as 1904 Joyce claimed to be a socialist and even attended a few of their meetings in Dublin.[8] Only three years before he had begun "The Day of the Rabblement" with "No man, said the Nolan, can be a lover of the true or the good unless he abhors the multitude; and the artist, though he may employ the crowd, is very careful to isolate himself" (CW 69). It remains a mystery how he could believe that the artist's autonomy would be better protected in a socialist state with this very same multitude at the helm. Nevertheless, in 1915, shortly after Italy entered the war, Joyce reaffirmed his position in a remark to Alessandro Francini:

> My political faith can be expressed in a word: Monarchies, constitutional or unconstitutional, disgust me. Kings are mountebanks. Republics are slippers for everyone's feet. Temporal power is gone and good riddance. What else is left? . . . Do you believe in the Sun of the Future [i.e. socialism]? [9]

Three years later he wrote:

> As an artist I am against every state. Of course I must recognize it, since indeed in all my dealings I come into contact with its institutions. The state is concentric, man is eccentric. Thence arises an eternal struggle. The monk, the bachelor, and the anarchist are in the same category.[10]

What Joyce had to gain by his flirtation with socialism is made clear by Richard Ellmann, who says that Joyce did indeed hope to secure for himself a subsidy from the state.[11] His socialist friends "encouraged him in his feeling that socialism should come,

for how else should he be fed? He needed a redistribution of
wealth if he was to be a spendthrift." [12] It is apparent that Joyce
is closer in his thinking to anarchy than socialism, though he does
not advocate the overthrow of any government. What he desires
is to preserve his autonomy at the cost of some state, and, if it
becomes necessary, to gnaw the red hand that feeds him. In short,
Joyce wished to become an institution dedicated to the subversion
of anti-Joycean institutions.

Joyce contented himself with opposing the forces that made
his exile necessary; that those same forces (British imperialism, a
Church hierarchy preoccupied with its own power, provincial
narrowness of mind) had been condemned by his fellow Irish
socialists as largely responsible for the poverty, emigration, and
spiritual stagnation of the Irish people during past centuries was
for him merely coincidental. Under these circumstances it makes
little sense to whitewash Joyce by pointing out that he detested
tyrants such as Hitler and Mussolini, or that he used his influence
to gain exit visas for several Jewish acquaintances from Nazi-held
territory.[13] He could not identify with the oppressed rabblement
anywhere, and sought either to withdraw from or soar beyond
the ugliness of conflict until it became a personal matter.

Admittedly indifferent to the outcome of both world wars (in
1939 he was apprehensive lest World War II deaden the impact
of *Finnegans Wake* and prevent it from becoming a best-seller),[14]
Joyce's political viewpoint is nowhere more humorously expressed than in his broadside "Doolysprudence":

> Who is the man when all the gallant nations run to war
> Goes home to have his dinner by the very first cablecar
> And as he eats his canteloup contorts himself in mirth
> To read the blatant bulletins of the rulers of the earth?
>
> It's Mr Dooley,
> Mr Dooley,
> The coolest chap our country ever knew

'They are out to collar
The dime and dollar'
Says Mr Dooley-ooley-ooley-oo.

Who is the funny fellow who declines to go to church
Since pope and priest and parson left the poor man in the
  lurch
And taught their flocks the only way to save all human souls
Was piercing human bodies through with dumdum bullet-
  holes?

　　　　It's Mr Dooley,
　　　　Mr Dooley,
　　　　The mildest man our country ever knew
　　　　Prays Mr Dooley-ooley-ooley-oo.
　　　　'Who will release us
　　　　From Jingo Jesus'

Who is the meek philosopher who doesn't care a damn
About the yellow peril or the problem of Siam
And disbelieves that British Tar is water from Life's fount
And will not gulp the gospel of the German on the Mount?

　　　　It's Mr Dooley,
　　　　Mr Dooley,
　　　　The broadest brain our country ever knew
　　　　'The curse of Moses
　　　　On both your houses'
　　　　Cries Mr Dooley-ooley-ooley-oo. (CW 246–7)

There are three more equally humorous verses, verses which
tempt us once again to embrace our lovable Mr Dooley, that jolly
wag, until we are reminded of the inherent lack of interest in the
human condition.

One may object to this line of reasoning by arguing that Joyce
was in fact living under a constant threat to his liberty as an
artist, that he *was* shamefully mistreated by his publishers, tormented in his personal life, plagued with blindness, and thus had
no opportunity to look beyond his immediate interests; or that
the lesson of Parnell *had* taught him the price of political in-

volvement. I can only say that at an early age Joyce carefully
defined his relationships with his countrymen and their institutions and lived throughout his life according to them. He chose
his enemies with great care and would under no circumstances
have made peace, believing perhaps rightly that peace would have
meant oblivion. Joyce created the conditions out of which he
was to create.

As Plato foresaw in his *Republic*, the artist has throughout
much of history been a subversive element in the political state,
and countless minstrels were probably beaten for saying less
than the Fool says to King Lear. Eccentricity (in two senses),
flamboyance and satire are, of course, tools of the trade, and
Joyce's case was no more extreme than many others. It differs,
however, in that it was not merely a defensive mechanism, not
entirely a mask that he could throw off at any time, but finally
an illness that prevented him from meeting other men as equals
in an atmosphere of mutual trust, prevented him from seeing
the world as anything more than grist for the mill of his art, made
it extremely difficult for him to understand that other men had
aspirations independent of his own, and absolved him from the
responsibility of feeling or loving in an unselfish way. Joyce
lived much of his life like some guilt-ridden Trotskyite, sleeping
with one eye open, waiting for the knife to fall, receding always
into the world of his family and his mind, yet relentlessly forging
in the smithy of his soul immortal works in a language increasingly his own.

Of course, Joyce did drink, sing, laugh, and do his "spider
dance"; he had great insight into his own problems and was
healthy enough mentally to indulge in self-ridicule; and he did
to a great extent transcend his bitterness by using it as the fuel
for his art. But his only real happiness came from the recreation
of life, not from the living of it. When the fun of the *Wake*
ended in 1939 he lapsed into stunned silence, already too remote

from the balanced equanimity of Leopold Bloom's world to comprehend why others might not comprehend.

For all of this I would not change a word that Joyce wrote and much prefer the moral neutrality of his works to the sentimentality and didacticism of lesser writers; but one still hopes somehow to reconcile the man, the work, and the age in which he lived. Perhaps the trouble is that we know too much about Joyce. I don't know. I honor him for every sacrifice he made in the name of Art except the sacrifice of his humanity, for with this loss he doomed himself to the fate of Milton's Satan, whose every triumph and failure produces only a bitter-sweet monotonous despair. We who devote much of our lives to the study of Joyce's work fare little better than Joyce's friends did in coming to terms with the man, but this is perhaps as he would have wished it.

In the meantime students are questioning us about relevance. If Joyce "waged literature like a battle," [15] they want to know what he had to gain beyond vengeance, the glory and the medals. They ask what motivated the sound and fury of his satirical indignation if it was not reform of the conditions that nauseated him. Joyceans like myself who are adequately repaid by the richness, the beauty, and above all the humor of his works, and who are happy if we can communicate our satisfaction to others, often go numb when our best student asks us whether, like Oscar Wilde at the customs barrier, Joyce had nothing to declare but his genius.

NOTES

1. See, for example, J. E. Cirlot, *Dictionary of Symbols* (New York, 1962), p. 231.
2. Homer, *The Odyssey* (Baltimore, Penguin Books, 1946), p. 142.
3. *The Odyssey*, p. 146.

4. Ellmann, pp. 113–14.
5. Ellmann, pp. 246–47.
6. Ellmann, p. 605.
7. Cf. "I hope that the day may come when I shall be able to give you the fame of being beside me when I have entered into my Kingdom." (*Letters II*, p. 309)
8. Ellmann, p. 147.
9. Ellmann, p. 394.
10. Ellmann, p. 460.
11. Ellmann, p. 204.
12. Ellmann, p. 147.
13. Ellmann, p. 722.
14. Ellmann, p. 733.
15. Ellmann, p. 215.

Some Psychological Determinants of Joyce's View of Love and Sex

Darcy O'Brien
POMONA COLLEGE

I WISH TO ESTABLISH certain psychological links between Joyce's life and work. Perhaps such connections can tell us something of the sources of Joyce's creative energy.

Rarely in Joyce's work can we find a representation of that unity of sensuality and affection which we like to call love. Notice that I am not referring to sensuality alone, nor affection alone, but to unity of the two. Instead of joining sensuality and affection, Joyce continuously depicts either desire without tenderness or tenderness without desire. The fragile love lyrics of *Chamber Music* embody much tenderness but only a veiled, furtive sort of sensuality, much like that of the "Hail Mary" or the litany of the Blessed Virgin. Stephen Dedalus venerates virgins but spends his lust on whores. In "The Dead," Gabriel Conroy admits to himself that his desire for his wife cannot be called love and that he has never known love. Richard Rowan, in *Exiles*, sustains sexual interest in his wife only sado-masochistically and homosexually, by inviting his own cuckoldry. In *Ulysses*, Bloom's sexual fantasies and actions are chiefly voyeuristic and masochistic; and as for Molly Bloom, she longs for love, she retains a certain affection for Poldy, but she gets sexual pleasure only from Blazes Boylan, who is less a character than a personified penis. The sexual elements of *Finnegans Wake* astound in their variety, but such harmony of sensuality and affection as can be found in the book is rare, tentative and, as in *Ulysses*, voiced only by the major female character, Anna Livia Plurabelle. The sexual life of Joyce's principal male characters is invariably grotesque, either pathetically or comically so, or both. Gabriel considers himself cuckolded, in effect, by a dead man, and feels his own identity dissolving from this recognition. Stephen Dedalus's fleshy amours are confined to nighttown. Richard Rowan is tormented by the adulterous situation he has brought about. Similarly, Bloom acquiesces to Molly's adultery largely because he takes painfully perverse pleasure in it. As for Earwicker, Joyce's gigantic figure of Everyman, his Joycean original sin is an act of sexual perversion, because of which he stutters with guilt and is comically reviled by all the world.

As I attempted to show in *The Conscience of James Joyce*,[1] the sexual puritanism of his Irish Catholic background instilled sexual fears in Joyce. And the division of womankind into virgins and whores, so striking in the *Portrait*, together with the later division of womankind into whores, coquettes, and adulteresses in *Ulysses* —all this is characteristically Irish. "I hear, sir," begins a sour old Irish joke, "that you value a woman no higher than a horse in Ireland." "Ah no," comes the reply, "we value horses very highly indeed in Ireland." But when Joyce writes about sex, he exhibits fears and hostilities far more complex than those of a typically puritanical Irishman. His emphasis on perversion and cuckoldry amounts to an obsession, the sources of which are more psychological than cultural.

A careful reading of Joyce's letters to Nora, particularly of those portions still withheld from publication by the Joyce Estate, reveals considerable sexual confusion and distress. From this correspondence we can gain an intimate sense of Joyce's moral repugnance at his own sexuality as well as insight into the complex nature of that sexuality. The letters describe a complete dissociation between what Joyce calls his love for Nora, on the one hand, and his sexual desire for her, on the other. The evidence suggests that for Joyce a union between affection and sensuality was impossible, or to put it more precisely, that such a union was impossible without the aid of certain kinds of fantasy.

Joyce used these letters partly to indulge in masturbatory fantasies about Nora, but they show also that he used Nora to indulge in masturbatory fantasies. Although the writing is often carefully structured and literary, it comes as close as we are going to get to Joyce's own internal monologue. When he proclaims that Nora is to his manhood what the Blessed Virgin was to his boyhood, and then goes on to reveal the intense sexual excitement he derives from defiling that virginal figure with his lust, only to be plunged into remorse and self-hatred once the act is complete, we can begin to perceive the psychological origins of Joyce's fictional representations of sexuality. Time and again he confesses what to him are brutal, bestial, obscene impulses; then he begs forgiveness by pointing to a purer, more spiritual love, which he associates with sacred images and cloistral hymns.

Joyce is disgusted by sexual impulses regarded as normal by most standards of behavior, and his more perverse desires and acts terrify him. He asks Nora to soil her letters with excrement, and he recalls with guilty pleasure her urinating on him. Desire joins with shame, and he craves flogging. In Nora he found the Virgin Mother he needed. He could adore her and defile her, and she could punish him. He gets tortured punishment from her participation—her murmuring of an obscene word, for example. Here the virgin is made whore, fit object for his mingled lust and shame. Be my whore, he says to her, you are still my schoolgirl, my flower, my virgin. What she can never be is simply and completely herself.

The configurations of Joyce's sexuality, while distinctly Irish Catholic in certain particulars, are hardly unique to him or to any national or religious group. He suffered from a Hibernian version of Portnoy's complaint, that is to say, from the difficulties of male sexuality predominant in the Western world. No phenomenon is more familiar to the psychoanalyst than the inability to unite feelings of tenderness and sensuality toward the same object. Freud was convinced that all civilized men share this disability to some degree, and he thought it the primary cause of psychic impotence. Causes elude precise identification, but, from a Freudian point of view, failure to overcome the incestuous fixations of early childhood plays the major role. That is, the more the mother retains her erotic sway over the adult, the more difficult it is for the mature man to combine tender love with sexual love. The mother is forbidden as an object of sexual desire but to her the child directs his emotional impulses and from her he receives his emotional comfort. Sexual difficulties arise when, later in life, the wife assumes so much of the maternal role toward her husband. Unconsciously the husband cannot accept this mother-figure as a sexual object. He tries to escape his conflicts by finding a psychologically more suitable sexual object—a prostitute, a mistress—or by taking refuge in fantasy. Sexual relations with the wife may come to be regarded as brutal assaults upon her purity and, if they are to be successful, may involve the husband's lowering her in his esteem by imagining her as a women of looser character, as a whore or as an adulteress. Her imaginary involvement with another man or men also serves to reproduce, for purposes of titillation and gratification, the primary Oedipal situation, where another man (the father) poached at will on what the child claimed as his estate.[2]

Prostitutes gave Joyce all his early sexual experience. So far as we know, he had no sexual experience of any kind with girls who were not prostitutes, until Nora. He visited nighttown with such friends as Gogarty, who described him ironically but acutely as "the virginal kip-ranger" (kip being slang for bordello). Joyce's habits were of course typical for young men until fairly recently and could only serve to reinforce the distinction between a woman fit for sex and one fit for marriage, to arrest the flow of mingled feelings toward a single object. Strolling through St. Stephen's Green one day with the seventeen-year-old Joyce, Francis Skeffington asked him whether he had ever been in love. Joyce replied with a defensive question: "How would I write the most perfect love songs of our time if I were in love?" And he later derided what he considered the stupidity of Skeffington's question. Joyce was however not writing the most perfect love songs of his or any other time, he was writing lyrical but thin and other-worldly abstractions, hymns to flesh-less beauty. Skeffington's question touched on the virginal kip-ranger's inexperience.

Suddenly at the age of twenty-two, less than a year after his mother's death, he encountered Nora Barnacle by chance in Merrion Square. Within four months' time, he took her to Europe to live with him for the rest of his life. She was the first and only woman with whom he was to share his sexual life—the first and only, that is, who was not a prostitute. There is a feverish panic in all this. Why Nora Barnacle? And why the need for this extraordinarily rapid escape with her? Much of the answer to both these questions lies in the effects of Joyce's mother's death on him.

For some time before her death, Joyce was conscious of the growing offense to his mother that his convictions and actions were becoming. Leaving Mother Church and Mother Ireland meant leaving his actual mother as well, for she was a conventional woman who feared openly for the salvation of her son's soul. Yet Joyce had depended greatly on his mother's love. He had, in fact, been something of a mama's boy until his university years—not only a brilliant student but, more important to a mother, a diligent and obedient one as well. On family outings he would work away at his lessons for a time and then bring them to his mother for examination. And to win his successive prizes in English composition, not only his grammar but his thoughts had to be orthodox. As he began to rebel, he frightened and confused his mother—and he suffered for it. During his first trip to Paris, his letters to her resemble a kind of emotional blackmail, asserting independence but demanding approbation and pity for his self-inflicted plight. Returning home to watch her die, he would not give in to her wishes that he make his confession and go to communion, but again he paid a price of guilt and remorse, of "agenbite of inwit." Later he listed his own "cynical frankness of conduct" as a contributing cause to her death.[3]

As Ernest Jones suggested in "The Island of Ireland," [4] the term "mother country" has more psychological force for the Irishman than for the citizen of most other lands: as powerful a symbol as Britannia or Italia or Germania or Columbia might be, none equals the specifically maternal symbolic force of Cathleen ni Houlihan—or, if you like, Erin, Dark Rosaleen, or any of the other dozen or so feminine names by which Hibernia is known to her sons. Traditionally her poets have personified Ireland as a virginal mother-figure, loverless and alone, or loved only by the poet. Think of the most famous example of all, Yeats's Cathleen ni Houlihan, the maternal aristocrat who inspires young Irishmen to follow her, even on their wedding days, and to die for her. She is maiden, old woman, and queen all together: she is mother. For centuries Irish poets have sung of the motherland as though it were the earthly paradise, one of the Fortunate Isles where all wants are satisfied. The poets sing this of what has been the most unfortunate country in Europe because Erin is mother. The praises, melancholy plaints, take on familiar aspects of womb-fantasies. No wonder the Irish have clung to the Catholic cult of the Virgin Mother, tend not to marry until their mothers are dead or dying, and hold virginity in such high esteem. No wonder that the myth of a United Ireland, antithetical to political, social and religious realities on the island, appeals so strongly to the Irish Catholic imagination: John Bull's presence in the North is unconsciously felt as a rape of mother.

If we combine these aspects of national psychology with

Joyce's personal psychology, we can understand better the bitterness of his struggle to set himself free. Exile meant separation from the tripartite womb of mother, nation, and Church that nurtures all Irishmen and stifles so many of them. To ease the anxiety of this separation Joyce found a substitute for mother, nation and Church in Nora, the ignorant Galway girl to whom he pleaded, "Guide me, my saint, my angel. . . . O that I could nestle in your womb like a child born of your flesh and blood, be fed by your blood, sleep in the warm secret gloom of your body!" [5]

Nora gave to Joyce what he required, but if we understand his escape with her as a way of not escaping, as a way of returning to the womb, then the perverse side of this relationship becomes manifest. In this light we can comprehend his feeling that to sleep with her was to assault her purity, that such an assault aroused masochistic lusts for punishment in him, and that often he had to see her as a whore, as no better than all the other women he had had, in order to gain physical pleasure from her.

Likewise the peculiar nature of Joyce's sexual interests in other women becomes clear. I am thinking of Amalia Popper, his pupil in Trieste, and of Martha Fleischmann. Signorina Popper excited him because of her virginity and her Jewishness, the one touching his need for a madonna and the other his need for the exotic, the forbidden. As the fantasies he recorded in *Giacomo Joyce* attest, he both venerated Signorina Popper and feared the "liquorish venom" of this "starry snake," and he took pleasure in feeling abject and inferior before her.[6] The attraction to Martha Fleischmann was analogous: her lameness supplied the helplessness of virginity, he invented her Jewishness, and she was already someone else's mistress. Joyce's pathetic letters to her—cries of weakness and self-castigation—are sexual fantasies, diminishing in vividness and intensity as soon as he discovers her name: as soon, that is, as reality begins to intrude. We can assume that Joyce derived pleasurable torment from similar fantasies about many other women, although no recorded evidence has come to light. There can have been no rest for his thwarted and compulsive spirit, surely, as we have seen, none with Nora. He was searching for something that has its roots in the unconscious recollections of childhood—something unfathomable and irretrievable that finds its resolution only in the final return of death.

There is an apparent contradiction in the fact that Joyce, who boasted of his monogamy and whose wife was wholly faithful to him, should have been obsessed in his fiction with cuckoldry and sexual perversion. The contradiction is merely apparent because often what appears consciously as two contraries is unconsciously a united whole. Joyce's art makes the unconscious conscious. Thus he gives us Richard Rowan, in *Exiles,* who struggles with a desire to be betrayed by his madonna-like wife, whom, he tells himself, he has robbed of "the virginity of her soul." Richard tries ineffectually to mask his motivations with talk of principles of sexual liberty, but like Joyce, he senses his perversity. Again like Joyce, he feels he has sinned against his mother by leaving Ireland and her Church and, most painful sin of all, by living with Bertha. His mother, recently dead, scorned his union with Bertha as sinful and scorned the son of that union as a child of sin. All this is Joyce's projection of his own anguish and guilt: his mother had died before he met Nora, but her spirit brooded over him, just as the ghost of Stephen's mother haunts him in *Ulysses.*

When Richard tries to make it simple for Bertha to cuckold him, this too is Joyce's self-projection, as he allows his sexual fantasies to work their way into his art. The idea of cuckoldry titillated Joyce as it does Richard for at least three reasons: it debases the beloved into a sexually acceptable object, it provides punishment for the sin of debauching the beloved, and it holds out the possibility of vicarious homosexual union with the beloved's new partner, who in an Oedipal sense assumes the role of the father. Richard, moreover, finds himself attracted to another woman, the icily virginal Beatrice, not only because of her purity but becaues she has been involved in some way with his friend Robert. Joyce was aware of the homosexual theme, for he alludes to it in the notes for *Exiles* and dramatizes it in several ways, notably when Richard and Robert take each other's hands and when Robert admits, "You are so strong that you attract me even through her."

Here Joyce was probably thinking of his erstwhile friend Vincent Cosgrave, who tried and failed to win Nora away. Perhaps now we can understand how ready Joyce was to believe Cosgrave's outrageous tale of Nora's unfaithfulness. In his troubled, complicated way Joyce wanted to believe Cosgrave, was attracted to the idea of being cuckolded at the same time as he was repelled by it. Even after he was convinced of Nora's innocence, his letters pursued with relish the details of whatever experience she had had with other men.[7] Perhaps too Joyce's refusal to wed Nora, until legal problems made marriage a necessity, was more than just the defiance of the rebel against social convention. The illegitimacy of his union was probably sexually exciting to him, a spark, like his fantasies, to his desire.

The erotic themes of *Ulysses* continue along the same lines, though more explicitly. The act of cuckoldry is completed. Bloom becomes a parody or caricature of his creator's own sexual oddities—whether writing a sado-masochistic letter to his Martha, pleading for the birch, masturbating at the sight of the lame and virginal Gerty (who reappears in nighttown as a whore), offering his wife to all strong-membered males, or clasping himself gleefully at a fantasy of Molly in bed with Blazes Boylan.

Although the sexual themes are more explicit in *Ulysses* than in the earlier works, Joyce disguised the close relationship between himself and his fictional character by making Bloom a Jew and a cuckold and by treating him with outrageous humor.

Joyce had many reasons for giving Bloom the characteristics he did, but psychologically he needed to place Bloom at a certain distance. In this way Joyce could more easily release and give form to his observations and judgments about perverse and unhappy aspects of his sexual life.

Like all obscene jokes, *Ulysses* overcomes inhibitions to expose what is hidden and repressed. What Joyce cannot or does not wish to deal with directly he displaces onto more remote, unlikely, and acceptable figures and symbols.[8] Bloom, so unlikely a psychosexual mirror-image of his creator, enables Joyce to explore himself while avoiding the embarrassment and bad taste of public confession. The fact that Bloom turned out to be an entirely plausible character shows how typical Joyce's sexual nature actually is, at least in the Western world,[9] and how logical a step it was for Joyce to name his next and last major male character HCE, or Here Comes Everybody. Sex for HCE is again tormented and perverse, and in *Finnegans Wake* there is again a notable scarcity of that union of tenderness and affection we call love. Whether we think of HCE watching the girls pee in the Phoenix Park or of Shem looking up the maidens' dresses or of Shaun aghast at his mother's "safety vulve," sex for the Joycean male is still a joke, often cruel.

Joyce gradually developed the idea, I think, that sexual love, as opposed to sex and love as separate entities, was something only women knew about and were capable of, though constantly denied it because of the nature of male sexuality. I doubt that this notion had evolved by the time he was writing "The Dead": Gretta Conroy's love for Michael Furey seems remote, disembodied, as ethereal as *Chamber Music*.[10] But Bertha, in *Exiles*, when she pleads for Richard's love, seems to speak out of a wisdom which is to him inscrutable but which he senses must be true, a sexual wisdom beyond Richard's compulsive, destructive manipulations. Unfortunately Joyce was too unsure of his themes (and of his sexual nature) at the time he wrote the play to give adequate realization to Bertha as a character. Like Richard, he was in a state of "restless living wounding doubt."

Through Molly Bloom, Joyce began to give form to his idea of what a woman can feel and know. The last two pages of Molly's monologue are the only truly positive passages in *Ulysses*, and they are about love and sex combined. Molly's lyrical burst is melancholy, however, because it celebrates not the present but the past and not even the recent past but childhood and adolescence, glimpses of things lost. Remembering at once her first, unconsummated love affair and the day of Bloom's proposal to her, when she was thinking both of Bloom and of that older love, Molly intertwines love and lust and a feeling of oneness with the natural world, flowers, sun, sea and sky; and at this moment in the book, Joyce says yes to her and with her. But he could say yes only through her, only through a woman, because he believed that only a woman could know affirmative sexuality. For himself, for any male, it was no, and as Bloom's perversions and Boylan's brutishness suggest, the male no was always a threat and a frustration to the female yes. Molly's dissatisfactions with Bloom and Boylan dramatize Joyce's idea that love and sex are one in woman, toward whom man strives and swives and never attains.

In *Finnegans Wake*, Anna Livia is to Molly as HCE is to Bloom, a universalization of the particular. In her guise as the Prankquean, she asks to be taken in, but the man will not take her in; she asks why it is that she looks like Shem and Shaun, who are opposite aspects of all men, but the man cannot answer her because he does not understand her. She is the life-stream, wherein all things mingle and are one. Like Molly, unlike Bloom and HCE, she is sexually amoral and guilt-free, and her soliloquy celebrates the natural world while lamenting man's inadequacy to it, to her, to woman.

Man wills, woman is. Man is a creature cast out from woman, wishing always to return, cast out from life, wishing death, sexual and actual. It is then insufficient to say that Anna Livia's voice is Joyce's, though certainly her watery moaning carries along in its sweep Joyce's sense of separation, of exile, and his melancholy longing to rush again into the arms, into the womb from which he had wrenched himself. Her voice is Joyce's idea of the nature of woman. Like Bloom, at times Joyce longed to be a woman, to be able to feel and know as he imagined a woman does. Given his view of man, who can blame him? He accomplished the feat through his art, but in life he was stuck with himself, until his final return to the earth-womb.

NOTES

1. (Princeton, 1968).

2. Essays specially pertinent to these phenomena include Freud's "Degradation in Erotic Life" and "Contributions to the Psychology of Love. A Special Type of Choice of Object Made by Men," *Collected Papers*, IV (London, 1925).

3. Letter to Nora of August 29, 1904 (*Letters II*, p. 48).

4. *Essays in Applied Psychoanalysis*, I (London, 1951).

5. Letter to Nora of September 5, 1909 (Letters II, p. 248).

6. I have referred to Amalia Popper as the pupil whom Joyce depicted in *Giacomo Joyce*, although there is still some debate as to her identity. Who she actually was does not matter in the present context: indeed she may have been no one. What does matter is the peculiarly Joycean element of sexual fantasy in the depiction. Joyce's model or models may have been Jewish or gentile, dark or fair, sweet or sour: but Joyce stressed and imagined the qualities demanded by his mind and art.

7. Ernest Jones's "Jealousy," *Papers on Psychoanalysis* (London, 1948), is remarkably applicable to the Joyce-Cosgrave incident. Joyce would appear to have been suffering from a neurotic form of jealousy based largely on his own fears about his masculinity and probably complicated by a repressed homosexual attachment to Cosgrave: "I do not love him, she does," says the jealous man.

8. Joyce did not of course have to resort to such indirections when he wanted to parody someone other than himself—Gogarty, for example, who can hardly be distinguished from Buck Mulligan.

9. I cherish the probably indefensible notion that the people of

the East enjoy a different psychosexual makeup from ourselves and
that there is no such thing as a Chinese Portnoy. One always hopes
that what one knows nothing of must be profoundly different from
what one knows.

10. Joyce's choice of the song that triggers Gretta's memory of
Michael Furey, however, prefigures his later development of the
theme of woman as the source and embodiment of life, spurned and
misunderstood by man. "The Lass of Aughrim" tells just such a tale.

Joyce and Gogarty

James F. Carens
BUCKNELL UNIVERSITY

H AD OLIVER ST. JOHN GOGARTY not existed, James Joyce
would have invented someone else to play the role of friend
and betrayer in life and in fiction. But had Oliver Gogarty not
existed, had a different rival been found at the appropriate moment, *Ulysses* would not be precisely the book that it is. Joyce's
comic masterpiece, in mood and motif, bears some significant
traces of the man who served as the model for Buck Mulligan.
Gogarty's relation to Joyce and his work—he was once described
as "accessory before the fact" of *Ulysses*—deserves another look.

The time is long since past when it was possible to regard the
Portrait or *Ulysses* as fundamentally "autobiographical" works in
such a way as to identify Joyce fully with Stephen Dedalus, or
to ascribe Stephen's aesthetic theories to the mature Joyce. Yet
the relation of Joyce to his fictive world is no simple matter.
Wayne Booth, picking up Richard Ellmann's suggestion that
Joyce in *Ulysses* "hit upon the . . . radical device of the unde-
pendable narrator," [1] suggested that, though concealed behind
multiple narrators, the authorial voice was never really silent.[2]
And a recent work by another critic went beyond Booth to suggest that the implied author of *Ulysses* is Stephen, not as we see
him in the novel but as he would be many years later when a mature artist.[3] I have even read one essay by a critic, apparently
steeped in the phenomenological thought of Merleau-Ponty, who
argues that the author of *Ulysses* is entirely concealed since the

28

novel's techniques exist to give a phenomenological rendering of experience.[4] (Stephen Dedalus might have been startled by that notion.)

Perhaps a consideration of the relation that the actual man Oliver Gogarty bears to the novel *Ulysses* can lead us to some conclusions, or confirmations of existing views, about the relation of Joyce to his work. That Joyce intended an unflattering characterization of Gogarty was assumed as early as 1905, when Vincent Cosgrave remarked to Stanislaus Joyce, "I wouldn't like to be Gogarty when your brother comes to the Tower episode. Thanks be to God I never kicked his arse or anything." [5] And Gogarty himself apparently assumed that Dublin's Dante would eventually consign him to one of the circles of hell, when, according to Joyce's account of their last interview, in 1909, the doctor asked, "Well, do you really want me to go to hell and be damned?" [6] Oddly enough, given the months of their companionship, one searches in vain for any comment by Joyce that would imply affection for Gogarty. The epiphany of 1903 or 1904 is (as Scholes and Kain have remarked) designed to reveal Gogarty's "self-assurance and smugness"; the Gogarty passage from the Trieste Notebook is a catalogue of errors, wrongs, slights, and sins; the Doherty fragment from a late *Portrait* manuscript is ironically hostile; and comments in the letters to Stanislaus from 1904 to 1909 are consistently bitter, even when Joyce was actually responding to Gogarty's overtures for a reconciliation.

How odd it is then that Frank Budgen, recording his impression of the opening chapters of *Ulysses*, should have written: "Every reader of *Ulysses* is captivated from the start with the wit and high spirits of Buck Mulligan. . . ." and that one should feel Budgen did not entirely exaggerate. Yet Budgen has also recorded for us this intriguing conversation concerning the Library episode:

> "What do you think of Buck Mulligan in this episode?" said Joyce when I returned the typescript.

"He is witty and entertaining as ever," I said.

"He should begin to pall on the reader as the day goes on," Joyce said.

"The comic man usually wearies," I said, "if he keeps it up too long. But I can't say that Buck Mulligan wearies me."

"And to the extent that Buck Mulligan's wit wears threadbare," Joyce continued, "Bloom's justness and reasonableness should grow in interest. As the day wears on Bloom should overshadow them all." [7]

True enough, after Scylla and Charybdis, Bloom does overshadow all. But it is not so much that Buck Mulligan's wit wears threadbare as that we see rather little of him after the Library episode. There is his very brief betrayal scene with Haines in The Wandering Rocks; and in Oxen of the Sun there is his dramatic arrival at the hospital, when his wit is as effervescent and as pointed as ever. There are brief appearances in the phantasmagoria of Nighttown, conspicuously in Mulligan's hilarious, psychically true account of Bloom's sexual abnormalities, and in the bestialities of the Black Mass. In short, Mulligan pretty well departs from the novel as an actual presence in Chapter 14; and he figures very little in the more than three hundred pages that follow.

Were one reckless enough to hazard the intentional fallacy and the eternal damnation of Wimsatt, some of this evidence might lead one to assume that Joyce intended a most unflattering portrait of Gogarty, that having brought him vividly to life in the novel, often quoting him almost verbatim as we know he did, he produced an effect on Budgen and most of the rest of us that he did not wish to achieve. Such a line of reasoning might lead one to conclude that Joyce then chose to leave us with a most unpleasant final impression of Mulligan, derived from the Black Mass in Nighttown. Actually the situation is rather more complex than this, and I think that neither the ordinary processes of biographical criticism nor absolutistic formalist standards will explain just what Joyce has done.

In the opening chapter of *Ulysses,* while Stephen is sullenly silent, Buck Mulligan is all volatility, energy, and satire. He is also, at a number of key moments, quite open, generous, and kind, even according to the author's narration:

> Buck Mulligan suddenly linked his arm in Stephen's and walked with him round the tower, his razor and mirror clacking in the pocket where he had thrust them.
> —It's not fair to tease you like that, Kinch, is it? he said kindly. God knows you have more spirit than any of them.
> (7)

Yet the dominant impression we gain from the opening of the novel is that Mulligan is sponging. Mulligan borrows money from Stephen. He has permitted Stephen to pay the rent of the Tower, even though he demands that he be given the key; and he assumes that Stephen will pay for drinks later in the day. Most readers are consequently both amused and puzzled when they discover, during the course of the second chapter, that Stephen's main indebtedness, in a substantial catalogue, is to Mulligan for "nine pounds, three pairs of socks, one pair brogues, ties" (31). Are we to assume that one of Mulligan's main offenses in the first chapter is that he subtly and cruelly reminds Stephen of that debt by borrowing from him? Even more curious, in Chapter One, is the appearance of "The Ballad of Joking Jesus," a work we know was in actuality composed by Oliver Gogarty and not by a fictional character. As we read the three stanzas Joyce uses, they seem a clever piece of blasphemy of just the kind we might expect from Mocking Malachi Mulligan. Oliver St. John Gogarty's poem, read in its entirety, is quite another thing. "The Song of the Cheerful (But Slightly Sarcastic) Jesus" was a poem of nine stanzas; its central theme is found in the stanzas Joyce does not quote.[8] These are the words of Gogarty's sarcastic persona:

> Whenever I enter in triumph and pass
> You will find that my triumph is due to an ass.
> (And public support is a grand sinecure

When you once get the public to pity the poor.)
Then give up your cabin and ask them for bread
And they'll give you a stone habitation instead
With fine grounds to walk in and raincoat to wear
And the Sheep will be naked before you'll grow bare.

The more men are wretched the more you will rule
But thunder out 'Sinner' to each bloody fool;
For the Kingdom of God (that's within you) begins
When you once make a fellow acknowledge he sins.[9]

It would be possible to quote more of this very funny poem but
the additional stanzas would only further demonstrate that Oliver
Gogarty wrote what he described, in an unpublished letter of
1905, as "a delightful satire on Commercial Christianity." [10] One
would not want to say his poem was untouched by blasphemy.
Still, one would have to conclude that it is basically an anti-clerical
ballad in which Gogarty ridiculed the allegiance of the clergy
to a repressive status quo. Excerpting from the poem and altering the final stanza for instance so that one line reads not "Goodbye, now, goodbye, you are sure to be fed" but instead "Goodbye now, goodbye. Write down all I said" (19), Joyce concealed
the actual theme of the original. It may be that he modified the
poem as he did so that it would suit a number of his central
themes, as it beautifully does. But it also seems that life and art
are mingling with one another in rather special ways and that
Joyce's personal feelings have something to do with the altera-
tions he made in Gogarty's poem.

In *Surface and Symbol*, Robert Adams observed that "there is
no proper fictional reason for some of the things that are said,
thought, and done in *Ulysses*. Autobiography," he wrote, "has
evidently usurped over narrative. . . ." [11] In the process of arriving at this conclusion, Mr. Adams cited Joyce's interesting list
of the bicycle riders in Trinity College Park, among whom we
find one J. A. Jackson. "To at least one alert student of *Ulysses*,"
Adams said, "this name had seemed to conceal a reference to the

author himself, James Augustine, son of Jack Joyce." Amused by
this notion, Adams granted that Joyce was fond of enigmas, but
added, if Jackson has a covert meaning in this instance must it not
also have a covert meaning when George A. Jackson, who produced the ballet-pantomime *Sinbad the Sailor,* in 1892, is alluded
to later in the novel? Should we assume a covert reference to
James's dead brother George Alfred? When a Dublin newspaper
revealed that one J. A. Jackson did in fact win a race on June 16,
1904, Robert Adams concluded that in this instance Joyce was
utilizing both names for surface realism rather than for enigma.[12]
But I am not so sure. Autobiography might be impinging again
on narrative; enigma, upon fact. Oliver Gogarty was also a prize-
winning bicycle racer at Trinity, though he seems not to have
competed in 1904. A "cyclist," Joyce once wrote contemptu-
ously, describing Gogarty.[13] Jack-son does indeed suggest St.
John. Moreover, Gogarty composed an epic piece of bawdry,
"Sinbad, the Sailor," which was known to Joyce and many others
in Dublin; and Sinbad emerges in the Eumaeus chapter and elsewhere as a comic analogue to Bloom and Ulysses. Frankly, I see
here enigma rather than symbol, a set of zany correspondences
Joyce has seized upon with delight. And I see more wish-fulfill-
ment fantasy than anything else, for in the race of *Ulysses* it is a
surrogate cyclist who rivals Gogarty at his own sport and a surrogate younger brother, his death avenged, who anticipates his
elder, that is Gogarty, in devising scenery for Sinbad. (Indeed if
any full copy of Gogarty's "Sinbad" has survived—we have only
short fragments of this—it seems imperative that it be published
at once not only for its intrinsic comic merit but for its possible
bearing on the novel.)

Joyce alludes to a second Gogarty poem in *Ulysses,* the su-
perbly obscene "Song of Medical Dick and Medical Davy"; or
rather he permits Buck Mulligan to sing two lines from the song
and to introduce the two medicals into the mock-drama he produces at the end of the Library episode. Gogarty sent this song

to Joyce—it is item #523 in the Cornell collection—some time
about 1902–1904 in a letter of extraordinary scatalogical vivacity.
This piece of bawdry is embellished with drawings of winged
male genitalia and prefaced, in parody of Swinburne on Baudel-
aire, by an address to Joyce as "the holder of the highest of contemporary names and the longest of contemporary tools." As innocent as Chaucer, I merely repeat another's words:

SONG

I
The first was Medical Dick
The second was Medical Davy
The first had a Bloody Big Prick
The second had Buckets of Gravy
To show—to show—to show what medicals are.

II
Then out spoke Medical Dick
To his comrade Medical Davy
'I'd swap my Bloody Big Prick
For you with your buckets of Gravy.'
To show etc.

III
'Steady Medical Dick'
Said Sturdy Medical Davy
'There's very little value in a prick
When ye haven't got the passage of the gravy.'
To show etc.

IV
'Every bullock were a bull
But for the little matter of a ballocks
If your prick can keep the women full
You'll find they'll never grumble at its small looks.'
To show etc.

In a mock-scholarly analysis of the poem's symbolism, Gogarty
points out that "the stones of David" overcame "the ponder-
ous Goliath." I believe that the entire letter and the genital
distinction that is made between Dick and Davy implies a joke

shared by Joyce and Gogarty. And I believe that the poem (and for that matter the comic allusion to David's triumph) is reflected in *Ulysses* in the blunt physiological contrast Molly Bloom makes between the divergent potencies of Poldy and Blazes, the latter of whom is, after all, associated with Mulligan as Bloom is with Stephen. Furthermore, both the bull motif and Bloom's combats with gigantic males—Blazes and the Citizen—are foreshadowed in the Gogarty letter.

Mrs. Glasheen's *Second Census of Finnegans Wake* draws our attention only to one specific allusion to the name Gogarty; and the *Wake's* exegetes seem to agree that "Stainusless" Joyce, other actual rivals long since dispatched, was the chief inspiration for Shaun the Post. But Gogarty was not entirely forgotten. Joyce's memory was a long one. "Bloody Big Bristol," an insult hurled at Earwicker (421.13), echoes very closely one of the bawdy phrases in the "Song" and also puns on pistol—Gogarty's famed revolver. And the two medicals, Dick and Davy, themselves put in an appearance in the *Wake*, reminding us of Mulligan's mockdrama in *Ulysses:* "a reiz every morning for Standfast Dick and a drop every minute for Stumblestone Davy" (210.28). Allusions to Oliver or to Roland's horn, harking back to the horn and hornblower motif of *Ulysses* and to one of Mulligan's names—Roland—, probably indicate that Gogarty, his song, and its implication of the Bloom-Blazes, Stephen-Mulligan, Joyce-Gogarty rivalry are still on Joyce's mind. (James Stephens—the one man Joyce thought might be able to complete the *Wake* and with whom he imaginatively identified himself in the *Wake* period—wrote the following curious little note to Gogarty, in April, 1930: "Dear Oliver: Here's the appropriate Roland, but tis I have the Oliver; by which two unchristian names you must be the sick man—still, haven't we proved in these that verse and versing is lovely. My love to you.") [14] "The Ballad of Persse O'Reilly" even seems to associate Gogarty with Earwicker, for it alludes in extended simile to Lord Olofa Crumple, to Gogarty's

interest in public health ("Mare's milk for the sick"), to the
Boylan-Mulligan horn motif, and to the "blue butter" [15] that
Gogarty prescribed as a prophylactic to fellow students ("Butter
his horns!"), and possibly even to the burning of Gogarty's
Renvyle House: "So snug he was in his hotel premises sump-
tuous / But soon we'll bonfire all his trash. . . ." (45.3–46).

These grotesque links, allusions, and speculations lead not to
any assurance that biographical details explain either *Ulysses* or
the *Wake*, but to the conclusion that absolutist formalist assumptions must be cast off if we are to *see* Joyce's major works as they
really are: not as expressions of a detached, classical temperament
that has refined itself out of existence but as an expression of a
comic sensibility that conceals but manifests itself everywhere,
even indulging in enigmas and private jokes. Consider the concluding passages of Oxen of the Sun. How are we to take a line
like "Landlord, landlord, have you good wine, staboo?" (426–7).
It makes some kind of sense in its drunken context, I suppose.
But who says it, who asks it, and why? Joyce knew, Gogarty
knew, Stanislaus knew, as he revealed in an open letter, that it was
a song Oliver Gogarty composed and sang as a young man.[16]
Take disjointed phrases like "and snares of the poxfiend," "Thrust
syphilis down to hell and with him those other licensed spirits"
(427). These fragments can be traced to Roman Catholic prayers
that they seem to parody and Joyce so explained them to his
German translator. However, in *It Isn't This Time of Year At
All!* Gogarty wrote of Joyce: he "could parody every prose style
and get an equivalent sound for every word. It was chiefly the
Collects of the New Testament he chose to parody." Curiously
enough, a detached manuscript sheet has survived from Gogarty's
draft of his autobiography; and on this sheet Gogarty goes on to
quote the following Joycean parody of a prayer after the Mass,
differing only slightly from the *Ulysses* fragments:

> Blessed Michael, the ass angel, propel us in the hour of our
> contact; be our safeguard against the wickedness and snares
> of the Syph Fiend; May God rebuke him we humbly pray

and do Thou, O Prince of the Heavenly Host, thrust Syphilis down to Hell and with him all the wicked spirits who wander through the world for the ruin of tools. Amen.[17]

One other detail: In a letter of February, 1907, Joyce reminded Stanislaus of this parody and said it had just come into his mind and made him laugh. To an understanding of the central theme and symbolic import of Joyce's fiction, a fortuitous discovery like the Gogarty manuscript page may mean little: but it does indicate a significant stratum of buried personal meanings and private allusions.

An only slightly reconstructed disciple of the aged New Criticism myself, I do not mean to dismiss the primacy of the tale and the duplicities of tellers. It does not matter to me in the least that T. S. Eliot composed the *Waste Land* while having a nervous breakdown or that Joyce had a rather sick-making interest in soiled undies. But it does matter that in *Ulysses* and the *Wake*, the teller is, in fact, *in* the tale. It is indeed possible to read *Ulysses* entirely on the level of action, symbol, and correspondence, ignoring the author's presence in his techniques and in the disposition of his materials. But let us at least admit that Joyce did not compose his last major works on pure formalist assumptions, that he was *not* an impersonal artist.

If Joyce in his art brought the real and the virtual into a unique relationship, his critics have often confused life and art. Thus a number of years after Hugh Kenner, reflecting some of the prejudices of early interpreters of Joyce, described Buck Mulligan as a "stage Irishman," a lead article in the *Times Literary Supplement* absurdly enough referred to Oliver St. John Gogarty, using the same expression.[18] Even Richard Ellmann's massive and impressive biography seems so committed to the values and genius of Joyce that it is quite prejudiced in its treatment of Gogarty and seems to assume that whatever criticisms Joyce made of Gogarty must be applicable to the character Buck Mulligan and must have been true of Gogarty himself. So we find Ellmann writing: "Stephen's charge against Mulligan is that Mulligan is

brutal and cruel" and adding in a footnote, "Joyce completed in
this his analysis of Gogarty." [19] And Ellmann's analysis of the
friendship and break between Joyce and Gogarty rises to a
climax when he writes: "they took part in a lifelong battle in
which Gogarty was severely worsted." [20] I am not sure that a
statement like that really makes any sense at all, given the very
great differences between the men, their interests, their careers,
the kind of works they produced, and their talents. Ellmann himself has drawn our attention to the notes for *Exiles*, which indicate that Joyce "regarded the relation of protagonist and antag-
onist as complicated by admiration as well as repugnance for each
other" [21] and it would seem that both biographers and literary
critics should keep this in mind.

The truth is that, given the contradictions in the surviving
evidence concerning the Joyce-Gogarty break, we cannot explain
motive or apportion blame with any real certainty. The most
one can say with any degree of positiveness is that two such
individual and brilliant natures should *never* have shared quarters
with one another and that they both may have made impossible
claims on the ideal of friendship. In June of 1904, Gogarty wrote
his friend G. K. A. Bell an account of Joyce's doings and concluded, "Isn't Joyce delightful?" [22] By the end of August, Gogarty knew that Joyce had written "The Holy Office." Under-
standably he was provoked by the contempt Joyce there expressed, and he wrote: "I have broken with Joyce, his want of
generosity became to me inexcusable, he lampooned AE, Yeats,
Colum and others to whom he was indebted in many ways. A
desert was revealed which I did not think existed amid the seeming luxuriance of his soul. . . ." [23] According to Stanislaus Joyce's
Dublin Diary, Gogarty wanted to put Joyce out of the Tower;
and Jim was "determined that if Gogarty puts him out it will
be done publicly." [24] On the night of Trench's nightmare, did
Gogarty fire his revolver into the shelf of pans over Joyce's bed
as therapy for the neurotic Trench (who later blew out his

brains), or as a practical joke against Joyce (who had pawned Gogarty's rifle), or in a deliberate attempt to force Joyce's departure? We do not know, even though Richard Ellmann now writes as if he had certain knowledge.[25] Years later, when he had some severe things to say about Joyce, Gogarty also admitted to faults: "My cavalier treatment did nothing to help. . ." and "Maybe I was wrong to try to make him genial." [26]

That intense emotions were involved in the friendship and its dissolution, there is no doubt. Richard Ellmann quotes two of Joyce's poems written at the time the two young men were drawing apart: "He who hath glory lost, nor hath / Found any soul to fellow his. . . ." and "He is a stranger now / Who was my friend." [27] And at just about the same time that Cosgrave was writing Joyce that Gogarty desired a reconciliation, Gogarty was writing G. K. A. Bell:

> There is in all human society the original sin arising from our frailty—little shynesses which prevent our daring to be sincere, false shame[s] which mentally withhold men from each other—and yet, perhaps, if one was too sincerely outspoken time would have nothing to confirm and nothing to teach—the object would be gone out of life. I do not know how it is!—The Stars are surrounded with darkness on all sides, if they blend they become diffused and diminished; if they would shine they must be separate and lonely. I suppose it is the same with men. . . . The original sin is in my nature, particularly [in] the Celtic nature.[28]

"Alone, what did Bloom feel? / The cold of interstellar space. . . ."

According to Joyce's account of his last meeting with Oliver St. John Gogarty, in 1909, though he had turned on his "spiritual-heroic refrigerating apparatus," he did say to the doctor, "I bear you no ill will. I believe you have some points of good nature." [29] Perhaps Joyce changed his mind later, after he began to believe that Cosgrave and Gogarty were linked in a plot to destroy his love for Nora; and perhaps he did set out, as Ellmann argues, to

associate Gogarty-Mulligan with "unconscionable power" and
Bloom, Stephen, and Molly with "casual kindness." [30] (One
knows what that would mean in the case of Bloom and Molly.
But Stephen?) Joyce's own formula of admiration and repugnance would seem better to illuminate the ambivalent handling
of Mulligan. For though, as I have suggested, there are apparent
inconsistencies in the characterization of the Buck, Frank Budgen's response to his wit was a valid one. In fact, given the prig-
gish solipsism of Stephen, Mulligan's irreverent sallies are telling
and true. The drama with which he deflates Stephen's Shakespeare theory—"Everyman His Own Wife"—pierces right to the
core of Stephen's intellectual onanism. Mulligan may be a mocker
when he ridicules "bonzes" and irresponsible when he celebrates
potency (in the Oxen of the Sun) but he is going to the heart
of Stephen's, Bloom's, and the nation's problem: sterility. Little
wonder that Father Noon should write, "This much at least
must be said for Buck Mulligan, that he is on the side of community." [31] Stephen harbors many resentments against Mulligan,
but too little attention has been paid to a central cause—his emotional ambivalence, his sexual uncertainty, and his jealousy of
Haines. The fundamental ambivalence of Joyce himself is made
manifest in the Black Mass of Nighttown, not the character's hallucinations for the most part but the author's own expressionist
drama about his characters. Fiction and autobiography jostle one
another. Father Malachi O'Flynn, the Mulligan who is paradoxically both priest and pagan in Stephen's imagination and who
has driven him from his residence in the tower, is assisted by the
Reverend Mr. Haines-Love—another landlord, who is a combination of the usurping Englishman, the French word for hate,
and an actual Anglican clergyman named Love with whom
Joyce's family had some difficulty. Stephen's homosexual fears
and uncertainties are projected into the monstrous perversities of
the celebrants. And Joyce's own love-hate attitude toward Mulli-
gan-Gogarty reaches its apotheosis.

During the course of the last meeting between Joyce and Gogarty, at least according to Joyce's account, Gogarty declared, "I don't care a damn what you say of me as long as it is literature." But it is hard to see how the doctor could have accepted some of the details in *Ulysses* with equanimity. In 1932 he fired his first public fusillade, declaring that Joyce was no mocking Dante but a mockery of him.[32] (To Dublin friends he had already said plenty!) Even more interesting was a play that Gogarty wrote, of which only a tantalizing fragment survives. *Wave Lengths* was probably written at the very close of the 'thirties; the manuscript was unaccountably lost, and it was rewritten in a shorter and inferior version after Gogarty settled in America. The fragment, like the later version, is based upon the notion that "theoretically every sound made on earth could be recovered from the ether provided that you had the necessary apparatus. . . ."[33] At least in part, I think Gogarty was scoring a point or two against Joyce, by alluding to the latter's extraordinary interest in lingerie and to certain transvestite details in *Ulysses*. When the voice machine's inventor picks up the voice of an advertising man named Leopold, we hear the following:

> "Fifi, darling, I didn't mean to tear your stocking. I was only putting it on for a joke."
> A woman's aggrieved voice. "A joke indeed with those toenails. Why don't you get yourself pedicured? Why don't you leave my undies alone?"

Ulick O'Connor has pointed out that by the time *Ulysses* was published, Gogarty was a public figure in Ireland, a practicing surgeon, deeply involved in political affairs, and that he regarded the portrait of Buck Mulligan as profoundly compromising, given the attitudes of the day. At the very moment that the national temper was turning to the Right, he was revealed as a "heretic." *Wave Lengths* supports the view that what incensed Oliver Gogarty was that his own words seemed to be used to mock him.

As the Professor of the play expostulates, his invention could be used so that "Every idle word that man uttered would be brought up against him." So the inventor insists that no one use his device to intimidate or "make a show of some poor silly mortal whose youth or whose tongue ran away with him."

Gogarty's sharpest assaults on Joyce were produced during his later American years. Two essays in the *Saturday Review,* one in 1941, and another in 1950, created a flurry in the academic-literary world. In both of these, Gogarty had some generous things to say. He responded well to the lyrical element in Joyce's art—to *Chamber Music* and "Anna Livia Plurabelle." Yet he left no dobut that he felt Joyce had abandoned himself to unintelligibility, choosing not "the Logos, the Divine Word," but instead "the senseless mutterings of the subliminal mind's low delirium. . . ." [34] In "They Think They Know Joyce," reacting more against Joyce's American admirers than against Joyce himself, he sharpened his attack, arguing that Joyce regarded only "the gargoyle and the grotesque instead of anything that might exalt and beautify life." [35] As did Joyce, Oliver Gogarty embraced contradictions. His 1904–07 letters to G. K. A. Bell reveal him as both naturalist and transcendentalist. His sensibility ranged from the Rabelaisianism of Medical Dick and Medical Davy to the delicate charm of a lyric like "Golden stockings you had on" and from the ribald opening of "Ringsend" to its exquisite closing image. In a notebook dating from 1904, he wrote the following passage: "The world stinks? Your standpoint is a dunghill." [36] Gogarty's ideal was an art that would elevate the spirit. He could never have taken "away the palm of beauty from Argive Helen and handed it to poor Penelope." So for him, in *Ulysses* and the *Wake,* Joyce was inscribing his name "on the backside of beauty. . . ." [37] In dismissing a book like *Ulysses* as a "gigantic hoax" and as "one of the most enormous leg-pulls in history," [38] Gogarty was terribly wrong. In another sense he was quite right, for he was doubtlessly responding to the play ele--

ment, to the level of private allusion. But Oliver St. John Gogarty could not see that Joyce's work might transcend its separate elements.

Seeing his former friend as a monkish soul, enslaved by hatred of a Church that had wounded him, embittered by poverty and rejection, and neurotic to the point of schizophrenia, Gogarty ascribed these qualities to Joyce's works. Much of the harshness of his judgments on Joyce's character was mitigated by the comic sense of his unpremeditated autobiography (1951). "I do not wish to pose as a blameless observer of my friend Joyce. . . . After all, who am I to talk about sanity? Out of four of my friends, two committed suicide, one contracted syphilis, and the fourth was a schizophrene. Show me your company! I am showing them to you, for I would not have you think that I wasn't as good or bad as any of them. . . ." [39] One can only regret that Gogarty, feeling himself betrayed by *Ulysses,* never saw that the contrary Joyce had created an image of him as Mulligan, insulting in its imputation of vulgar materialism, to be sure, but far more human and attractive than the image of Stephen. Bernard Benstock has pointed out how at points throughout *Finnegans Wake* "harmony concludes the brother conflict," as Shem and Shaun are "unified into a single figure." And he has shown how the Roland and Oliver pair "becomes another parallel of the friendship motif that assimilates the antagonistic brothers. . . ." [40] It was Joyce's genius that in the isolation of his craft he could transform the conflicts of his experience. But for Gogarty poetry was a social act, as he revealed in his early associations with Joyce and G. K. A. Bell and Dermot Freyer and later in his associations with friends at the Bailey, with Lord Dunsany, and with Yeats. He might have been amused that Stanislaus, who admittedly set out to destroy the Joyce-Gogarty friendship, later displaced him as the main rival; but it is very doubtful that he could have responded to the artistic reconciliation of Roland and Oliver. At the conclusion of his chapter on Joyce in *It Isn't This Time of Year at All,* Gogarty wrote: ". . . he sent two poems ("The Holy Office" and "Gas from a Burner") to his aquaintances— he would not admit a friend." [41]

NOTES

1. Richard Ellmann, *James Joyce* (New York, 1959), p. 367.
2. Wayne C. Booth, *The Rhetoric of Fiction,* 1st text ed. (Chicago and London, 1963), p. 300n.
3. Louis D. Rubin, *The Teller in the Tale* (Seattle and London, 1967), p. 160ff.
4. F. R. Jamieson, "Seriality in Modern Literature," *Bucknell Review,* XVIII (Spring 1970), 63–80.
5. Ellmann, p. 215.
6. Ibid., p. 287.
7. Frank Budgen, *James Joyce and the Making of "Ulysses,"* Midland Book ed. (Bloomington, Ind., 1964), pp. 115–116.
8. Note Joyce's significant refashioning of Gogarty's title.
9. Ellmann, pp. 213–214.
10. Oliver St. John Gogarty, *Many Lines to Thee: Letters to G. K. A. Bell, 1904–1907,* edited with a commentary by James F. Carens (Dublin, 1971), p. 133.
11. Robert M. Adams, *Surface and Symbol,* Galaxy ed. (New York, 1967), p. 34.
12. Adams, pp. xvff.
13. *Letters III,* p. 233.
14. The James Stephens letter is in the Gogarty Collection of Bertrand Library, Bucknell University, Lewisburg, Pennsylvania.
15. See Oliver St. John Gogarty, *Tumbling in the Hay* (London, 1939), p. 235.
16. Stanislaus Joyce, "Open Letter to Dr. Oliver Gogarty," *Interim,* IV, 1 and 2 (1954), 54.
17. Gogarty Collection, Bucknell University.
18. "From Sligo to Byzantium," *Times Literary Supplement,* 31304 (June 24, 1965), 530.
19. Ellmann, p. 390n.
20. Ibid., p. 215.
21. Ibid., p. 389.
22. *Many Lines to Thee,* p. 11.
23. Ibid., p. 33.
24. Stanislaus Joyce, *The Dublin Diary,* ed. G. H. Healey (Ithaca, N.Y., 1962), p. 69.

25. Richard Ellmann, *James Joyce's Tower* (Dublin, 1969).

26. Oliver St. John Gogarty, *It Isn't This Time of Year at All!* (London, 1954), pp. 72–3.

27. Ellmann, p. 180.

28. *Many Lines to Thee*, p. 57.

29. *Letters II*, p. 231.

30. Ellmann, p. 390.

31. William T. Noon, S. J., *Joyce and Aquinas* (New Haven, 1957), p. 95.

32. Marvin Magalaner and Richard M. Kain, *Joyce, the Man, the Work, the Reputation*, Collier ed. (New York, 1962), pp. 283–4.

33. The fragment of *Wave Lengths* is in the Gogarty Collection of Bucknell University.

See Ulick O'Connor, *Oliver St. John Gogarty*, Jonathan Cape (London, 1964), p. 61.

34. Oliver St. John Gogarty, "The Joyce I Knew," *The Saturday Review Gallery* (New York, 1959), p. 260.

35. Oliver St. John Gogarty, "They Think They Know Joyce," *The Saturday Review Gallery*, p. 264.

36. Gogarty Collection, Bucknell University.

37. *Saturday Review Gallery*, p. 264.

38. Ibid., p. 262.

39. *It Isn't This Time of Year*, pp. 72ff.

40. Bernard Benstock, *Joyce Again's Wake* (Seattle and London, 1965), pp. 18ff., p. 178.

41. *It Isn't This Time of Year*, p. 79.

Mind Your Genderous:
Toward a *Wake* Grammar

Strother B. Purdy
MARQUETTE UNIVERSITY

C AN THERE BE awake grammar? Must you find a grammar asleep to prove it? I think not, for even a wake has a grammar. That is, a wake is an event having a repeatable form. That allows it to be identified as a wake even though all the actors, including the corpse, may be different from those taking part in any other wake, past or future. Such form is part of communication; that is to say, form that is repeated or repeatable communicates. The repetition is made communication in a given moment of time by a process of comparison, or relation, to a set of forms we carry in our heads—our experience. For that reason you cannot understand an Ife sculpture, or an English sentence, if you have never experienced one before, and a unique event is never decipherable. This relatability-to-comparable-form is called convention in many contexts; in language the rules of convention may be summed up by the term *grammar*.

In this sense both a wake and *Finnegans Wake* have a grammar, under the general rule: repeatable form is not without convention; convention is not without communication; communication is not without grammar. Whether or not *Finnegans Wake* is difficult to read is irrelevant to this basic fact—we can apply to it, after all, J. R. Pierce's maxim that the amount of information conveyed by a message increases in proportion to the amount of uncertainty as to what message will be produced.[1] *Finnegans Wake* as communication is anything but a failure on the cumula-

46

tive scale; there is no danger these days of our deriving too little information from it. I feel, rather, that we tend to derive too much, in too random a fashion, and this is because we approach the text with little or no concern for its grammar, for what kind of a grammar it may actually have. This paper is an attempt to move toward an identification of that grammar, with two main points in mind. First, that such an identification helps us avoid random overreading, the application, in effect, of the contents of our own lexicons to supplement that of the text. I think that a great deal of *Finnegans Wake* criticism has been overly word-oriented, seeking and finding words in the text without concern for the sentences that contain the words. A great deal of criticism has been written as well on *Finnegans Wake* as a drama, a novel, a myth, with the result that there has been full discussion of the two poles of its linguistic structure—word, and total form—but little discussion of the center, the sentence and its immediate constituents. Yet it is a basic linguistic assumption that neither the meaning of the words nor the identity of the whole discourse can be established in any other terms than that of the utterance unit, or sentence.

As far as I can discover, the general opinion of critics is that the syntax of the *Wake* is the same as that of conventional English. This is, of course, a far different opinion than "*Finnegans Wake* is written in conventional English," which to my knowledge is held by no one. The evidence of the notebooks and first drafts,[2] which contain a large proportion of normal English sentences, is advanced to support the common opinion and, indeed, there is also the support of the final text, which contains several hundred sentences with normal English patterns. Yet there is something counter-intuitive about this, for a very large number of *Finnegans Wake* sentences, those, in fact, we tend to characterize it by (the first and the second on the first page, for instance), will not be accepted or responded to if delivered to a normal speaker of English—as the totality of sentences in most

English novels, and perhaps 95 per cent of the sentences in *Ulysses,* would be accepted and responded to. The normal-syntax theory forces us to say that the individual words in the sentences are responsible for this rejection. Doubting it may seem absurd to some—after all, what is there to a sentence but the words in it? The answer is, "the structure in it," and it is to this structure, or syntax, that we as speakers of English are far more sensitively attuned than to individual words. We don't expect to recognize every word we hear, our individual vocabularies running somewhat below 5 per cent of all the words that may be considered to be "in" the language, but we do expect to be able to recognize an English sentence when we hear one—that is, recognize the structure. And we always can, for the language has no sentence patterns we don't recognize, they being the necessary basis of any spoken language at any moment. We call a sentence (S) an English S even of we don't recognize the words, as long as the structure is all right (The slithy toves did gyre and gimble in the wabe), and we reject an S even if the words are all right, as long as the structure is wrong (In found old cats are flats ladies usually).

The second point I want to make, then, is that the syntax most characteristic of *Finnegans Wake* is not that of normal English, and thus its rules for S formation, necessarily existent on the theoretical basis I have described, differ in important ways from those of English. They may be called a distortion of English rules to a certain extent, but it must be borne in mind that we could if we chose call the rules of any discourse a distortion of those of English.

But before I go further with my own views, I might review what has been already said on the subject. Joyce's own remarks are necessarily of great interest, though we cannot expect from him, any more than from any other great artist, both the work and the underlying theory—and that's on the assumption he ever intended to formulate a theory, or was aware of the inner consistency of what he was doing with language. He said he was "au bout de l'anglais" [3] with *Finnegans Wake,* but even while at work on *Ulysses* he had said he needed a "language which is above all languages" [4] to escape the impossibility of expressing himself in English. He emphasized sound in composition, defending *Finnegans Wake* as music,[5] and astonished the Italian translater of ALP, whom he was assisting, by "caring more for sound and rhythm than sense." [6] Certain revisions testify to this: "Death banes and the quick quoke" (595.1–2) was first "Death banes and the still quoke"; then, presumably for internal rhyme, "Death banes and the unquick quoke"; the final change, "unquick" to "quick," improving the sound again but reversing the meaning. He clearly made use of Vico's assertion of history within language, the "use of etymology . . . to uncover the significance of events." [7] On this basis *Finnegans Wake* has from the beginning been compared to Vico's "ideal language." [8]

At the same time Joyce referred repeatedly to the language of *Finnegans Wake* as being that of sleep or dream: Ellmann tells us he defended the language of the book "in terms of the appropriateness of linguistic distortion to a book which traced the distortion of dreams," and stated that "I have put the language to sleep." [9] To Harriet Shaw Weaver he wrote, "One great part of human existence is passed in a state which cannot be rendered sensible by the use of a wideawake language, cutandry grammar and goahead plot." [10] *Finnegans Wake* itself tells us, with typical ambiguity, "this is nat language at any sinse of the world" (83.12). This concept of a night language has at least three aspects: it may be taken as essentially a Viconian language behind all languages; as the language of the unconscious, which is quite parallel if we take the unconscious in the Jungian collective sense; and as the language perceived in dreams (it is commonly asserted that the language of dreams is the language of the unconscious). From Jolas on, with his call for a "language of night" (*transition* 23.101) and the "word of the dream" (*transition* 15.15), on the basis that "obviously we do not use the same words while asleep as those we employ when awake," [11] this has become a critical commonplace—Hugh Kenner, for instance, calls *Finnegans Wake* language "largely the speech of dreams"; [12] F. G. Asenjo calls its sentences "oneiric"; [13] and Michel Butor calls the *Wake* "le langage du rêve." [14]

As a critical approach to the book, however, all this is unhelpful, perhaps even intellectually confused. If there is a language of the unconscious, collective or individual, no one has yet discovered it. The language of dreams is, on the other hand, very real—something many of us experience regularly, and it is used as a key to the unconscious by psychiatrists. But it is not a language, in any recorded case I can find, of any resemblance to *Finnegans Wake* language. The words and sentences dreamers hear are usually quite normal; I might even point out that this is the case when Joyce himself dreamed he saw Molly Bloom, for she said to him, "And I have done with you, too, Mr. Joyce." [15] It certainly is true, on the other hand, that *Finnegans Wake* contains *sleepy* speech, the relaxed articulation of those who are falling asleep, as in the case of the Washers at the Ford ("My foos won't moos," 215.34). It would hardly be possible to so characterize a large number of *Finnegans Wake* sentences. If Joyce meant, as some of his remarks might be interpreted, that he was writing a sleep or dream *of* the language, rather than the dream language of a human dreamer, he slips out of our hands— we can make no more comment on that *terra incognita* than on the collective unconscious as a linguistic source. But we can, and I suggest that we do, stop our blithe reference to *Finnegans Wake* as "dream language," as if there were such a thing in the outside world to which the novel at all corresponded. [16]

Of far greater interest is the episode from the making of *Ulysses* that Budgen reports, in which Joyce said he had the words, but was working on their order, to get "Perfume of embraces all him assailed. With hungered flesh obscurely, he mutely craved to adore." [17] What Joyce was doing was putting normal English words in an abnormal order, forming a deviant utterance by altering English syntax. Or was he? We cannot assume that he started with a normal English sentence; he may have started with the idea of using the syntax of another language, like Latin, or with a syntax of his own invention. *Ulysses* is only distantly comparable to *Finnegans Wake*, but I think this testimony is valuable for its indication that Joyce was not always putting together English S over which he then laid ambiguities. Clive Hart says Joyce worked from "relatively plain English" in the early chapter drafts, to "the complexities of the final text," but he notes at the same time that "many highly complicated sentences appear to have been written down in their final form without prior commitment to paper," [18] that is, without any demonstrable "plain English" starting point.

Early statements about *Finnegans Wake* language, some made during its composition by friends and acquaintances of Joyce, vary widely in accuracy and usefulness. The writers of *Our Exagmination* offer comments the more valuable for Joyce's assistance in their composition (Ellmann, 626), but while they proclaim a "new language" [19] they give very few specifics. Samuel Beckett is perhaps the least helpful with his display of what might be called the Fallacy of Direct Apprehension, the idea that you can, and should, bypass words to get direct apprehension of the things they somehow, artificially (by what Beckett calls "sophistication") conceal. Thus *dubitare* is better than *doubt* because it *is* more doubtful, as a word! Beckett holds up as an example of the method Shakespeare's use of "fat, greasy words to express corruption" (*transition* 16–17.249) in the line "Duller shouldst thou be than the fat weed that rots itself in death on Lethe wharf"—I suppose we could say that "fat" is a "fat" word, in which case it would have to be the greasy word too, unless we make "rot" greasy, for is there anything fat or greasy about Lethe, wharf, weed, or death? This kind of exaggerated phonetic symbolism has been reappearing, and being held up to ridicule, in every age; that Joyce appears to have toyed with it himself does not enable us to employ it on *Finnegans Wake*— we could only make discoveries like Beckett's about Shakespeare.

Eugene Jolas was capable of writing far more nonsense than Samuel Beckett ever was, but his "Revolution of the Word" theorizing is a mixture containing some perfectly good comment on artistic innovation in language. He too cites Shakespeare, but to make the point that the organic evolution of language is brought about by individual minds as well as by external conditions,[20] and he notes that Joyce's style is "aided by his idea to disregard the norms of orthodox syntax" (*transition* 11.114). Number seven of the twelve declarations in the Revolution of the Word proclamation reads "He [the literary creator] has the right to use words of his own fashioning and to disregard existing grammatical and syntactical laws." Jolas seemed unwilling to allow Marinetti any precedence in such theory, but there are striking and insufficiently explored resemblances here to the "parole in libertà" of the futurists and the attack on the "vecchia sintassi ereditata" of the 1912 *Manifesto . . . della letteratura futurista*.[21]

Other *Exagmination* writers, like William Carlos Williams, Robert Sage, and John Rodker, had parallel sentiments on the rightness and necessity of the new word,[22] while Robert McAlmon added a form of Language as Gesture theory by comparing *Finnegans Wake* to the dance, pure form that bears subconscious, rather than conscious, relations to meaning. "To him [Joyce] language does not mean the English language," says McAlmon, but he does not continue his argument in linguistic terms, except to pose an "esperanto of the subconscious" that escapes analysis.[23]

I might also mention Padraic Colum, whose "Notes on *Finnegans Wake*" (1941) [24] offer as explanation of the form of the novel the idea that it adds "a new dimension, the dimension of speech, to literature," and that a great part of this (human) speech is, in the normal course of events, nonsense. To continue Colum's argument, we might say that *Finnegans Wake* gives us speech communication as it really is, rather than as it traditionally has been in literature—full of redundancies, meanderings into side issues, and syntactic breaks, what H. A. Gleason calls Consultative Key.[25] This gives us a kind of start toward *Finnegans Wake* from ordinary speech, and it bears interesting possibilities for relating it to other modern art—specifically, the theory of repeated sentences that led Gertrude Stein into *The Making of Americans* and *A Novel of Thank You*, and Luis Buñuel beyond surrealism to the triumph of *El Angel Exterminador*.

To jump ahead into contemporary criticism of *Finnegans Wake*, that generally of the 1960's, we find again a central interest in the word, with comment on syntax rather indirectly put. When David Hayman speaks of Joyce's "growing facility with the new idiom, the language of the *Wake*,[26] we may have an indication of explicit *Wake* composition-rules from one in a very good position to judge, but Clive Hart makes the assertion (which I have indicated I feel to be generally accepted) that "Joyce makes no attempt . . . to break up the normal processes of word-association, nor to dispense with clause-structure, as do Stein, Jolas, or the Dadaists." [27] W. I. Thompson has compared *Wake* language to "word sentences" from agglutinative languages, and offered "superject" as a unit characterizing its combination of subject-experiencing and subject-of-experience.[28] More suggestive of *Finnegans Wake* structure, to my mind, is F. G. Asenjo's 1964 comparison of its sentences to catenative strings in which many words are used successively as the subject.[29] His demonstration of this interesting idea is frustrated by lack of any illustrative examples. Richard Ellmann's biography contents itself with a general identification of *Wake* language with "the word- and image-formation in the unconscious mind" (729-30), while Hugh Kenner, besides supporting the dream-speech idea, lends weight to Colum's assertion that the novel bases its style on people talking.[30] This association with common speech is borne out by the many bits of slang and dialect worked into the text, as well as by Joyce's attitude to sound and to reading the book aloud, but I don't think it carries us to any general description of the text. Like Kenner's assertion that "one of Joyce's modalities of composition is to keep in constant touch with the normal pace of breathing," [31] it founders on the empirical test I suggested at the beginning. I think there is a contradiction in what appears to have been (from the uncertain sources we have) Joyce's thinking on the matter, one treated as non-existent by the critics I have so far mentioned. That is, to move toward the spoken word, to stress phonetic reproduction of dialect, is to move in a direction counter to that of night language, the language of history and the unconscious, which is not a dialect but a hypothetical meta-language. The two cannot be discussed as if they were going on at the same time.

Bernard Benstock's *Joyce-Again's Wake* (Seattle, 1965) should be mentioned here for its assertion of phonetic *leitmotiven* in *Finnegans Wake* language, but I'd like to end this survey with a look at the main counter-attitudes, or anti-*Wake* language theories. Sean O'Faolain's emotional outcry about the wellspring of pure English defiled [32] was, or should be understood to have been, answered by Jolas. F. R. Leavis' fulmination against destruction of language [33] is worth pausing over only because he has been the most able critic to apply to *Finnegans Wake* the Fallacy of Invisible Language, a concept that dogs criticism and has even been subscribed to by some linguists, notably Edward Sapir. It is the idea that the truly great writer displays his work in a medium so transparent that you are never aware that it is there; your attention is never drawn to the language but always through it to the subject, as if such a thing could exist apart from the language. This is finally a linguistic misconception, that language is a replaceable counter system for an independent reality, that thought may be separated from language. It is an insidious lure, having successfully disguised itself for a century or two as the doctrine of the *mot juste,* and thereby come to be taken as a part of artistic dedication or "sincerity." Joyce very consciously worked in the opposite direction, which of course can be over-done—anything can—to result in a fascination with the sound, shape, or other non-semantic qualities of words. But when he told Budgen that a novel described in terms of its situations with-out a description of its words is not made worthy of attention,[34] he was not so much indulging an idiosyncracy as demonstrating an awareness of the real nature of a literary composition.

Archibald Hill, one of the surprisingly small number of lin-guists to write on the linguistics of *Finnegans Wake,* directed, in 1939, a withering blast at the Fallacy of Direct Apprehension, what he called "the denial of the arbitrary and social nature of language, and an affirmation instead that sounds and words are naturally and universally connected with things." [35] This is a fair charge, but Hill's application of it to the *Wake* comes down heavily upon certain of Joyce's more fallible remarks about lan-guage,[36] and emphasizes the private qualities of the puns. That the associative pattern set up by the puns is artificially limited by phonetic similarity is another fair charge—"Wall-straight" can bring in Wall St., but not Battery Park—but Hill's setting as a standard against the *Wake* a "conventional and disciplined En-glish" is unimaginative and restrictive, uncomfortably close to the schoolmaster's infatuation with "correct usage." Hill is quite right to say that there is "childish amusement" in the *Wake*'s lan-guage trickery, but quite wrong to rest his case there, as if *Sylvie and Bruno* had never been written.[37]

The most reasonable negative approach, and the last I wish to take up, is that of A. Walton Litz, who gives Joyce the benefit of very thorough textual study before sorrowfully concluding that the linguistic theory on which the *Wake* is based is unwork-able, that Joyce brought "his aesthetic ideal of 'simultaneity'" into a finally insoluble conflict with "the consecutive nature of

language." [38] The Imagist simultaneity in the *Wake* "can only be
appreciated by the reader after laborious exegesis" (p. 62); its
compositional pattern of "prolonged expansion" robs it of "that
sense of 'inevitability' or 'rightness' which is the sign of a con-
trolled narrative structure" (p. 62). Litz's study of Joyce's revisions shows an enrichment of reference "only at the expense of
obscuring some of the original (and important) meanings"
(91–2), which can only be taken as "an inherent defect in Joyce's
method" (92). These criticisms are too well founded in textual
study to be dismissed, nor can they be attacked from a basis of
linguistic theory. Except in one case, where Litz leaves his guard
down by decrying the fact that in Joyce "techniques tend to
exist for their own sake, *imposing* order rather than reflecting it"
(123). Surely this is what any great art does; there being no
possibility of an art reflecting order when we have yet to discover what that order is. Or as Hugh Kenner put it in his discussion of *Finnegans Wake,* quoting Gilson, "The mind does
not perceive . . . connections, it *prescribes* them." [39] It would
be quite wrong to think that the elemental method of *Finnegans
Wake* is any different from that of *The Golden Bowl,* or even
that of writing this sentence—a guess at order, and an attempt to
embody it.

But this does not answer Litz's charges. If they are to be answered, it can only be by taking a more rigid view of the ontol-
ogy of the drafts and revisions, rejecting them both as the shad-
owing forth of some *Ur-Wake* that might have been written in
conventional English, and as indications of meanings within the
changed, and seemingly obscured, text of the final version.[40]

My review has not covered a very large body of theory; there
remains a good deal that is applicable, but so far unapplied. I
have said I think too much past criticism has been limited to the
word; even so, what there is might be enriched by some further
word-theory. Leo Spitzer, in his "Linguistics and Literary History," [41] describes the "autonomy of the word" as a principle of

Renaissance style, tracing its subsequent history and showing how it is essentially averse to the concept of the *mot juste* (in turn a stalking horse for the Theory of Invisible Language). I think this is a basis for a demonstration of the true likeness between Joyce and Rabelais, which has been obscured in the past by such formulae as that Rabelais came to words through things, but Joyce to things through words,[42] as well as a good basis for treating *Finnegans Wake* in its own terms, instead of attempting to apply the norms of social communication to it. It is what Jolas said about the "autonomous vocable" over again, but now in a linguistic and historical perspective, with something more to go on than "arousing the hidden sources of the wonderful in the listener." [43]

To suit the wider philosophical approaches to the language of the *Wake*, there is a body of work by Indian grammarians that exceeds anything done in the West for scale and complexity. This is Sanskrit *dhvani* and *sphoṭa* theory, embodied in such works as the *Dhvanyāloka* of Anandavardana, the *Sāhityadarpaṇa* of Viçvanātha, the *Kāvyaprakāça* of Mammaṭa, and the *Sphoṭa-vada* of Nāgeśabhaṭṭa. Here is an elaborate classification of word and phrase by levels of suggestion, sound, and meaning, with reference to the literature Joyce used in part to construct his *Wake* framework. Sanskrit doctrine also includes a view of the word as an apparition of divinity, Brahma as *çabda*, that offers intriguing parallels to HCE as universal name, as well as the "yes" of *Ulysses* as a kind of AUM. Perhaps this kind of thing has already gone far enough in the West, however, with Michael Stuart's evocation of what he considers to be the magic word of *The Book of the Dead*, Flora's "sacralità della parola" in *Ulysses,* and McLuhan's "submerged metaphysical drama" of the words at the wake.[44] I think *dhvani* theory could, however, give a more rigorous form to such comments as W. Y. Tindall's, that Joycean words "express the overtones of experience while they fix its meanings and quality by rhythms." [45]

Of most importance to my present topic are the newer American theories of grammar, which during the 1960's have been increasingly applied to the investigation of literary style. While the sentence analysis of traditional grammar could very well be applied to *Finnegans Wake,* such analysis is essentially static, and not easily reducible to economy of statement. Transformational-generative grammar is so reducible, and it employs a model of sentence composition by ordered rules, out of an immediate constituent (IC) subcomponent, that may very well be the most accurate model of speech and writing that we have to date. Its leading proponent is Noam Chomsky, and its terminology is on the way to becoming standard in the United States. There are other grammars on the theoretical horizon, but they lack the suggestiveness, and the range of application, the work of Chomsky, Katz, Postal, Fodor, and others has given to Transformational. I am therefore going to place my suggestions about the language of *Finnegans Wake* within its general boundaries.

Starting with phonology, can we imagine writing a set of phonemic rules that will produce any and all of the phonological sequences of the *Wake?* There are clearly phonemes, and phoneme sequences, particularly consonant clusters, that do not occur in English: on the first page we could single out the thunderclap (sequences -raghta-, -tuonn-, dependent on the phonetic values we assign) and the word *pftjschute* (phoneme and phoneme sequence); on the third page *choruysh* and *jpysian* (both sequence and possibly phoneme too); and so on. I doubt very much, though, that there are more than 200 phonemes in the whole text. As small as that number is, it would mean four times the number of phonemes that could represent the main dialects of English. All of Joyce's own English phonemes must be there, but unless the others could be posed as allophonic and allographic—not phonemes at all but the product of contextual rhyming and eye devices, a factor of the punning—we have at the outset of our grammar an indication that it may be strongly variant from English.

The morpheme stock of *Finnegans Wake* is as fully undetermined, even though it has been the subject of a great deal of study. For I use *morpheme* in the sense "smallest meaningful unit"; figuring out what the words mean is therefore a process of assigning readings to morphemes. In using our own language this is a matter we handle with varying success: so many speakers conduct the "in" of "inflammable" with the "in" of "infirm" rather than with that of "inflammation" or "inflammatory," that most danger signs for combustibles now read "flammable." Yet our morpheme "in" can only be given two readings, location and negation; a speaker of English giving a reading to an unfamiliar word containing it has a 50 per cent chance of being right. A word like "chortle" poses many more possibilities, several hundred if it is understood that it is composed of English phoneme sequences taken out of context, but kept in left-right order. "Chuckle" and "snort" are its components, but we could guess "church," "wart," "turtle," "chart," "horticultural," and so forth. What then, if we were told we could draw on the morpheme stock of 29 languages (FW 470–1), that the phoneme sequences need not be in left-right order (as "eat" for "tea" or "corpse" in "cropse"), *and* that word boundaries will not necessarily be indicated? I don't think it is sufficiently appreciated that under such conditions the guesses we could make are quite astronomical in number. If we take "redissolusingness" (143.14) as an example, we have 17 letters (the problem of phoneme identification set aside), of which one occurs 5 times, 3 occur twice, and the others once. The total number of permutations, or ways these seventeen letters can occur together, is then

$$\frac{17!}{5! \times 2! \times 2! \times 2!}$$

or 370 billion, 515 million, 717 thousand six hundred. Unreal, isn't it? No one has yet directly suggested that Joyce permuted on the order of 17; if they do, they might keep that figure in mind! The common form that reading such words takes is pulling out shorter sequences, those we presume to be the parts of a compound, as we might feel ready to identify the "un, -im-, -peach-, -able" of "unimpeachable" in other combinations. If we approach "redissolusingness" in this way, and limit each combination to three letters as a typical syllable, we then have $(17P3 = 17 \times 16 \times 15 =)$ 4,080 possibilities, or, if we allowed no syllable to repeat a letter, $(10 \times 9 \times 8 =)$ 720. That is still impossibly large. Let's take the extreme simplification of reducing "redissolusingness" to the six left-right syllables we would count if it were a standard English word. If we then set out to match those six to the phonemic/graphemic shapes of like morphemes in the 29 other languages Joyce is known to have used at one point or another in the text, taking a figure of 10^5 morphemes in each language, of which we count on 100 bearing similarity to any one of the six syllables, we would have a network of nearly 20,000 morphemic items *bearing on each other*. The possibilities are again impossible to visualize. There must be some way to keep the process in bounds, other than running out of paper on which to write, or saying "No, Joyce couldn't have had that in mind." Joyce had obviously so much in mind that many critics seem to welcome an infinity of readings: Campbell and Robinson assured us that "there are no nonsense syllables in Joyce! His language means so much that any intelligent reader can shave off some rewarding layers of meaning. The clarity and scope of the discoveries will depend almost wholly on the perception brought to bear"; [46] Bernard Benstock tells us the word "Joax" has "infinite possibilities" of interpretation; [47] Clive Hart, in a discussion that expresses "dismay at the incoherencies" of unscholarly readings, can nevertheless assure us that there is "ultimately . . . no such thing as an incorrect reading of FW," for it contains "an infinite regress of planes of meaning." [48] Talk about infinity upsets me; I find perfectly finite numbers like 370 billion already far beyond anything that can make sense in *Finnegans Wake*. There is nothing in such theory to prevent me from finding the contents of my 1968 income tax return in *Finnegans Wake*. Common sense generally prevents such aberrations; it governs the principles Professor Hart sets out at the end of the passage I quoted from above. But there is, it seems to me, a way of incorporating a limitation on morpheme identification into a *Finnegans Wake* grammar. That is, to refuse all readings that treat a word as if it had no context, to force the *Finnegans Wake* word back into the *Finnegans Wake* sentence. I propose the following rule:

> No reading may be assigned to a morpheme unless such reading satisfies the selection restrictions (SR, both semantic and structural) of another morpheme on the same or higher level in the constituent structure. That structure may be numbered up to the longest S form without regard to textual punctuation, and in cases of phonetic similarity may be considered to include S of greater distance from the morpheme in question.

This is best illustrated by examples: in "O, felicious coolpose" (618.1), *culpa* cannot be assigned without the support of "felicious" on the same level. Then, with "O" on a higher level, we have a three part structure of phonetic resemblance to several other occurrences, equally derived

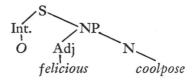

from "O felix culpa," in the text. The rule would allow, with this information, the reading of "culpa" from a single occurrence of "coolpose" elsewhere in the text, but not in any other circumstance. In "the tembo in her tumbo" (209.11), the example that has engaged the attention of Messrs Hart, Dalton, and Wolff, the SR would allow any noun (N) that can co-occur with "the" and "in her N_2." Phonetic similarity with Swahili "elephant" then allows that reading, along with the SR of "game" (N-animate, non-human) in the preceding S. That "tumbo" may be read as another Swahili word gives equal level support, though once we find that "palmwine" is another possibility for *tembo*, we may drop "elephant" and its "game" collocator for this choice, referring to the SR of "pepper-," "Saas," and "specis" to derive more comfortable contents for a stomach. The rule allows either reading, but would strongly resist either "elephant" or "palmwine" if the S had "I tembo red" without any support from elsewhere in the text.

When we have readings for morpheme strings the reinforcement is a simpler matter: "dimdom done" (594.6) has a slight phonetic resemblance to "kingdom come" but the rule will not allow such a reading unless something as close as "*dumdim dung" appeared elsewhere in a clearly religious and Christian passage. Actually the religious context is here; the next (equal level) IC is "till light kindling light has led." So with "brid and breakfedes" (597.16–17), where phonetic similarity to "bed and breakfast" is far from convincing, but the matching SR of "bread" [brId] and "coushcouch" (bed), and the higher level constituent ". . . a story" allow it.

What of a one word S, like "Svap" (595.30)? A Sanskrit reading, "sleep," has been offered here, but nothing in the surrounding S supports it, though they can't help but allow it, since they have independent IC trees. The occurrence of "svapnasvap" (597.4) with the full Skt. noun, and supported by "sleep" and "rolywholyover" in the preceding two lines, establishes it there, and on that basis the rule allows the reading at 595.30.

What kind of reading will the rule reject? One like "punkah wallah" from "the penic walls and the ind" (156.3),[49] where the superior C, "he reproved it . . . by the binomial dioram and . . ," are hardly satisfied by such a reading, there is no phonetic resemblance, and the more distant C reinforce Egyptian rather than Indian reference. The lexicons of non-English words that have been published for *Finnegans Wake* are apt to give further negative examples because they do not deal with sentences, and their authors have a natural tendency to find what they set out to find. Brendan O'Hehir's preface to his *A Gaelic Lexicon for Finnegans Wake* (Berkeley, 1967) states that he finds he can keep adding to his word list, and that it is not his responsibility to prove the relevance of what he finds. What he has given us is very good, but a word list sustained on such principles could grow indefinitely, as I hope I have shown. Helmut Bonheim's *A Lexicon of the German in Finnegans Wake* (Berkeley, 1967) makes very reasonable statements in the preface about employing the context when in doubt about a reading, but the entries themselves proceed to make assignments on the basis of phonetic likeness alone. To derive *lottern* "loaf" (V) from "clottering down" (5.3), which follows "clittering up" (the skyerscape) is to ignore the SR of every C in the S so that a phonetic resemblance may be followed. So *Räder* "wheels" for "raiders" (6.18) of "There was plumbs and grumes and cheriffs and citherers and raiders and cinemen too." The equal level C all dictate N-animate (they all joined in the wake), and the phonetic distortion indicates food; the insertion of *Räder* gives it a double plural and goes against every SR. *Held* "hero" from the "beheld" of 55.24 is just as unconvincing; "beheld" there is acting as the normal English V-trans., with an object. To read something like "be a hero" would be to break up the sentence.[50] To the objection "Why can't it be both at the same time?" I can only answer that that way lies the land of the 370 billion.

Under the same heading I would consider Lith. *bulve* "potatoes" for "bullugs" (180.24).[51] Not only is phonetic resemblance slight, but we are here in a long list where the equal level SR indicate "part of the body," as "the lump in his throat . . . the itch in his palm . . . the tickle of his tail . . . the bane in his bullugs." Couldn't we settle for "ballocks" and go on from there?

Several other matters involved in the grammar should be noted before I go on to the sentence, such as what exact form the SR would take. It is obvious that they cannot be nearly so restrictive as those in a grammar of English, for they have to allow totally deviant readings of morphemes when those readings are founded in a phonetically similar sequence elsewhere in the text. This can be done because *Finnegans Wake* is a closed system; it has to be done because of the way Joyce uses repeated word and phrase themes. Secondly, do the morpheme sequences like compound words have a regular structure; is their composition a matter of statable rules? Again, I feel sure that it is, that there are such rules: Professor Litz, for instance, states that "The compounding of words in *Finnegans Wake* followed a number of rigid self-imposed 'rules' which Joyce seldom violated." [52] He gives two of them, but also shows how Joyce did violate the second, "the original or 'base' words must not be completely obscured in the process of deformation." [53] I think further rules are behind the relation of compound-formation to the stress pattern of the including sentence ("halfaloafonwashed" 159.27), the use of phonetic spelling, generally in the direction of folk etymology ("Mildew Lisa" 40.17), and relaxed articulation ("respassers" 594.14, "addle" 4.28), as well as a recursive introduction of similar sounds ("anzanzangan" 389.01, "wickerworker" 559.06, "rhubarbarorum" 555.24).

Third, what form do *Finnegans Wake* phrase structure (PS) rules take? That they diverge from those in any natural language grammar follows from *Finnegans Wake* sentence form, as I hope to outline; I think they always allow variation so as to incorporate titles, sayings, poetic lines, songs, and names into the surface structure, carrying on the principles laid down by Lewis Carroll: "Happy, happy, happy Small! . . . None but the Short, none but the Short, none but the Short enjoy the Tall!" [54] In the matter of *Finnegans Wake* poetic prose, however, I find that the principle on which assignment of poetic form is currently made can, once again, lead us into a near-infinity of readings. If the last line in a section of ALP is "rare dactylic octometer," with no support from the next-to-last line, and the "basic verse structure for the *Wake*" allows "almost infinite variation within the line," [55] we might better pause to consider the few thousand poetic patterns, a foot or so at a time, to be seen in the text of this paper, or in the telephone book. A rule like the following is stringent, but it provides convincing readings:

> A *Finnegans Wake* stress or pitch pattern may be identified with a poetic line if either of the following conditions are satisfied: (a) it is repeated in 3 or more contiguous S nodes, (b) it carries morphemic resemblance to a line or lines of poetry within a poetic tradition on which *Finnegans Wake* draws in at least 2 other instances.

The second condition includes the numerous poetic parodies, like "old stile and new style and heave a lep onwards" (347.13–14); the first will exclude stray half-lines with only pitch/stress resemblance to poetry.

Since the sentences of the *Wake* are so far from normal English sentences, I have made use of Chomsky's criteria of *grammaticality* and *acceptability* to divide them into types, adding to those another, *understandability*, to suit the nature of a work of literature. The combinations into which these three fall are the following:

$$
\begin{aligned}
&\text{(a)} \quad G \ \ A \ \ U \\
&\text{(b)} \quad {-}G \ \ {-}A \ \ {-}U \\
&\text{(c)} \quad {-}G \ \ A \ \ U \\
&\text{(d)} \quad G \ \ {-}A \ \ {-}U \\
&\text{(e)} \quad G \ \ {-}A \ \ U \\
&\qquad \ \ \ G \ \ A \ \ {-}U \\
&\qquad \ {-}G \ \ A \ \ {-}U \\
&\qquad \ {-}G \ \ {-}A \ \ U
\end{aligned}
$$

I shall use the prefixed lower case letters as shorthand for the S types; "—" means "lacking quality so prefixed"; the last three types are unassigned because you do not fail to understand an S that you accept, nor do you understand one you fail to accept. This is why Chomsky does not need the third criterion, it being linked to the second in speech situations. Reading a text of great complexity brings in a type (e) that requires the distinction.[56]

Type (a) G A U are those S grammatical, acceptable by a native speaker, and understandable: "John plays golf"; "Sincerity frightens John"; "Cats are usually found in old ladies' flats"; "Read next answer" (167.26–7). For *Finnegans Wake* a type (a.2) must be added, that is (a), now (a.1), with morpheme distortion—by compounding, semantic overlay, and such: "Toumbalo, how was I acclapadad!" (347.26–7); the only difference here is that the understanding is a little more difficult. In the case of "But what a neats ung gels!" (361.16–17) we are on the borderline of losing the U.

Type (b) —G —A —U, ungrammatical, unacceptable, and nonsensical, for which in *Finnegans Wake* we shall substitute "fully difficult to understand," must also be subdivided. Chomsky's "Furiously sleep ideas green colorless" I shall call (b.1), morphemes and lexical items recognizable, but they could not be used in any other structure to derive an acceptable sentence. The form (b.2) is the same but with morpheme distortion, lexical items unrecognizable: "Reebly lup tomps frzz ardless"; (b.3) has recognizable lexical items, and could be rearranged to form an acceptable S: "In found old cats are flats usually ladies." *Finnegans Wake* is well provided with such (b) types: "Be who, farther potential?" (115.20) is (b.1); "Whilesd this pellover his finnisch" (325.12) is the more common (b.2), as is "Thingman placeyear howed wholst somwom shimwhir tinkledinkledelled" (346.26–7); "Not offgott affsang is you, buthbach? (346.23); and "A hov and az ov and off like a gow!" (346.21–2). In none of these can an English structure be derived, because the morphemes identifiable as English in each contain conflicting SR—in that sense such S are "ungrammatical," not in the sense of failing to meet some standard of usage. The form (b.3) is uncommon in *Finnegans Wake* because of the amount of morpheme distortion; examples like "He jumps leaps rising" (363.10) and "Harkabuddy, feign!" (346.25) must serve as partially conforming. In the latter, if we take "feign" as an English morpheme we are prevented from assigning a structure because that verb does not form an imperative. Taking "hark" and "buddy" as English verb and noun only makes it worse, but on the other hand we can rearrange the order of these items to get a grammatical, if unacceptable, string: "Feign harkabuddy," where "harkabuddy" would be made an NP by position.

Type (c), —G A U, ungrammatical but acceptable (because) understandable, includes Gleason's Consultative Key, common enough in spoken English. In shorter spoken examples, no IC tree may be derived, yet if a man crawled up to you in the desert and cried "Help water drink!" you would both understand and accept his sentence. Longer spoken examples have two or more IC structures that clash; there is a break in the middle, a changing-horses-in-midstream effect. An example I recently heard is "Remember when McCarthy was for president, at the convention, that night I watched TV for three nights in a row?" FW 360.19, "To which yes he did, capt, that was the answer" is a good example: the structure-break is easily bridged in the context; a speaker of English almost automatically derives "To which (question) he answer(ed), 'Yes, he did, Captain.' " Type (c) is thus like (a) in being typical of English speech and accurately reported English speech; type (c) is also fairly common in English novels. Note that such S cannot be very long, and cannot contain very much morpheme distortion; otherwise the lack of a grammatical derivation would quickly prevent understanding.

Type (d) G —A —U, grammatical but unacceptable (because) nonsensical (for which again we pose "difficult to understand" in *Finnegans Wake*), contains three subclasses: (d.1), without morpheme distortion but breaks in semantic SR (or lexical classification), contains S like "Golf plays John"; "Colorless green

ideas sleep furiously"; "John frightens sincerity." English structure is present—NP-Vtrans.-NP; NP-Vintrans.-Adv—and so
grammaticality, but rules like "N inanimate (Golf) does not take
V animate-actor (play)" are broken, so a hearer considers them
nonsense and will not accept them. FW 112.4, "It is a puling
sample jungle of woods," is an example: all C are recognizably
English and in place, but "a puling sample" and a "sample jungle"
are semantically divergent in the same way "frightens sincerity"
is.

Type (d.2) is the same as (d.1) but for morpheme distortion,
which in turn makes it difficult to comment on the SR. "The
slithy toves did gyre and gimble in the wabe," as I mentioned
earlier, is clearly grammatical English, but until we got help from
Humpty-Dumpty we'd assign it —U, or call it nonsensical. The
line between (a.2) and (d.2) can be difficult to draw, but such is
the nature of assigning readings in a living language. I find "Luck-
ily there is another cant to the questy" (109.01) a (d.2), along
with "Ere ore or ire in Aaarlund" (69.08) and "Het wis if ee
newt" (21.2). These could be assigned (a.2) on the basis of morpheme recognition those more skilled in reading the *Wake* might
find a simple matter, but we are not talking about understandability in the context "after special training."

Type (d.3) includes those grammatical S, with little or no
morpheme distortion or SR breaks, that are unacceptable because too difficult to understand, yet are possible to assign readings on a contextual basis. In speech situations some of these verge
on being an ambiguous (a.1) merely, like "John was frightened
by the new methods," or "The shooting of the men was awful."
A sentence like "We were in Tibet tonight" differs in that it is
not so much ambiguous as nonsensical—hearing it anywhere but
in a very restricted environment leads to annoyance and rejection, annoyance not dispelled, but replaced by contextual acceptability, when we find that the speaker is using a coy way of
telling us she and others saw a movie about Tibet from 9 to 11

that evening. Contextuality is also what operates to gain acceptability for most (c) types, and it is the principle I wish to note here, for *Finnegans Wake* has few (d.3)'s ("Your feet are in the cloister of Virgo" 26.13; "Now by memory inspired, turn wheel again to the whole of the wall" 69.5–6).

Type (e), G —A U, is grammatical but unacceptable, *although* understandable, a type of S that rarely occurs in speech. It deviates by demanding too much from memory; it can be understood by working out its parts on paper or in mental repose. It has two kinds, based on the two directions in which any English S may be developed: progressive or right-branching ("He knows what should have been included in the box he brought from the station"); and regressive or left-branching ("Very clearly projected pictures followed").[57] Right-branching gives structural cues as it goes along, but left-branching forces the hearer to store morphemes he cannot translate into a structure until the later parts of the S appear. An abuse of right-branching produces type (e.1), which must be a sentence that is simply too long to keep track of, since the structure is not hard to interpret. The amount of structural deviation in *Finnegans Wake* is such that most of its longer S fall into other categories, but that which travels from an uncertain start on page 287 to a kind of finish on page 292 ("you must, how, in undivided reawlity draw the line somewhawre") is (e.1), for it's generally not hard to understand, keeps to English structure, and develops it left-to-right as it progresses. It is totally unacceptable, however, as a spoken sentence. The first of the twelve questions in Shaun the Post, which runs from 126.10 to 139.13, is another example.

A type (e.2), on the other hand, need not be very long to be unacceptable, since it abuses left-branching. Witness "The man the boy who the students recognized pointed out is a friend of mine"; "What what what he wanted cost in New York would buy in Germany was amazing." "The howtosayto itiswhatis hemustwhomust worden schall" (223.27) is typical of shorter examples of left-branching in *Finnegans Wake* because it mixes in distorted morphemes and ungrammaticality (here German syntax); in the longer S, however, clear (e.2)'s occur as constituents. Question nine on page 143 has a leftward "if" clause that is developed for 225 words before we reach the head node of the question itself, "then *what* would that fargazer seem to seemself to seem seeming of, dimm it all?"; question eleven on page 148 develops 4 leftward "if" clauses for 13 lines before reaching the head node; the S "So in the names of the balder and of the sol . . . whimwhim" on page 331 never does reach a clearly superior node, but it repeats leftward elements for 13 lines again.

A closer look at the structure of some typical longer sentences can give further illustration of the types mentioned: following "So in the names of the balder . . ." we find structure assignable to a left-adverbial C until we arrive at "mensuring the megnominous . . . [comma] the myrioheartzed. . . ," where there seems little choice but to take what follows as further objects of the verb "mensuring." But that brings us to the last C, "how Big Bil Brine Borumoter first took his gage . . ." with no way of deriving a total structure, since Adv-*how*-NP-VP-NP is deviant and unacceptable. *How*-NP-VP-NP has a leftward tie, but the leftward part of this S does not fit it. The type is thus (b.1).

The S in Butt's speech (345.30–3) is a good example of how semantic layering in the *Wake* style causes shifts in structure derivation. It reads "Theres scares knud in this gnarld warld a fully so svend as dilates for the improvement of our foerses of nature by your very ample solvent of referacting upon me is boesen fiennd." For "Theres scares knud" two constituents immediately assert themselves for the speaker of English: "There is" and "scares knud" with "knud" as N-obj. This gives the highest level of ungrammaticality. A rereading of "scares knud" as "scarce enough" gives a grammatical leftmost C, "There's scarce enough in this gnarled world," but it cannot be joined in upward branching to the rightmost C, "is boesen fiennd." The type is thus (b.2).

Joyce's revisions are generally taken to indicate a steady progression away from normal English, and on the whole this is true. The chronologically arranged versions of ALP that Professor Higginson has prepared [58] show mostly types (a) and (c) at the beginning, while the last additions, including those made after the Higginson F text, are more often (b.2), like "We'd be bundukiboi meet askarigal" (201.24–5), or (d.2) "But the majik wavus has elfun anon meshes" (203.31). Higginson's D text, page 48, has a type (a.2), starting "Well, old Humber was as glum as a grampus. . . ," which retains its progressive structure throughout the revisions, but by the time it appears in FW 198.29–199.9 so many C have been added that it is type (e.1), and barely that considering the difficulties of its distorted morphemes. The S that ends as FW 202.23–6 is a somewhat parallel example. In the Higginson A text it reads "She says herself she hardly knew who he was or what he did or where he crossed her" (p. 25). The first change comes in the C text (p. 39), where we find the object of V-t "know" has been expanded from 3 clauses to 4 by "or how young she was," and the last clause has grown from "where he crossed her" to "when and where and how often he crossed her." The S remains (a.1) and progressive, but grows more complex. The D text (pp. 50–1) introduces the first structural anomaly: "how young she was" becomes "how young she played," which can be assigned a grammatical reading, "how young she pretended to be," without much hesitation. In the E text, however, morpheme distortion occurs, along with SR breaks, and reading becomes much more difficult: A text "who he was," in texts B-D "who her graveller was," now becomes "whuon the annals her graveller was, a dynast of Leinster, a wolf of the sea"; while "how young she played" has become "how blyth she played," and "how often he crossed her," "jumped her" in D, has become "jumpned her." The F text makes this "jumpnad her" and the reading "V-t" can now be made by position in the string alone. Finally, we have the addition "jumpnad her and how it was gave her away"—a new C with no clearly assignable subject. The S is now strung between (c) and (b.1): "She sid herself she hardly knows whuon the annals her graveller was, a dynast of Leinster, a wolf of the sea, or what he did or how blyth she played or how, when, why, where and who offon he jumpnad her and how it was gave her away." It has employed a PS rule of the recursive type NP (in string VP [V-t plus NP]) → NP plus NP to expand rightward, and shed the grammaticality of its first version by subject deletion and morpheme distortion.

The ALP section was from the beginning one of the simpler and linguistically more normal sections of the *Wake;* readers have managed to get the gist of it from the beginning. It is worth noting that in the first drafts of other sections there are numerous (b), (d), and (e) sentences along with the (a) and (c) types. The first question in I,vi, previously mentioned as an (e.1), is an (e.1) in the first draft, running on for 26 lines, but in *Finnegans Wake* it has grown to enormous length by another recursive PS rule, of the form VP (in string NP-VP) → VP plus VP; VP→VP plus VP. Butt's speech of FW 346–7 occurs in the first draft as two S, the first (a.2), "It was somewhile in Crimealian war, somewhere in Ayerland"; the second (d.2), "And I was during me weeping stillstumns . . . and heave a lep onward." [59] In the final version S$_1$ has been expanded to (e.1) by the addition of clauses, and the same process had made S$_2$ an extended (d.2). The common element here is expansion, the ungrammaticality being original. A first draft (a) that is still (a) in the final text is rare.

The variations *Finnegans Wake* plays upon its quotation from Edgar Quinet give another view of Joyce's practice with sentences: the original [60] appears on page 281; its structure is easily reproducible in English syntax. A temporal C (*Aujourd'hui*) plus a comparative (*comme aux temps de Pline . . .*) plus NP—Vintrans—locative, which is echoed twice (*la jacinthe se plaît dans* . . .), this making up an inner S_1 connected by *et* to an inner S_2, which is temporal C (*pendant qu'autour* . . .) plus subordinate NP—Vtrans—NP plus NP (*les villes ont changé* . . .), paralleled by a second NP—VPpass—Vpp (*civilisations se sont choquées* . . .); then NP (*générations*) plus Vtrans—NP (*traversé les âges*) paralleled by Vintrans—loc (*arrivées jusqu'à nous*), the *nous* serving as a semantic tie to the beginning of S_1 (an improvement introduced by Joyce), with an ending of Pred Adj (2) (*fraîches* . . .) plus Temp-comp (*comme aux jours* . . .). The first parody, FW 14–15, "Since the bouts of Hebear and Hairyman . . . ," follows the Quinet structure quite closely, but carries on the process we have seen in the revisions of Joyce's own S: another NP—VP constituent is added in S_1, and its V is distorted ("fairygeyed"); S_2 opens with a C unassignable to its structure ("though for rings round them") and adds two new NP—VP elements to Quinet's two after the temporal clause.

"Since nozzy Nanette tripped palmyways . . ." (117.16–30), the second parody written, begins and ends in the Quinet manner but severely deviates from the inner structure by introducing both regressiveness and IC breaks. The latter prevent part-of-speech identification of the ambiguous or distorted morphemes like "wet . . . eve . . . talkatalka . . . smelt." Structure ties have given way to semantic ties, of the form "*Aujourd'hui . . . nous,*" but extended. The main one is fire . . . turf . . . peat . . . clay; one of the secondary ones is (naughty) . . . peaties . . . pot/ wet . . . poules . . . (rear)end . . . marryings. The third parody, "Since the days of Roamaloose and Rehmoose . . ." (236.19–32), is closer to the original than the first or the second; it develops the same IC expansion as the first but does not introduce IC breaks. The fourth (354.22–36), "When old the wormd was a gadden . . . ," makes five S out of Quinet's one and only shows it is a parody at all by word-echoes like "plinnyflowers." Nevertheless, it breaks structure in four out of the five S, mainly by morpheme distortion. The last parody, "Our wholemole mill-wheeling vicociclometer . . ." (614.27–615.10), takes Joyce's other main tack, lengthening out in the direction of (e.1).

The last parody is also truffled with HCE tags, "heroticisms, catastrophes and eccentricities . . . highly charged with elec-trons . . . hophazards can effective," and it might be claimed that they do as much to unite sound with sense as the undermined IC structure can manage. They extend outward through many other *Finnegans Wake* sentences, and in so doing serve as inter-S ties. To that extent, some readings that we cannot derive from the S themselves may be derivable from elsewhere in the book. There is a parallel to this in the type (c) and (d.3) situation already de-scribed; information from surrounding S can even provide partial readings for (b.2)'s like "With my how on armer and hits leg an arrow cockshock rockrogn" (353.20–1), where left and right C contain suggestions of shooting and the victim's identity. But Joyce did not write such S just to throw the weight of reading onto word association, acronymic tags, and the structural con-text. One reason I think he might have had for doing it was to prevent unconscious reading, the careless absorption of his text. If the syntax were normal in *Finnegans Wake,* one could read the words, both normal and abnormal, into the usual IC structure slots, making filler identification by slot knowledge. The struc-ture, and thus predictability, of the slots must therefore be broken up to enforce attention upon the semantic layering that is going on. *Finnegans Wake* is set against the invisibility of language, and also against the invisibility of the structure of language. In that Joyce took the extra step beyond Dodgson, Nabokov, or Ionesco.

More to my point in this paper is that, with the restriction of (a) and (c) types to short sentences, the many short sentences that are (b) or (d), and the inclusion of all longer sentences in (b), (d), or (e), it must be concluded that *Finnegans Wake* is strongly deviant from English. Although it uses the syntax of other languages, it is probably closer to English than to any other language, and therefore it cannot be considered to be written in any real, or natural, language, in the speech of any group. The *Exagmination* writers were not so far from the truth: *Finnegans Wake* is qualitatively different, with a grammar of its own, not cutandry English grammar decorated with polylingual puns, and until we establish its rules we cannot move on to a mastery of the whole. "Don't start furlan your ladins till you've learned the lie of her landuage!"

NOTES

1. J. R. Pierce, *Symbols, Signals and Noise* (New York, 1961), p. 23.
2. Notwithstanding Clive Hart's point, that "many highly complicated sentences appear to have been written down in their final form without prior commitment to paper" *A Wake Digest* (Sydney, 1968), p. 5.
3. Ellmann, p. 559.
4. Ellmann, p. 410.
5. Ellmann, p. 393.
6. Ellmann, p. 646. In a similar vein, A. Walton Litz, in his *The Art of James Joyce* (London, 1961) says "*Finnegans Wake* is not 'like' music, it is a kind of music" (p. 71), and quotes Daiches' remark that "Joyce endeavours to use words like musical chords"; he concludes "Joyce has relied almost entirely upon the 'musical' qualities of his language to establish initial communication" (p. 126).
7. Ellmann, p. 565.
8. So Stuart Gilbert, writing in *Our Exagmination . . .* (Paris, 1929), stated that *Finnegans Wake* is the "mental vocabulary" Vico attempted, "whose object would be to explain all languages that exist by an ideal synthesis of their varied expression"—so Joyce achieved the "synthesis of language and history" that Vico dreamed of (p. 54).
9. Ellmann, pp. 716, 559.
10. *Letters* III, 146.
11. "The Revolution of Language and James Joyce," in *Our Exagmination*, p. 91.
12. *Dublin's Joyce* (Bloomington, Ind., 1956), p. 278.
13. "The General Problem of Sentence Structure: An Analysis Prompted by the Loss of Subject in *Finnegans Wake*," CRAS, VIII (1964), 398–408.

14. "Esquisse d'un Seuil pour Finnegan," NNRF, 60.1033–1053 (Dec., 1957).

15. As related by Gorman, *James Joyce* (New York, 1948), p. 283. I have come to this conclusion by questioning individual dreamers, including practicing psychiatrists, who listen to many thousands of other dreamers' dreams. My own survey of the literature gives me no grounds to doubt their report: the dreams related in Freud's *Traumdeutung*, for instance, contain sentences like "Ich sage ihr: Wenn du noch Schmerzen hast, so ist es wirklich nur deine Schuld" (edition Fischer Bücherei, 1961, p. 98), "Ihr Mann fragt: Soll man das Klavier nicht stimmen lassen" (p. 162), "Es ist doch merkwürdig, daß auch Leute, die sonst tutelrein sind, solche Angelegenheiten nicht zu behandeln verstehen" (p. 249). The indirect discourse Freud uses to report many dream speeches is perhaps indicative of the experience many, if not nearly all, dreamers have of understanding, rather than hearing, the speeches. The dreams Jung published appear equally normal in syntax; recent publications like L. L. Altman, *The Dream in Psychoanalysis* (New York, 1969) lists many dreams containing speech, but all normally patterned sentences.

16. Margaret Schlauch made this point in 1939; she has not been sufficiently attended to—see her "The Language of James Joyce," *Science and Society*, III (Fall 1939), 482–497.

17. *James Joyce and the Making of Ulysses* (London, 1934), p. 20.

18. *Wake Digest*, p. 5.

19. E.g., Marcel Brion, "Joyce has created his own language" (p. 29); Eugene Jolas, "language is being born before our eyes" (p. 89); Robert Sage, "it is not surprising that Joyce should have had the idea of . . . creating a language" (p. 157).

20. *Our Exagmination*, pp. 80, 84.

21. Reprinted in Verdone, *Cinema e letteratura del futurismo* (Roma, 1968), pp. 213–18.

22. See Harry Crosby, "The New Word," *transition*, 16–17 (June, 1929), p. 30.

23. "Mr. Joyce Directs an Irish Word Ballet," in *Our Exagmination*, pp. 105–116.

24. In *Yale Review*, XXX (March, 1941), 640–645.

25. *Linguistics and English Grammar* (New York, 1965), p. 359.

26. *A First-Draft Version of Finnegans Wake* (Austin, Texas, 1963), p. 8.

27. *Structure and Motif in Finnegans Wake* (Evanston, Ill., 1962), p. 31.

28. "The Language of *Finnegans Wake*," SR, 72 (1964), 78–90.

29. See note 13.

30. *Dublin's Joyce*, pp. 304, 319.

31. *Dublin's Joyce,* p. 309.
32. "The Cruelty and Beauty of Words," *Virginia Quarterly,* IV (1928), 208–225.
33. "Joyce and 'The Revolution of the Word'," *Scrutiny,* II (1933), 193–201. "Mr. Joyce's liberties with English are essentially unlike Shakespeare's. Shakespeare's were not the product of a desire to 'develop the medium to the fullest,' but of a pressure of something to be conveyed. . . . That is Shakespeare's greatness: the complete subjection—subjugation—of the medium to the uncompromising, complex and delicate need that uses it. Those miraculous intricacies of expression could have come only to one whose medium was for him strictly a medium, an object of interest only as something that, under the creative compulsion, identified itself with what insisted on being expressed. . . ." A better example of "The message is not the Medium" and Thought-as-having-nothing-to-do-with-Speech could hardly be found in 20th-century criticism.
34. *James Joyce and the Making of Ulysses,* p. 180.
35. "A Philologist Looks at *Finnegans Wake,*" *Virginia Quarterly,* XV (1939), 650–656.
36. Such as that about *Leib.* It's only fair to Joyce to say that there is some conscious, and some unconscious, association of sound to thing in natural languages, and also a good deal of support for rather exaggerated views of its extent and importance from linguists. For a good survey see Roger Brown, *Words and Things* (Glencoe, Ill., 1958), pp. 110–156.
37. Hart, *Wake Digest* p. 6, gives a good reply to such criticism of *Finnegans Wake,* which he sees lurking within even the appreciative writings of Professor Jack Dalton.
38. *The Art of James Joyce,* p. 56. Further reference in text parentheses.
39. *Dublin's Joyce,* p. 317.
40. Brushing aside the fact that some of the revisions go beyond the final version, since they were misplaced and never incorporated!
41. In *Linguistics and Literary History* (New York, 1962), pp. 1–29.
42. J. M. Cohen, as quoted by Ellmann, p. 2. The opinion is common, and is founded on a type of the biographical fallacy.
43. *transition,* 16–17 (June 1929), p. 29.
44. Michael Stuart, "Mr. Joyce's Word Creature," *Symposium,* II (Oct., 1931), 459–469; Francesco Flora, *Poesia e Impoesia nell' Ulisse di Joyce* (Milano, 1962), p. 194; Marshall McLuhan, "James Joyce: Trivial and Quadrivial," *Thought,* XXVIII (1953), 75–98.
45. *James Joyce* (New York, 1950), p. 3.
46. *A Skeleton Key to Finnegans Wake* (New York, 1944), p. 360.
47. *Joyce-Again's Wake* (Seattle, 1965), p. 203n.

48. *Wake Digest,* pp. 4, 8, 12.

49. *Joyce-Again's Wake,* p. 34n.

50. Hart, *Wake Digest,* p. 7, speaks of parsing as "a grave literary sin," so perhaps he would take the opposite view here. If that is his meaning, I would only point out that such a view amounts to allowing any reading, and throwing away the one safeguard against formlessness.

51. M. J. C. Hodgart, *Wake Digest,* p. 61.

52. *Art of James Joyce,* p. 71.

53. *Art of James Joyce,* p. 72. Cf. p. 92.

54. *The Works of Lewis Carroll* (London, 1965), p. 498.

55. *Joyce-Again's Wake,* p. 157, with quote from William Troy.

56. Clive Hart's statement (*Wake Digest,* p. 7) that acceptable readings need not make sense (in any ordinary way) would require using the first two of the types I have left empty—if it were applied rigorously. I prefer to leave it in a gray area, along with the question of whether or not "every *Wake* syllable is meaningful" (Campbell and Robinson; Hart).

57. Examples adapted from Victor Yngve, "Computer Programs for Translation," *Scientific American,* 215 (1964), 68–76.

58. *Anna Livia Plurabelle: The Making of a Chapter* (Minneapolis, 1960).

59. Hayman, *First Draft,* pp. 183–6.

60. The original, that is, with some misquotations. For this information and the chronology of the parodies I have drawn on Hart, *Structure and Motif,* pp. 182–200.

Characteristic Sentence Patterns in Proteus and Lestrygonians

Erwin R. Steinberg
CARNEGIE-MELLON UNIVERSITY

W HEN AN AUTHOR uses the stream-of-consciousness technique for several characters in a novel, he presents the reader, presumably, with the unique contents of the individual mind of each character. It is simple enough for an author to provide different ideas for the mind of each character, just as authors have always had particular characters voice particular ideas. Thus, just as Joyce has Stephen talk about philosophy, so he has him think about it; just as he has Bloom talk about Molly's tours, so he has him think about them.

To what extent, however, does Joyce simulate a different cognitive style for each character? To what extent does his individuation of his characters depend upon his using special language or a unique rhetoric for the stream of consciousness of each? To answer this question, I have examined and compared two stream-of-consciousness chapters in *Ulysses:* Proteus, for Stephen's stream of consciousness; and Lestrygonians, for Bloom's. That examination showed very clearly that the streams of consciousness of Stephen and Bloom both evidence characteristic—indeed, highly idiosyncratic—sentence patterns.

For example, Lestrygonians has many examples of a type of sentence that one usually associates with the Irish, in which part of the predicate of the sentence comes at the beginning rather than at the end of the sentence.

Forty-one instances of this type of sentence appear in Lestry-gonians:

149.26	151.26 [1]	Phosphorus it must be done with.
150.07	152.08	Underfed she looks too.
150.08	152.09	It's after they feel it.
150.34	152.37	The flow of the language it is.
151.10	153.12	Live on fleshy fish they have to . . .
151.25	153.28	Good idea that.
152.15	154.18	Powerful man he was at storing away num-ber one Bass.
152.19	154.23	Like that priest they are this morning . . .
152.39	155.02	Well out of that ruck I am.
152.39	155.02	Devil of a job it was collecting accounts of those convents.
153.28	155.34	Rabbit pie we had that day.
153.30	155.35	Snug little room that was . . .
153.33	155.38	Funny she looked soaped all over.
155.21	157.29	Pleasure or pain is it?
156.27	158.38	Philip Beaufoy I was thinking.
157.34	160.04	Wrote it for a lark in the Scotch house, I bet anything.
158.21	160.33	Strong as a brood mare some of those horsey women.
158.24	160.36	Stonewall or five-barred gate put her mount to it.
158.28	160.41	Didn't take a feather out of her my handling them.
158.32	161.02	Mayonnaise I poured on the plums thinking it was custard.
158.41	161.11	Hardy annuals he presents her with.
159.10	161.22	Three days imagine groaning on a bed with a vinegared handkerchief round her fore-head . . .
159.12	161.24	Dreadful simply!
159.14	161.26	Kill me that would.
159.17	161.29	Nine she had.
159.30	162.01	Funny sight two of them together, their bel-lies out.
160.05	162.18	Mackerel they called me.
160.20	162.34	Pupil of Michael Balfe's wasn't she?
160.26	162.39	That horse policeman the day Joe Chamber-lain was given his degree in Trinity he got a run for his money.

163.36	166.08	Those literary ethereal people they are all.
164.23	166.40	Terrific explosions they are.
165.36	168.12	Thick feet that woman has in the white stockings.
166.03	168.21	Great chorus that.
168.39	171.16	Hot fresh blood they prescribe for decline.
169.23	172.01	Hygiene that was what they call now.
173.25	176.05	Pillowed on my coat she had her hair . . .
173.29	176.08	Ravished over her I lay . . .
173.34	176.13	Flowers her eyes were . . .
179.01	181.27	Weight. Would he feel it if something was removed.[2]
179.02	181.28	Queer idea of Dublin he must have, tapping his way round by the stones.
180.17	183.03	Power those judges have.

This Irish type of sentence is to be expected of Bloom, who was educated in regular Irish schools, who mixed in every-day Irish circles, and who was seldom subjected to accents other than the Irish. Although the reader may not be aware of it, this type of sentence in Bloom's stream of consciousness provides a distinguishing characteristic. The Irish flavor that it imparts is one of the many features that go to make up in the reader's mind the pattern that is Bloom.

The thoughts of Stephen, who had a more formal education, who had teachers and acquaintances who were English, who had read considerably in English literature, who traveled generally in educated circles, who spoke of his nationality and language as nets he would "try to fly by," and who had been abroad—Stephen's thoughts show, as might be expected, very few sentences of such a construction—in fact, only three in the whole of *Proteus*:

38.07	37.07	Bald he was and a millionaire . . .
42.18	41.20	About the nature of women he read in Michelet.
48.20	47.27	Morose delectation Aquinas tunbelly calls this . . .

Another characteristic of the structure of a good many sentences in Bloom's stream of consciousness is what may be described as condensation. Each of the sentences below, all of the examples of this type found in Lestrygonians, reads as if it were composed of the main elements of ideas that would normally be expressed in several sentences; in each of these condensations, however, these elements have all been rolled together awkwardly into a single sentence:

149.21	151.22	Where was that ad some Birmingham firm the luminous crucifix?
150.25	152.28	Elijah thirty-two feet per sec is com.
154.04	156.10	Windy night that was I went to fetch her there was that lodge meeting on about those lottery tickets after Goodwin's concert in the supper room or oak room of the mansion house.
159.22	161.34	Whole thing quite painless out of all the taxes give every child born five quid at compound interest up to twenty-one, five per cent is a hundred shillings and five tiresome pounds, multiply by twenty decimal system, encourage people to put by money save hundred and ten and a bit twenty-one years want to work it out on paper come to a tidy sum, more than you think.
163.37	166.09	I wouldn't be surprised if it was that kind of food you see produces the like waves of the brain the poetical.
165.03	167.19	The full moon was the night we were Sunday fortnight exactly there is a new moon.
168.11	170.29	John Howard Parnell example the provost of Trinity every mother's son don't talk of your provosts and provost of Trinity women and children, cabmen, priests, parsons, field-marshals, archbishops.
168.28	171.05	After all there's a lot in that vegetarian fine flavour of things from the earth garlic, of course, it stinks Italian organgrinders crisp of onions, mushrooms truffles.
172.06	174.25	Wine soaked and softened rolled pith of bread mustard a moment mawkish cheese.

173.18	175.40	Glowing wine on his palate lingered swallowed.
173.20	175.41	Seems to a secret touch telling me memory.
173.21	175.42	Touched his sense moistened remembered.
173.25	176.05	Pillowed on my coat she had her hair, earwigs in the heather scrub my hand under her nape, you'll toss me all.
174.12	176.34	Lovely forms of woman sculped Junonian.
174.16	176.38	Bend down let something fall see if she.
177.17	179.41	They could: and watch it all the way down, swallow a pin sometimes come out of the ribs years after, tour round the body, changing biliary duct, spleen squirting liver, gastric juice coils of intestines like pipes.
179.22	182.06	The voice temperature when he touches her with fingers must almost see the lines, the curves.
180.01	182.28	All those women and children excursion beanfeast burned and drowned in New York.
180.03	182.30	Karma they call that transmigration for sins you did in a past life the reincarnation met him pikehoses.
180.42	183.27	Sir Thomas Deane was the Greek architecture.
181.05	183.32	He thrust back quickly Agendath.
181.11	183.38	His hand looking for the where did I put found in his hip pocket soap lotion have to call tepid paper stuck.

Much the same effect is given by sentences from which some of the words seem to be missing and seem, therefore, also to be condensations. Lestrygonians has five examples of this type of condensation:

150.01	152.03	A housekeeper of one of those fellows if you could pick it out of her.
153.23	155.29	She didn't like it because I sprained my ankle first day she wore choir picnic at the Sugarloaf.
168.09	170.27	Suppose that communal kitchen years to come perhaps.
171.41	174.18	Will I tell him that horse Lenehan?
172.26	175.04	Perhaps he young flesh in bed.

The awkwardness and the confusion of the condensation has even infected the omniscient author's sentences in Lestrygonians in four instances:

151.20	153.23	His eyes sought answer from the river and saw a rowboat rock at anchor on the treacly swells lazily its plastered board.
152.07	154.10	Mr. Bloom smilled O rocks at two windows of the ballast office.
165.12	167.28	With a keep quiet relief, his eyes took note: this is street here middle of the day Bob Doran's bottle shoulders.
174.19	176.41	A man and ready he drained his glass to the lees and walked, to men too they gave themselves, manly conscious, lay with men lovers, a youth enjoyed her, to the yard.

All of Proteus shows only two examples of condensation (as opposed to the twenty-nine in Lestrygonians):

42.41	42.01	Hunger toothache
49.03	48.11	Thanking you for hospitality tear the blank end off.

The difference in the frequency of this type of sentence in the two chapters again indicates for the reader a difference between Stephen and Bloom. It creates the effect of much more muddled thinking by Bloom.

A third type of sentence found often in Bloom's stream of consciousness, somewhat similar in effect to the condensed sentence but recognizably different in construction, is the accumulating sentence. Many of this type are merely a listing of perceptions, items, or ideas, generally with but sometimes without punctuation. The following are all the examples of the accumulating sentence in Lestrygonians:

PERCEPTIONS PILED UP
162.13	164.27	Houses, lines of houses, streets, miles of pavements, piledup bricks, stones.

162.18	164.32	Piled up in cities, worn away age after age. Pyramids in sand. Built on bread and onions. Slaves. Chinese wall.[3] Babylon. Big stones left. Round towers. Rest rubble, sprawling suburbs, jerrybuilt, Kerwan's mushroom houses, built of breeze.
165.35	168.11	Muslin prints, silk, dames and dowagers, jingle of harnesses, hoofthuds lowringing in the baking causeway.[4]
166.36	169.12	Perched on high stools by the bar, hats shoved back, at the tables calling for more bread no charge, swilling, wolfing gobfuls of sloppy food, their eyes bulging, wiping wetted moustaches.
167.12	169.30	Spaton sawdust, sweetish warmish cigarette smoke, reek of plug, spilt beer, men's beery piss, the stale of ferment.

No punctuation

154.13	156.19	Corner of Harcourt road remember that gust?
156.19	158.28	Pungent mockturtle oxtail mulligatawny.
165.28	168.03	She was twenty-three when we left Lombard street west something changed.
169.21	171.41	Cauls mouldy tripes windpipes faked and minced up.
173.04	175.24	Just as well to write it on the bill of fare so you can know what you've eaten too many drugs spoil the broth.
178.32	181.16	Keep his cane clear of the horse's legs tired drudge get his doze.
180.13	182.41	Police chargesheets crammed with cases get their percentage manufacturing crime.

Some of these sentences are accumulations of just visual perceptions: 162.13/164.27; 162.18/164.31; 173.12/175.33. Others are accumulations of several types of perception (i.e., visual, auditory, olfactory): 165.35/168.11; 166.36/169.12; 167.12/169.30. Of the sentences without punctuation, some seem to be a cross in effect between condensations and accumulations, single sentences that could properly be written as two sentences if portions of them were set off by terminal punctuation; for example:

165.28   168.03   She was twenty-three when we left Lombard street west something changed.

Or: She was twenty-three when we left Lombard street west. Something changed.

There are also sentences in Bloom's stream of consciousness in which words have been wrenched out of their normal order, but which seem to fall into no discernible pattern:

166.19   168.37   Perfume of embraces all him assailed.
166.19   168.37   With hungered flesh obscurely, he mutely craved to adore.
170.26   173.04   His midriff yearned then upward, sank within him, yearned more longly, longingly.
172.26   175.03   Was he oyster old fish at table.[5]
174.19   176.40   Dribbling a quiet message from his bladder came to go to do not to do there to do.

Where the accumulating sentences in Bloom's stream of consciousness are composed of items jumbled together without any apparent pattern, the accumulating sentences in Stephen's stream of consciousness are composed of parallel items in series—usually in threes—a characteristic of formal prose. Once again, then, the sentence structure aids in giving the reader different impressions of the personalities of Stephen and Bloom. Where the jumbled accumulating sentences of Bloom's stream of consciousness create the impression of muddled thinking, the nicely balanced parallels of Stephen's accumulating sentences give the impression of a person who thinks more carefully and more coolly. The parallel construction also suggests a more trained mind. Following are all the examples of accumulating sentences in Proteus:

38.02   37.02   Signatures of all things I am here to read, seaspawn and seawrack, the nearing tide, that rusty boot. Snotgreen, bluesilver, rust: coloured signs.
39.07   38.07   Belly without blemish, bulging big, a buckler of taut vellum . . .
39.19   38.19   With breaded mitre and with crozier, stalled

upon his throne, widower of a widowed see, with upstiffed omophorion, with clotted hinderparts.

39.23 38.23 The whitemaned seahorses, champing, brightwindbridled, the steeds of Mananaan.

40.33 39.23 Houses of decay, mine, his and all.

40.40 39.40 The oval equine faces. Temple, Buck Mulligan, Foxy Campbell.[6]

41.04 40.04 A choir gives back menace and echo, assisting about the altar's horns, the snorted Latin of jackpriests moving burly in their albs, tonsured and oiled and gelded, fat with the fat of kidneys of wheat.

41.08 40.09 And at the same instant perhaps a priest round the corner is elevating it. Dringdring! And two streets off another locking it into a pyx. Dringadring! And in a ladychapel another taking housel all to his own cheek. Dringdring! Down, up, forward, back.[7]

41.39 40.41 His boots trod again a damp crackling mast, razorshells, squeaking pebbles, that on the unnumbered pebbles beats, wood sieved by the shipworm, lost Armada.

42.04 41.06 Broken hoops on the shore; at the land a maze of dark cunning nets; farther away chalkscrawled backdoors and on the higher beach a dryingline with two crucified shirts.

43.23 42.25 Gold light on sea, on sand, on boulders.

43.24 42.26 The sun is there, the slender trees, the lemon houses.

43.26 42.28 Moist pith of farls of bread, the froggreen wormwood, her matin incense, court the air,

44.12 43.14 Maud Gonne, beautiful woman, *La Patrie*, M. Millevoye, Felix Faure, know how he died?

44.23 43.25 Got up as a young bride, man, veil, orangeblossoms, drove out the road to Malahide.

44.26 43.28 Disguises, clutched at, gone, not here.

44.36 43.38 Loveless, landless, wifeless.

44.38 43.41 Peachy cheeks, a zebra skirt, frisky as a young thing's.

45.17 44.19 Blue dusk, nightfall, deep blue night.

46.13 45.15 . . . my people, with flayers' knives, running, scaling, hacking in green blubbery whalemeat. Famine, plague and slaughters.[8]

46.18	45.21	The dog's bark ran towards him, stopped, ran back.
46.19	45.22	I just simply stood pale, silent, bayed about.
46.22	45.25	The Bruce's brother. Thomas Fitzgerald, silken knight. Perkin Warbeck, York's false scion, in breeches of silk of whiterose ivory, wonder of a day, and Lambert Simnel, with a tail of nans and sutlers, a scullion crowned.
46.42	46.04	Waters: bitter death: lost.
47.06	46.11	He turned, bounded back, came nearer, trotted on twinkling shanks. On a field tenny a buck, trippant, proper, unattired.
48.33	47.42	Bridebed, childbed, bed of death, ghostcandled.
49.28	48.37	She, she, she.
50.21	49.30	Vehement breath of waters amid seasnakes, rearing horses, rocks.
50.27	49.38	Day by day: night by night: lifted, flooded and let fall.
50.31	49.42	To no end gathered: vainly then released, forth flowing, wending back: loom of the moon.
50.37	50.05	Driving before it a loose drift of rubble, fanshoals of fishes, silly shells.
51.03	50.13	God becomes man becomes fish becomes barnacle goose becomes featherbed mountain.
51.14	50.25	My cockle hat and staff and his my sandal shoon.
51.35	51.04	Moving through the air high spars of a threemaster, her sails brailed up on the crosstrees, homing, upstream, silently moving, a silent ship.

Proteus begins and ends with these balanced accumulating sentences.

One other type of sentence is typical of Stephen's stream of consciousness—the appositive. Something like Bloom's Irish sentence in that it rises, pauses, and then falls, it is distinctly different in that the relative shortness of the appositive and the quick falling off tends to make the pause in Stephen's sentence much more abrupt. Where Bloom's Irish sentence goes ⸺⋀⸺ ,
Stephen's appositive sentence tends to go ⸺⋀ .
Lestrygonians has only one such appositive sentence (Nectar,

imagine it drinking electricity: gods' food [9]—174.11/176.33) as
opposed to the following twelve instances found in Proteus:

38.04	37.04	Snotgreen, bluesilver, rust: coloured signs.
38.07	37.07	Bald he was and a millionaire, *maestro di color che sanno*.
38.33	37.34	They came down the steps from Leahy's terrace prudently, *Frauenzimmer* . . .
39.06	38.06	Spouse and helpmate of Adam Kadmon: Heva, naked Eve.
39.18	38.18	In a Greek watercloset he breathed his last: euthanasia.
39.22	38.22	They are coming, waves.
40.40	39.40	The oval equine faces. Temple, Buck Mulligan, Foxy Campbell.[10]
46.11	45.14	Then from the starving cagework city a horde of jerkined dwarfs, my people . . .
47.34	46.41	Something he buried there, his grandmother.
48.05	47.12	With woman steps she followed: the ruffian and his strolling mort.
50.10	49.19	The foot that beat the ground in tripudium, foot I dislove.
50.33	50.01	Weary too in sight of lovers, lascivious men, a naked woman shining in her courts, she draws a toil of waters.

The steady rise and rapid fall of Stephen's appositive sentence
helps further to characterize Stephen. It supports the suggestion
of an ordered and efficient mind that the reader gets from the
accumulating sentence; for it shows a mind that gathers in a group
of people and then characterizes them precisely and efficiently
(38.33/37.32), a mind that views a scene or remembers an action
and comments on it neatly "in a formulated phrase" (38.04/37.04;
50.10/49.19).

Joyce's use of the colon in the two chapters adds to the impression that one gets from the appositive sentences that Stephen's
mind tends to observe or gather information and then comment,
characterize, or expand. In the fourteen pages of Proteus, Joyce
uses a total of fifty-eight colons, or slightly more than four to a

page. In the thirty-two and a half pages of Lestrygonians, however, he uses only seventy-five colons, or about two and a quarter colons to a page.[11] Thus, although Joyce seems to use the colon relatively heavily in both chapters,[12] he uses it much more heavily for Stephen's stream of consciousness than he does for Bloom's.

Most of the instances of the use of the colon by Joyce are aptly described by the following statements about the colon:

> The colon is a mark of anticipation, indicating that what follows the mark will supplement what preceded it. Its function differs from that of the semicolon, which is a stop, almost a period.[13]

> A colon is used between clauses when the following one is either an illustration of the first, a restatement in different terms, or an amplification of the first. . . .[14] [Joyce also uses the colon this way between words and phrases.]

This pause of "anticipation" is much like the pause in the appositive sentence described above. Indeed, three of the appositives in the list of sentences above contain colons to indicate the point of pause.

There are other examples of unusual usage, or sentence construction in both chapters:

BLOOM

155.07	157.14	womaneyes
165.10	167.26	quick breathing
165.12	167.28	a keep quiet relief
168.35	171.13	sheepsnouts bloodypapered snivelling nosejam on sawdust
169.22	171.41	windpipes faked
170.30	173.07	smellsipped

STEPHEN

38.05	37.05	Then he was aware of them bodies before of them coloured.
39.10	38.10	Wombed in sin darkness
39.17	38.17	contransmagnificandjewbangtantiality
39.23	38.23	brightwindbridled

41.02	40.02	see him me clambering down
43.07	42.09	loudlatinlaughing
47.09	46.15	His snout lifted barked
47.10	46.16	wavenoise
47.10	46.16	seamorse
47.32	46.38	pissed quick short
47.41	47.06	I am almosting it
49.23	48.32	Our souls, shame-wounded [15]
50.20	49.29	fourworded wavespeech
51.15	50.26	his my sandal shoon

And of reversals in the usual order:

BLOOM

172.31	174.31	His eyes unhungrily saw shelves of tins

STEPHEN

42.38	41.40	Proudly walking
43.25	42.28	Paris rawly waking
49.26	48.35	her hand gentle

Thus in fewer than half the number of pages, Stephen's stream of consciousness contains more than twice the number of unusual usages as Bloom's. The comparison again indicates a difference between the two men. To the careful reader, Stephen's playing with words suggests a man interested in language, a suggestion reinforced by other aspects of Stephen's stream of consciousness. Even the casual reader must pause long enough at such combinations as *contransmagnificandjewbangtantiality* and *loudlatinlaughing* to realize that here is a mind with interests different from Bloom's—and possibly from his own.

From the lists and discussions above, it is obvious that the streams of consciousness of Bloom and Stephen have different patterns. Over Bloom's Irish sentences, which serve as the underlying framework of Bloom's speech and thoughts, giving them some base, Joyce has poured jumbled sentences, sentences into which words and phrases seem to have been poured helter-skelter,[16] and sentences in which the normal word order seems purposely to have been violated.[17] Therefore, although Lestrygonians has, in

the arrangement of its omniscient author's sentences (which keep
the reader oriented) and in Bloom's Irish sentences, a basic framework, its immediate impact on the reader is one of disorder and
sometimes even confusion. The sentences characteristic of Stephen's stream of consciousness, however, have a very definite—
and usually measured—pattern: the a, b, and c type parallel construction, usually in triads. Above this basic pattern, other minor
patterns appear. Some sentences have a measured balance of rise
and fall: "Their blood is in me, their lusts my waves" (46.15/
45.17). Others have a more involved form, rising, pausing, falling,
and continuing on to rise and fall again: "He rooted in the sand,
dabbling, delving and stopped to listen to the air, scraped up the
sand again with a fury of his claws, soon ceasing, a pard, a pan-
ther, got in spousebreach, vulturing the dead" (47.35/46.41). The
effect of the carefully planned complexity of these sentences,
reminiscent, appropriately, of the classical languages, is broken on
occasion by the rapid fall of the end of an appositive sentence:
"They are coming, waves" (39.22/38.22). But even here, though
the break is sharp, it is orderly and not at all like the shifts in
Bloom's stream of consciousness, which often herald sharp changes
in direction or mere lumping together of ideas. Thus, what little
pattern there is in Bloom's stream of consciousness (the Irish sentence) is a folk pattern, whereas the pattern in Stephen's stream
of consciousness is an indication of training and education.

Further adding to the difference in effect between the two
streams of consciousness, the relative awkwardness of the structure of the sentences representing Bloom's thoughts as compared
to the balanced flow of Stephen's, is the fact that Bloom's are
shorter and thus give the effect of being more elementary. The
mean number of words per sentence in Lestrygonians is only
6.63, as compared to 8.14 for Proteus.[18]

What the critics have long indicated about the differentiating
"rhythms" or "styles" of Stephen's and Bloom's streams of con-

sciousness (but have not documented), this analysis thus finds evidence for. For example, in an early discussion of *Ulysses* (in 1931), Wilson said:

> Thus the mind of Stephen Dedalus is represented by a weaving of bright poetic images and fragmentary abstractions, *on a rhythm sober, melancholy and proud;* that of Bloom by a *rapid staccato notation,* prosaic but vivid and alert, *jetting out in all directions* in little ideas growing out of ideas.[19]

Some years later, Toynbee commented:

> In the early passages of *Ulysses* we have seen that there are already two distinct styles; there is the "high" language of Stephen, rich, *supple,* and poetical, and there is the "low" language of Bloom, earthy, colloquial, and *disjointed.*[20]

And a few years later, Tindall noted that:

> The monologue of each has a tone by which the quality of individual experience is discovered and *each has a proper rhythm.*[21]

The total effect of Proteus on the reader *is* different from the total effect of Lestrygonians. And this analysis shows that the difference is partly a result of the difference in distinguishing or typical sentence patterns—what the critics seem to be referring to when they speak of different "rhythms" or "styles."

At present it would be impossible to determine whether Joyce assigned in advance to Stephen and Bloom the sentence structures and patterns outlined above and then proceeded to employ them. None of his reported remarks or his available letters bears witness in this matter. We do know from his reported conversations and his letters that he was a painstaking workman, compared often to another master-craftsman and word-weigher, Flaubert, whose every line he had read,[22] of whose works he knew whole pages by heart,[23] and who he felt had done the best work in the novel.[24]

That Joyce felt that he was a master of the word is born out by such remarks as "I can do anything with language" [25] and by the audacity of *Finnegans Wake.*

Whether or not it can be said that Joyce intended to distinguish his characters by giving them different and characterizing sentence patterns, however, it can be said that the strong predominance of different types of sentence pattern for each of the two chapters helps to project for the reader different personalities for the two chief male characters of *Ulysses.*

And if there is no evidence of Joyce's intent here, there is evidence that bears not only on Joyce's interest in language in general, but on his writing of some of the specific sentences discussed above as characteristic. There is, for example, Budgen's well-known report of the following discussion with Joyce:

> I enquired about *Ulysses.* Was it progressing?
> "I have been working hard on it all day," said Joyce.
> "Does that mean that you have written a great deal?" I said.
> "Two sentences," said Joyce.
> I looked sideways but Joyce was not smiling. I thought of Flaubert.
> "You have been seeking the *mot juste?*" I said.
> "No," said Joyce. "I have the words already. What I am seeking is the perfect order of the words in the sentence. There is an order in every way appropriate. I think I have it."
> "What are the words?" I asked.
> [Joyce] ". . . there is a seduction motive in the Odyssey, the cannibal king's daughter. Seduction appears in my book as women's silk petticoats hanging in a show window. The words through which I express the effect of it on my hungry hero are: 'Perfume of embraces all him assailed. With hungered flesh obscurely, he mutely craved to adore.' You can see for yourself in how many different ways they might be arranged." [26]

We know, therefore, that the violation of the normal word order in at least two of the sentences listed above as wrenched sentences was deliberate.

The myriad changes in the Rosenbach [27] manuscript and in the galley proofs at the Houghton Library [28] supply further evidence that Joyce constantly sought the *mot juste* and was always experimenting with sentence structure. But they also show that, whether Joyce was conscious of it or not, his revisions strengthened the distinctive elements of Bloom's stream of consciousness, sentence patterns found typically in Lestrygonians but not in Proteus. Thus, of the forty-one instances of the Irish sentence culled from Lestrygonians, twelve were added either in the Rosenbach manuscript or later.[29] Had Joyce not added these sentences in revision or had he removed sentences of this pattern instead of adding them, Lestrygonians would have been less distinguishable from Proteus than it is. By that much, therefore, Bloom would have been less distinguishable from Stephen. Six of the condensations and accumulating sentences were also added between the time of the writing of the final handwritten draft and going to press.[30] Once again, therefore, Joyce's revisions served to strengthen two typical patterns of Lestrygonians. There is considerably less rewriting of Proteus in the manuscript and galleys, but even in that chapter, some of the sentences listed above as typical of Stephen's stream of consciousness were adjusted and revised.[31]

Perhaps a few striking examples of addition and revision would be helpful here:

IRISH SENTENCES

150.34	152.38	The flow of language it is [added in first galley].
160.05	162.18	Mackeral they called me [added in second galley].
179.01	181.27	Weight would he feel it if something was removed. [Reads this way in first galley, but Rosenbach manuscript reads: "Weight a line if something blackened man in dark. Wonder if he'd feel it if something was removed."].

CONDENSATIONS

| 173.25 | 176.05 | Pillowed on my coat she had her hair, ear- |

wigs in the heather scrub my hand under her nape, you'll toss me all [not in Rosenbach manuscript, but in first galley].

174.12   176.34   Lovely forms of woman sculped Junonian [read originally: Lovely form of woman bodies: "Junonian" substituted for bodies in Rosenbach manuscript; "sculped" added in second galley].

OTHER

174.11   176.33   Nectar, imagine it drinking electricity: god's food. [Sometime between the Rosenbach manuscript and the first galley, the word "like" was deleted from between "it" and "drinking."]

39.10   38.10   Wombed in sin darkness I was to . . . [changed in first galley from: "Wombed in darkness sin . . ."].

The point of this discussion is not merely that Joyce added and revised endlessly, but that he made many and significant additions and revisions of sentences and paragraphs that now seem to be characteristic of the stream of consciousness of Bloom and that these additions and revisions strengthened the patterns typical of Lestrygonians rather than weakening them. All this of course still does not prove that Joyce was aware of the difference between the two over-all patterns that he was building, but it does suggest that the possibility of such awareness might profitably be considered in the light of new evidence as it arises.

NOTES

1. Means page 149, line 26 in the 1934 Random House edition of *Ulysses* and page 151, line 26 in the 1961 edition.
2. The 1934 edition reads: Weight would he feel it . . . .
3. The 1934 edition reads: Slaves Chinese wall.
4. The 1934 edition reads: Muslin prints silk . . . .
5. The 1934 edition reads: Was the oyster . . . .
6. The 1934 edition reads: The oral equine faces, Temple . . . .
7. This passage is not a single sentence, of course. It illustrates, how-

ever, the use of three parallel items in series characteristic of Stephen's stream of consciousness.

8. The 1934 edition reads: and slaughter.

9. The 1934 edition reads: god's.

10. The 1934 edition reads: The oval equine faces, Temple . . . .

11. Joyce's revisions helped to increase this difference in the number of the uses of the colon between the two chapters. In the manuscript and galleys, Joyce changed two semicolons in Proteus to colons (50.13/ 49.22; 50.28/49.38), but did not strike out any colons or change them to any other type of punctuation. In Lestrygonians, however, Joyce changed one comma to a colon (164.24/166.41) and added a colon (165.12/167.28); but he also changed a colon to a semicolon (162.03/ 164.18), changed six colons to periods (150.05/152.06; 160.12/162.25; 163.16/165.30; 167.40/170.15; 170.33/173.10), and simply took out five other colons (162.04/164.18; 155.09/157.15; 168.09/170.27; 178.33/ 181.17; 179.22/182.06). His revisions, then, added two colons to the total in Proteus and subtracted ten from the total in Lestrygonians. (The page and line numbers given above in this note indicate the beginning of the sentence in which the punctuation referred to occurs and not necessarily the line on which the punctuation itself appears.)

12. That the colon is not necessarily a concomitant of the stream-of-consciousness technique can be seen by comparing the figures for the use of the colon in Proteus and Lestrygonians with the number of uses of the colon in the first section (sixteen and a half pages) of Virginia Woolf's *Mrs. Dalloway:* only three. Inspection of the rest of *Ulysses* indicated that the proportion of colons per page was about the same throughout.

Mrs. Woolf, however, used semicolons heavily in *Mrs. Dalloway:* 131 in the first sixteen and a half pages—almost eight per page. By comparison, Joyce used only four semicolons in the fourteen pages of Proteus and only four in the thirty-two and a half pages of Lestrygonians. A comparison of the use of the stream-of-consciousness technique by the two authors, a study beyond the scope of this one, might find this difference in punctuation a meaningful clue to differences between the authors' styles or concept formations. *Mrs. Dalloway* (New York: Harcourt Brace), 1925.

13. Porter G. Perrin, *Writer's Guide and Index to English.* (Fourth Edition) (Chicago: Scott, Foresman, 1965), p. 537.

14. Perrin, p. 537. Perrin also says, "Some writers prefer colons where most would use commas or semicolons" (p. 538). This statement applies to six of the fifty-eight colons in Proteus (41.30/40.31; 46.17/45.20; 48.22/47.30; 50.27/49.38; 50.28/49.39; 50.31/49.42) and to seven of the seventy-five colons in Lestrygonians (152.25/154.29; 155.28/157.37; 156.20/158.29; 162.12/164.26; 173.27/176.07; 178.23/

181.07; 180.05/182.32). Joyce's use of the colon where usage would call for a semicolon seems to indicate a fondness for the pause of "anticipation." In only one instance in the two chapters does Joyce use a semicolon where he could have used a colon (43.10/42.12).

15. The 1934 edition reads: shamewounded.

16. Condensations and accumulations.

17. Wrenched sentences.

18. These means were determined from six sample passages from each chapter. Statistical calculations show them to be significant on the .01 level. Such a level of significance means that we may be very confident that the difference is a true one and not attributable to sampling errors.

19. Edmund Wilson, *Axel's Castle* (New York: Scribner's), 1950, p. 204. The italics are mine.

20. Philip Toynbee, "A Study of *Ulysses*," in *James Joyce; Two Decades of Criticism*, edited by Seon Givens (New York: Vanguard Press, 1949), p. 271. The italics are mine.

21. W. Y. Tindall, *James Joyce* (New York: Scribner's, 1950), p. 42. The italics are mine.

22. Frank Budgen, *James Joyce and the Making of Ulysses* (New York: Harrison Smith and Robert Haas, 1934), p. 181.

23. Budgen, p. 176.

24. Budgen, p. 180. Many of the other major Joycean critics, Gilbert, Kain, Levin, Tindall, and Wilson, either compare Joyce's method of writing to Flaubert's, declare Joyce a student of Flaubert, or mention Joyce's high estimate of Flaubert.

25. Joyce is supposed to have made this remark to Eugene Jolas. Tindall, p. 95.

26. Budgen, pp. 19–20.

27. The original autograph manuscript of *Ulysses*, described in John J. Slocum and Herbert Cahoon, *A Bibliography of James Joyce, 1882–1941* (New Haven: Yale University Press, 1953), pp. 138–140.

28. See Slocum and Cahoon, pp. 141–142.

29. 150.34/152.38; 155.21/157.30; 158.28/160.40; 158.32/161.02; 158.41/161.11; 159.17/161.29; 159.30/162.01; 166.03/168.21; 173.25/176.05; 180.17/183.03.

30. 165.35/168.11; 169.21/171.41; 172.26/175.03; 173.04/175.24; 173.25/176.05; 180.13/182.41.

31. 39.10/38.10; 39.18/38.18; 39.19/38.19; 39.23/38.23; 44.12/43.14; 46.22/45.25; 48.05/47.12; 50.30/50.01.

The Text of *Ulysses**

Jack P. Dalton

HE MORE ONE VALUES a book, the more one should value an
authentic text of that book. After all, a book is first a collection of words, because "I gotta use words when I talk to
you." [1] We should want to know *what the author wrote*—which
is to say, what words he wrote and in what order, spelt how and
punctuated how. This concern has been well established for centuries in the case of classical texts, despite detractors, but it is
very far from well established in the case of modern texts. When

* I have delivered this paper on three occasions—on December 6-7, 1966
at Cornell University, as a lecture (entitled "Textual Criticism and James
Joyce") and a seminar; on May 10, 1969 at Marquette University as part
of the seventh annual American Committee for Irish Studies conference
(a 45-minute version); and on June 13, 1969 at Trinity College, Dublin,
as part of the Second International James Joyce Symposium (a 30-minute
version). The text printed here corresponds most nearly to that given in
Dublin, with documentation and some discursive comment added paren-
thetically and in notes. I have otherwise little altered its unabashedly
oral/aural nature.
   The research on which the paper is based was made possible almost
wholly by two Fellowships—1964-65 and 1966-67—granted me by the
John Simon Guggenheim Memorial Foundation, and by vital financial aid
extended both before and between the Fellowships by my parents, Dr
and Mrs Jack P. Dalton. For materials, facilities, and permissions I have
especially to thank the Lockwood Memorial Library of the State University of New York at Buffalo, as well as the British Museum, Cornell
University, the Rosenbach Foundation, the University of Wisconsin at
Milwaukee, Southern Illinois University, Eliot House Library (Harvard),
the Pierpont Morgan Library, John Hinsdale Thompson, Harvard University, Yale University, the University of Texas, and the James Joyce
Estate and the Society of Authors.

the classical scholar J. P. Postgate wrote on textual criticism for the 1911 *Britannica,* he concluded by saying: "In the newer texts, . . . as experience has already shown, it will have from the outset but a very contracted field." Postgate, I am afraid, was in effect speaking as "the average man" of whom A. E. Housman wrote (if we may merely change the word "ancient" to "modern"): "[The average man] believes that the text of [modern] authors is generally sound, not because he has acquainted himself with the elements of the problem, but because he would feel uncomfortable if he did not believe it; just as he believes, on the same cogent evidence, that he is a fine fellow, and that he will rise again from the dead." [2] What we casually assume of the text of a modern book is fairly well summed up by Thomas Marc Parrott in his handbook on Shakespeare: "Mr. Shaw, for instance, when he is ready to publish a play contracts for its appearance with a publisher, sends him a neatly typed manuscript, receives several sets of proof which he carefully corrects, and finally sees his work given to the world in a printed form as nearly accurate as human ingenuity and care can make it." [3] But it is a demonstrable fact that not all modern books were so lucky, and we can't tell which were and which weren't until we practice textual criticism on them. And Professor Parrott forgets reprint transmission, with its "remorseless corrupting influence" (in Professor Bowers's phrase).[4]

Several years ago I set out to do a certain job of work on *Ulysses.* Naturally I chose for my work a copy of the new, 1961 edition, for—so we were assured on the front flap of the dust jacket—this setting was "scrupulously corrected." Certainly it *needed* to be "scrupulously corrected," for the first American edition of 1934 could have come straight out of the bad old days and no questions asked. The learned judge handed down his famous decision on December 6, 1933, and Bennett Cerf says that ten minutes after he heard the good news he had his printers hard at work.[5] Unfortunately, the copytext which he had supplied them was afterwards discovered to have been a copy of Samuel Roth's type facsimile pirate edition, so much easier to come by in New York, where it was printed, than the authentic edition from France, and this pirate was one of the more notable scandals since Gutenberg started it all.[6] It contained thousands of corruptions, and few of them were removed by Cerf's printers and proofreaders. The ineffable nature of this edition should be clear to you from a noted corruption on the second page: the preposition "to" was left out (after "over") so that Buck Mulligan, from the top of the Martello tower, "went over the parapet, laughing to himself"—a surrealistic smashup for a major character who reappears in the next sentence, lathering up for a shave.

So, in 1961, after a quarter of a century, Bennett Cerf resolved to trade in his monster on a book. I bought a copy. I started to read. Hardly had I started to read before I found a word which appeared to be printed correctly in the old, corrupt edition and incorrectly in the new, "scrupulously corrected" edition. Presently I found another. In the meantime I had become greatly disturbed when I found the word "woeful" spelt without the "e."[7] This was ironic, for "woful" is common in England and turned out to be the spelling Joyce wrote. Anyway, it was new to me and I thought it looked awful, so I decided to see for myself what sort of "scrupulously corrected" edition this was. I read it through with care, noting things which seemed to me suspicious, and when these were checked against other editions and the autograph fair copy manuscript,[8] I had found almost 400 corruptions. I thought this a great number and prepared to publish them. Then I became busy with other things, and when I returned to that paper, I found myself very dissatisfied with the extent of my research, which had taken little more than a week. I set out to do more. Fifteen months later, I had increased my findings tenfold.

I had discovered some 4,000 corruptions in this "scrupulously corrected" edition.⁹ It was better than the old edition, yes, but it was certainly not good.

The situation, I found, was this: the old edition had been, of course, an early collateral descendant of the first edition, whereas the new edition was a lineal descendant. The new edition, far from being "scrupulously corrected," was merely a reprint, with some new errors, of the 1960 English resetting. It was the fifth successive resetting of type since the first edition; each edition had been copied from the one preceding. Some 1,700 errors had accumulated in thirtyfive years of resetting, and most of these errors were, in 1961, already at least twentyfive years old and had appeared in at least three successive settings. And then there were well over 2,000 corruptions which went back to the manuscripts, things which had *never* been printed correctly.

In other words, it was the kind of book you could use only a few minutes in a chemistry lab before blowing the place up. Do you think I exaggerate? Listen to this story from the *New York Times* of July 28, 1962: "FOR WANT OF HYPHEN VENUS ROCKET IS LOST. The omission of a hyphen in some mathematical data caused the $18,500,000 failure of a spacecraft launched toward Venus last Sunday, scientists disclosed today. The spacecraft, Mariner I, veered off course about four minutes after its launching from Cape Canaveral, Fla., and had to be blown up in the air." A hyphen! Not *precisely* relevant, of course, because none of the hyphens in *Ulysses* is worth $18,500,000 in hard cash. Too bad, because if they were, publishers would exert themselves with marvelous alacrity. In the reign of Charles I a Bible appeared in which the psalm ran: "The fool hath said in his heart there is a God." The printers were fined £3,000 and all copies were suppressed.¹⁰ Such stories are unfortunately very rare. Publishers are usually allowed to operate on the notion that to print up a thickish book with the word ULYSSES imprinted on its spine is to do the whole duty of man.

Let's look first at some of the things that reprint transmission has done to our book:

Early in the first episode Buck Mulligan leaves Stephen Dedalus alone on top of the Martello tower. The song he sings as he descends the stairs very powerfully brings to Stephen's mind obsessive memories of his dead mother. At the climax of this scene Stephen silently cries out to her, "No, mother. Let me be and let me live." The direct address becomes even more meaningful when we get to the end of the *Circe* episode, almost 600 pages away, where in a drunken hallucination the mother takes such possession of Stephen, she speaking to him and he to her, that he can exorcise her only by running amok and smashing a lamp. The 1960 printers, and therefore the 1961 printers, left out the comma between "No" and "mother," so that Stephen says, "No mother. Let me be and let me live." Without the comma, Stephen speaks not to the mother but to himself, saying that he will have no mother. "Only" a comma, you see, but its presence or absence determines the grammar of "mother," determines the syntax of the sentence, controls the meaning and tone of an intense page-long scene, and has considerable significance for a scene almost 600 pages away. Such is the effect of the first omitted comma, page 10, and I begin with it because of an observation a friend made on this paper: Well, you'll have to stay away from the commas and all, then, won't you?

So I won't. For example, Joyce wrote this sentence: "Funny, very." The 1926 printers left out the comma to read "Funny very," which is puzzling (629.19). Joyce wrote "whelks and money cowries and leopard shells," three kinds of shells, and the 1932 printers inserted a comma after "money" to read "money, cowries," which is puzzling indeed (29.38). And often more than literal sense is at stake. In the cemetery Bloom thinks: "Mamma, poor mamma, and little Rudy." The 1926 printers left out the first comma to read "Mamma poor mamma, and little Rudy." The sentence as Joyce wrote it is a profound sigh—"Mamma, poor mamma, and little Rudy"—and when the first comma was lost, most of the sigh was lost (111.13).

Before we leave punctuation I want to mention the exclamation mark with which Joyce ended the *Hades* episode (115.41). It hasn't appeared since the first printing of the first edition, 1922, when most of the stem was worn away. I won't say that the meaning of this powerful episode hangs on that final exclamation mark, nor the character of Bloom. Yet, once we're aware of it, it has a vital bearing on our grasp of both. Is this $18,500,000 worth? Not really. It's something better. It's priceless, because *Ulysses* is priceless.

Now for some words. Many people think of a misprint as being a non-word, perhaps because that's the only kind of misprint they ever notice. But non-words are rarely preserved in a text. The 1961 printers have Bloom beginning a *"long unintelligibe speech,"* but a succeeding printer could hardly fail to supply the missing "l" and set *"unintelligible"* (461.25). These misprints are not dangerous unless they allow of more than one resolution. The misprints that are most generally dangerous are the real words printed in place of other real words. The 1932 printers set "grilled beefsteaks" as "frilled beefsteaks," and the three succeeding printers have accepted this as perfect sense (108.17). The 1936 printers compare Molly's voice to a "thrust," where Bloom compared it to a "thrush" (93.28). The 1936 printers have Cashel Boyle O'Connor Fitzmaurice Tisdall Farrell "glasseyed": he is actually only "glassyeyed" (244.41). The 1936 printers have Mr Dedalus a "famous fighter": he is really a famous "father," as Lenehan has just said, the "famous father" of a "famous son" (262.33). The 1926 printers imagine a "Phila of cachous": it's a "Phial" (274.18). The 1936 printers attribute some infant mortality to "abnormal trauma": Joyce attributed it to "abdominal" trauma (419.8). The 1926 printers gave the two privates in *Circe* *"blond copper polls"*: Joyce gave them *"blond cropped polls"* (430.35). The 1926 printers have the Citizen imploring God to send down a "cove": the

Citizen wanted a "dove" (593.13). The 1961 printers write of conferring "a lasting boom on everybody concerned" rather than "a lasting boon" (633.23). The 1936 printers say that as a High School scholar, Bloom "had excelled in his table and protracted execution of the half lever movement on the parallel bars." The two succeeding printers have passed along this nonsense: what Bloom excelled in was his "stable" execution of that gymnastic feat (681.33).

Such changes are often the result of what is called trivialization or vulgarization. Here are some examples. Joyce wrote of Bloom "Drawing back his head and gazing far from beneath his vailed eyelids"—"vailed," a rare word meaning "dropped." [11] As is mentioned elsewhere (e.g., 57.12 and 71.28), Bloom is walking about in the hot, glary summer forenoon with dropped eyelids. But it was clear to the 1927 printers that no such word existed, so ever since, Bloom has gazed from beneath his "veiled" eyelids—whatever that could mean (74.6). In a passage of archaic English Joyce wrote of two nurses as "Watchers twey"—"Watchers twey there walk, white sisters in ward sleepless." The 1936 printers changed it to "they" (385.10). At one point in *Circe* Bloom "*Blushes furiously all over from frons to nates*"—from forehead to buttocks. The 1928 printers changed it to "*front,*" which ironically is cognate with "frons" (496.19).

A number of Joyce's special effects have been trivialized out of the text. For example, Bloom remembers his daughter Milly at the age of three lisping, "Me have a nice pace"—"pace" for "face." The 1926 printers "corrected" her defect (372.16). Stephen, wearing a pair of Buck Mulligan's castoff boots, thinks of his costume as "My cockle hat and staff and hismy sandal shoon"—"hismy." The 1926 printers split it into two words (50.26). In that part of *Circe* where Bella becomes a man and Bloom a woman and Bello puts Bloom up for auction, he, Bello, invites bidders to "examine shis points. Handle hrim," "shis" and "hrim" being amalgrams of the masculine and feminine pronouns, reflecting the momentary

ambiguity of Bloom's sex. The 1926 printers were not amused, so
ever since, the female Bloom has been referred to here with
masculine pronouns (540.8). A bit earlier in the episode Bloom
had gotten very bothered and confused and answered a question
with the reply "Nes. Yo." The 1936 printers knew one worth two
of that, and Bloom now answers "Yes. No." (527.28). In the last
episode Molly thinks about Paddy Dignam's funeral earlier in the
day and she names a few of those who attended. She begins with
"L Boom" and ends with "Fanny MCoys husband," both delicious
touches, for M'Coy wasn't there except in the newspaper and "L.
Boom" is the newspaper's styling and misprinting of her husband's
name. She saw the account, of course, in the paper Blazes Boylan
brought in, which is a touch, but not delicious. The 1936 printers
—butter, you know, wouldn't have melted in their mouths—set a
"correct" "Bloom" (773.26). One more example, from *Sirens:*
"Lydia for Lidwell squeak scarcely hear so ladylike the muse un-
squeaked a ray of hopk." This is supposed to be contrapuntal. Si
Dedalus is singing an aria from *Martha* in which the words "ray
of hope" have just occurred. One of the barmaids, Lydia, is
squeakily pulling a cork from a bottle. The work "hopk" is the
"hope" of the song combined with the work "cork," and very
nicely approximates—though better in the imagination than aloud,
perhaps—the sound of a cork being finally withdrawn. I don't
have to tell you that the 1926 printers changed it to "hope"
(275.2). Joyce's sketch for the word has been preserved: he wrote
down the words "hope" and "cork" and then began to scramble
their letters into a new word. The fourth experiment satisfied
him. This example has special interest because it points to *Finnegans Wake.*[12]

A number of words have been lost from the text in the course
of its transmission. For example, this passage from Stephen's
thoughts: "To Caesar what is Caesar's, to God what is God's. A
long look from dark eyes, a riddling sentence to be woven and
woven on the church's looms." ". . . to be woven and woven":

it suggests the hypnotic rhythm of weaving. But the 1961 printers lost it; it now reads quite matter-of-factly, "a riddling sentence to be woven on the church's looms" (26.17).[13]

Other words have been added *to* the text. For example, Buck Mulligan: "Joyfully he thrust message and envelope into a pocket." A "the" was added in 1961: "Joyfully he thrust the message and envelope into a pocket" (199.28). A small thing, at first glance, but the more you think about it the more you see how the most minute change blurs the unearthly precision of Joyce's prose.

I've picked these examples at random, with an eye only to their interest in the telling, but the sample has some statistical validity. In particular, it shows that many of the reprint transmission errors date from 1936, the first edition set in England. The publishers declared it "definitive." The 1932 edition had also been "definitive." And of course the 1961 edition is "scrupulously corrected." Right.[14] The mass of corruption introduced into that 1936 edition is now thirtythree years old, a third of a century, and has been faithfully preserved by the two succeeding printers. Before the limited 1936 edition was issued the following year in a trade edition, the publishers decided that their text fell short of "definitive," and they did considerable proofreading and correcting before photoreducing it. But when they came to reset it in 1960 they chose as their copytext the limited edition, no doubt because its type was so much larger and more readable. Thus the 1937 proofreading was bypassed and lost. One way or another, a mistake once is so often a mistake forever. This is what Professor Bowers means by "the remorseless corrupting influence that eats away at a text during the course of its transmission," and he is right in saying that "Only a practising textual critic and bibliographer knows."

You will remember I said that well over 2,000 corruptions had appeared in all editions from the first, in addition to the 1,700-odd corruptions which have accumulated since then. Practically speaking, these too—all but a handful of them—are errors of transmission. Transmission begins, actually, the moment the author makes a fair copy of a draft, and continues through typescripts and proofs into the first edition and then beyond. Now, *Ulysses* didn't have one of those modern publications of which Professor Parrott spoke so highly. First, the typescripts are a sickening lot. The typing is appalling, reflecting all too well the cheap labor and borrowed typewriters which Joyce scraped together here and there at odd times; and then Joyce made many, sometimes profuse, additions and revisions in his own ineffable handwriting. Second, the printing was done in Dijon, France, and, according to the foreman, not a single compositor (I have counted, incidentally, twentysix of them) knew English.[15] The foreman, Maurice Hirchwald, did, but not as a native speaker. He saw, what was true, that the typescripts could hardly be set as they were, with all their crude mistakes—misspellings, words run together, others pulled apart. He therefore began to edit them, and before long he had conceived himself God's gift to English literature. He laid a monstrously heavy hand on the book, and indeed continued to do so through the next decade as it went through eleven printings in two settings of type in the Darantière shop.[16] Joyce corrected many of Hirchwald's changes but missed many, many more. He received five successive sets of proof until the press of time cut it to three, and most of these proofs he loaded— often spectacularly—with additions, revisions, and corrections.[17] Had these French printers been provided typescript throughout, they would have given little trouble, but instead they were provided massive doses of Joyce's hand. Transcribing an unknown foreign language from cursive script—certainly Joyce's—is a job to make a man wish he'd never been born. The printers persistently misread a number of the letters, and these patches uncorrected look like nothing on earth.[18] Joyce protested that his words were being "crippled," [19] but the printers were doing their best— which was very, very good—with a bad job. Joyce did begin to write as plainly as he could. He even went so far as to notice that the printers were almost invariably misreading his "r," and he thereupon changed over, permanently, to the other form. But these measures did little good. By the end, as the bill records, the printers had spent nearly 2,000 hours in revising the proofs, all charged to Joyce, so that this single expense accounted for almost a fourth of the total cost of publishing the first edition. In the midst of this chaos Joyce was writing the last 120 pages of the book, *Ithaca* and *Penelope*. He described these labors in a letter: "I write and revise and correct with one or two eyes about twelve hours a day I should say, stopping for intervals of five minutes or so when I can't see any more. My brain reels after it. . . . I was going to take a fortyeight hour holiday somewhere but decided not to do so. If I lay down in some remote part of the country I am so tired that I should never have the energy to get up." In a later letter he said he was "nearly crazed with work," and in another that he was "working like a lunatic, trying to revise and improve and connect and continue and create all at the one time." [20] These descriptions can hardly be exaggerated. Week after week, month after month, the publication date was advanced, until Joyce at last fixed it on his birthday. It was a case of doing the impossible, and the first two copies arrived in Paris early that morning, only three days after the last batch of corrected proofs had arrived in Dijon. [21]

After being edified with this history you may wonder why there weren't *more* than 2,000 errors in the first edition. There were, hundreds and hundreds more, but they were removed through a geat deal of further checking by Joyce, Hirchwald, and others. But over 2,000 have remained to this day. Consider these few examples:

Bloom on the strand musing over the possibility of approaching Gerty MacDowell: "Suppose I spoke to her. What about? Bad plan however if you don't know how to end the conversation. Ask them a question they ask you another. Good idea if you're in a cart" (370.22–25). Do you follow that? Why is it a good idea if you're in a cart? I can worry a number of possibilities out of it, but they're all absurd. Here is the passage as the printers were given it in typescript: "Suppose I spoke to her. What about? Bad plan however if you don't know how to end the conversation. Ask them a question they ask you another. Good idea if you're stuck. Gain time. But then you're in a cart"; and the earliest manuscript reads: "Ask them a question they ask you another: then you're in a cart." [22] Both make it very clear what Bloom is getting at. He seems to think himself able to open a conversation, but he is held back by the fear of being unable to end it. You ask them a question, they ask you another: then you're in a cart. You know what the phrase means: an American equivalent is, you're in a jam. The compositor's eye skipped from the word "you're" in one line to the same word in the next line, losing the words between. Insofar as the present text makes any sense at all, its sense is opposite to the sense intended. Bloom naturally thinks it's *bad* to be in a cart. Our text says he thinks it *good*, with no explanation of why, nor of what sort of cart Bloom is supposed to have in mind.

The next example may seem at first sight a molehill by comparison, but I hope you'll perceive the mountain in it. It's the passage at the beginning of *Calypso* in which we first hear Bloom speaking to Molly:

> He said softly in the bare hall:
> —I'm going round the corner. Be back in a minute.
> And when he had heard his voice say it he added:
> —You don't want anything for breakfast?
> A sleepy soft grunt answered:
> —Mn. (56.20–25)

That is what Joyce wrote: "I'm going round the corner." But it's always been printed "I am going round the corner." Joyce wrote "I'm." His typist typed "I'am," an absurd but common error in these typescripts. The printers set "I' am." Joyce himself then deleted the apostrophe, in what he casually took for a routine proof correction.[23] But "I am" is not what Bloom said. This is not the way Bloom talks to Molly. If it were, we should have to revise our idea of their relationship. And the passage itself won't stand it. Bloom says "round," not "around." He says "Be back," not "I will be back." He says "You don't," not "You do not." What he says is, "I'm going round the corner. Be back in a minute. . . . You don't want anything for breakfast?"

Take this sentence from *Circe:* "*Pulling, the gasjet lights up a crushed mauve purple shade*" (584.18–19). "*Pulling*"? Joyce wrote "*Puling*," the sound the gasjet makes.[24]

Or the man searching his pockets for change to pay his outsider. Bloom, eager to watch the beautiful woman mount the car, impatiently wonders: "What is he fostering over that change for?" (74.14–15). "fostering"? Joyce wrote "foostering," a nice Anglo-Irish touch for Bloom. On the last set of proofs, after Joyce had read them, Hirchwald deleted one of the "o"s.[25]

Or this: "A warm shock of air heat of mustard hauched on Mr Bloom's heart" (172.42–173.1). "hauched"? There is no such word. Joyce wrote "hanched," a verb which means "to snap at or bite greedily or noisily" and fits perfectly into this episode, the *Lestrygonians,* even to the overtone of cannibalism: the typist simply read the "n" as a "u." [26] Bloom's heart is indeed being eaten, and not so much by the mustard as by the name "Blazes Boylan" in the preceding sentence. "A warm shock of air heat of mustard hanched on Mr Bloom's heart." Terrifyingly poignant.

Take this passage from *Eumeus:* "While the other [Stephen] was reading it [the newspaper] on page two Boom (to give him for the nonce his new misnomer) whiled away a few odd leisure moments in fits and starts with the account of the third event at Ascot on page three, his sidevalue 1000 sovs" etc. (648.15–18). One can only construe this as meaning that Bloom reads that one of the horses has a "sidevalue" of 1,000 sovereigns, and that "sidevalue" is a technical term in horseracing. But it isn't. In the two preserved manuscripts Joyce wrote "side. Value." The typist took the period for a hyphen and followed it with a small letter to read "side-value." Joyce corrected this on the three preserved copies of this typescript page, but either he failed to do so on the printer's copy or the printer failed to note the correction, because the printer set the typist's version—"side-value."²⁷ In the second setting of type in 1926 the hyphen was dropped, giving the present "sidevalue." Here it as as Joyce wrote it: "While the other was reading it on page two Boom . . . whiled away a few odd leisure moments in fits and starts with the account of the third event at Ascot on page three, his side. Value 1000 sovs" etc. Page three, in short, is on *his* side, which means he is sitting on Stephen's right.²⁸

Take this from *Eolus:* "Demesne situate in the townland of Rosenallis, barony of Tinnachinch" (119.1–2). There is no barony of "Tinnachinch." Joyce wrote, correctly, "Tinnahinch," but the printer read the "a" as a "c" and set "Tinnchinch." Joyce then directed that an "a" be substituted for the "c," but, since his substitution mark was a bit to the left, it seemed to the printer that Joyce wanted the "a" *inserted* before the "c." In "Tinnachinch," then, we have the correct "a" and the incorrect "c" preserved together, side by side.²⁹

And what of the "pasturelands of Lush and Rush and Carrickmines" in *Cyclops* (295.3–4)? Rush and Carrickmines, yes, but where is "Lush"? Joyce wrote "Lusk," correctly, but the typist read "Lush," and if you saw the manuscript you'd understand why.³⁰

In *Oxen of the Sun* we learn that Bloom as a youth lived in "Clambrassil street" (413.8). Joyce wrote it correctly, but it was mangled in the typing. Whether this was the typist's fault or the machine's I'm not sure, but there are two "n"s in the typescript, not one, the first extremely light. Joyce noted the mistake and crossed out the first "n" with a diagonal hyphen, his usual sign for closing up a space. The printer read it, however, together

with the second "n," as the ligature and first leg of an "m." Therefore "Clambrassil." [31]

What is one to make of this at the end of *Cyclops:* "And Ned
and J. G. paralysed with the laughing" (343.34)? Who is "J. G."?
And then you remember that one of the characters in the episode
is named "J. J." This, of course, is what Joyce wrote, what the
typist typed, and what the printer set. The type of the second
"J" was imperfect, however, so when reading over the last proofs,
Hirchwald crossed it out and wrote "J." The printer then read
this manuscript "J" as a "G." [32]

And what is one to make of this from *Lestrygonians*, Bloom
thinking about the blind stripling whom he has just helped across
the street: "Sense of smell must be stronger too. Smells on all sides
bunched together. Each person too" (181.40–41). Each person
what too? Bunched together? That's the best one can make of
the passage as it stands, and it's ridiculous. Joyce wrote, and the
typist typed, "Sense of smell must be stronger too. Smells on all
sides bunched together. Each street different smell. Each person
too." The printer's eye jumped from the first "Each" to the second, leaving out one sentence and thus making nonsense of what
remained. [33]

And all this mess is often vilely punctuated, whereas Joyce's
own punctuation, with the occasional careless lapse, was elegant.
Sometimes only the rhythm is destroyed, at other times the syntax
as well.

Did Joyce not see these corruptions in typescript and proof?
We can say only that they were present in the typescripts and
proofs he saw, and in the printed text when he read it after publication. He caught thousands and thousands of them, but he
missed some 2,000. I can show you many single words, misspelled
in several places, which Joyce corrected in one or two places but
not the others. [34] Joyce was always a poor proofreader, from the
beginning of his career to the end. Most writers *have* been poor

proofreaders. They are creators, not clerks.[35] Had you worked as long as I have among the manuscripts of *Dubliners*, the *Portrait*, *Ulysses*, and *Finnegans Wake*—and Joyce missed in *Finnegans Wake* over three times as many errors, at least, as he did in *Ulysses* [36]—you would find the whole question of his proofreading as silly and tiresome as I do. As Professor Bowers observes, the textual critic—one, at any rate, who has brains in his head instead of a cauliflower—realises that "approval by an author of a nonautograph copy can under no circumstances bestow on that copy the authority inherent in a true autograph original." [37] *Could it, we should be stuck with this hideously corrupt text almost as it stands, for Joyce also proofread the 1936 edition, and relatively few corruptions have been introduced since then.*[38]

What is to be done? I wish to say at this time only that I am under contract with Random House to edit the text of *Ulysses*. When this new edition will appear has yet to be settled. I have until 1979, if necessary, to perfect it.

Listen again, now, to J. P. Postgate's 1911 summation: "In the newer texts, . . . as experience has already shown, [textual criticism] will have from the outset but a very contracted field." It is precisely experience that shows us otherwise. Books of every age continue to need the skills and dedication of the textual critic, whose job is nothing more but nothing less than to rescue and protect from the injuries of chance and time those precious things which the makers have made.

NOTES

1. For the benefit of those who may not know, this engaging line is from T. S. Eliot's "Sweeney Agonistes."

2. Preface, Manilius I, p. xliii; also in *Selected Prose*, ed. John Carter (Cambridge: At the University Press, 1961), p. 43.

3. *William Shakespeare: A Handbook* (New York: Scribner's, 1934), p. 195.

4. Fredson Bowers, *Textual and Literary Criticism* (Cambridge:

At the University Press, 1959), p. 8. For two brief, authoritative accounts of textual criticism, both by Bowers, see the current *Britannica* and the Modern Language Association's booklet *The Aims and Methods of Scholarship in Modern Languages and Literatures.*

5. *Contempo,* 3 (February 15, 1934), 2.

6. R. F. Roberts, "Bibliographical Notes on James Joyce's *Ulysses*," *Colophon,* N.S., 1 (1936), 565–579.

7. At 4.25 (it also occurs at 25.32). The two words were "knifeblade" for "knifeblade" at 4.21 and "coat-sleeve" for "coatsleeve" at 5.31.

8. I.e., the manuscript in the Rosenbach Foundation, Philadelphia.

9. Obviously, not a precise figure. I know about how many file cards I have by the number of boxes they fill, I know that some of the cards represent multiple emendations, I know that some of the cards will be weeded out, and I know that I will be adding more cards to the lot.

10. It is known as the "Fool" Bible.

11. Undoubtedly one of the book's great number of *Hamlet* allusions: "Do not for ever with thy vailed lids / Seek for thy noble father in the dust" (1.2.70–71). Joyce used the same word in *Finnegans Wake* at 606.4, "when violet vesper vailed"—i.e., when evening fell.

12. Harvard proof 97.3 (i.e., third page of proofsheet bearing the handwritten number "97"), end of *Cyclops:*

> hope
> cork
>
> corpe [cancelled]
> p rh
> hoprk
> hopk

13. This passage is part of a series: "all them that weave the wind" (21.14) and "Weave, weaver of the wind" (25.20) precede it.

14. The 1936's flyer began with the words "Final and definitive edition." Authority unspecified. Notice that it was a throwaway, just as the dust jacket bearing the 1961's "scrupulously corrected" is a throwaway. The 1932 edition—the Odyssey Press edition—was bolder, printing on its copyright page this puff: "The present edition may be regarded as the definitive standard edition, as it has been specially revised, at the author's request, by *Stuart Gilbert.*" Joyceans have been glad to sink back onto this pneumatic bosom, seriously imagining Mr Gilbert to have collated manuscripts and otherwise filled the office of professional scholar. Mr Gilbert himself suffered under no such delusions. "As far as I recall I was asked to proofread the Odyssey

Press *Ulysses* by Holroyd Rees (owner of the flourishing Albatross Press, successor of Tauchnitz) or by his Paris manager, a youngish man called Wegner. . . . It was Joyce who advised the Odyssey Press (created ad hoc) to get me to look after the proofs. . . . I consulted Joyce re some of the doubtful points—including punctuation—when I was correcting proofs of the Odyssey Press *Ulysses*. I've no idea what's become of the proofs." So he wrote me on April 23, 1965. I returned him a xerox copy of the letter when requesting permission to quote, and after reviewing it he said, "it can stand." He added that "As far as I remember I used what was then the latest Shakespeare & Co edition and also my copy of the First, when correcting the Odyssey Press text of *Ulysses*. I certainly asked for, and received, revise proofs. The Albatross people did not, I think, try to rush me" (letter of December 27). But whatever Mr Gilbert did and didn't do, the word "definitive" is demonstrably farcical in connection with the Odyssey Press edition.

15. Letter from Maurice Hirchwald to Sylvia Beach of October 14, 1921: "our typesetters know no English."

A word of explanation is now called for. If the French printers knew no English, you may justly ask, how could they have "corrected" "vailed" to "veiled" in 1927 and "*frons*" to "*front*" in 1928 (changes patently deliberate, having been made on the *clichés*); and, in 1926, "pace" to "face," "hismy" to "his my," "shis" and "hrim" to "his" and "him," and "hopk" to "hope"? Obviously, with reference to these printings, I have used "printers" as a term of convenience. One need look no further than Hirchwald for the villain, but almost certainly there were other "helpers" (Sylvia Beach and Harriet Shaw Weaver, for example). In any case, a competent textual critic will be in no danger of thinking these changes authorial.

16. He reached his apogee, fortunately, as early on as the *Lestrygonians* episode—whose penultimate paragraph, for example, read this way before he mutilated it: "His hand looking for the where did I put found in his hip pocket soap lotion have to call tepid paper stuck. Ah soap there I yes. Gate" (Buffalo MS V. B. 6, p. 112). Compare *that* with 183.38–40!

17. See the pages conveniently reproduced in Sylvia Beach's *Shakespeare and Company* (New York: Harcourt, Brace, 1959), p. 59, and in the new edition of Margaret Anderson's *My Thirty Years' War* (New York: Horizon Press, 1969), among the illustrations following p. 54 (this latter substituted, as I suggested to Miss Anderson, for the *transition Finnegans Wake* proofs which she had paraded in the original 1930 edition as belonging to *Ulysses*). "*Penelope* in printed proof (the 4th)," Joyce wrote Harriet Shaw Weaver, "is so illegible with

interlineations that it would be useless to send it"; but this did not prevent him, of course, from sending it to the printers, who two months before he had suggested might "all leap into the Rhone in despair at the mosaics I send them back" *(Letters of James Joyce*, ed. Stuart Gilbert [New York: Viking, 1957], pp. 178, 172).

18. See, for example, Harvard 48.1, where "vavions" is set for "various," "vorth" for "with," "toacks" for "tracks," "Rathfaruham" for "Rathfarnham," "Dackey" for "Dalkey," "Dounybrook" for "Donnybrook," "Still" for "still," "Stackney cass" for "Hackney cars," "mailvrans" for "mailvans," and "broughanms" for "broughams"— all in five lines. Don't for a second imagine this a prize titbit: it's typical. A few other examples, picked up from these proofs at random, are "betholln" for "between," "Wattly Jrceman" for "Weekly Freeman," and "Yrceman's Journal" for "Freeman's Journal" in two lines of 39.2; "fuit or pook shop" for "fruit or pork shop" on 50.2; and "urbe" for "wife" on 60.1.

19. Preserved only as a quotation in Hirchwald's letter to Beach of October 14, 1921.

20. *Letters*, pp. 168, 172, 173. In the first passage Gilbert prints a hyphen in "fortyeight" which is not, of course, in the autograph.

21. This, incidentally, sounds a bit more heroic than it actually was: the book had been printed signature by signature as Joyce approved them, and all that remained to do at the end was print the last several signatures, gather and bind.

22. Buffalo MS V. B. 11. a, p. 15; Cornell MS 56, p. 26.

23. Rosenbach MS; Buffalo MS V. B. 3. a. & b, p. 2; Harvard 7.8.

24. Rosenbach MS.

25. Rosenbach MS; Texas proof p. 71 (first state).

26. Rosenbach MS; Buffalo MS V. B. 6, p. 106.

27. Buffalo MS V. A. 21, p. [39], Rosenbach MS; Buffalo MS V. B. 14. a, b, & c, p. 21, this page wanting in d, the setting typescript.

28. Needless to say, significant. Twelve pages later, for example, leaving the cabman's shelter, Bloom "skipped around nimbly, considering frankly, at the same time apologetic, to get on his companion's right, a habit of his" (660.23–25). The news story which Bloom reads is indeed on page 3 of the *Evening Telegraph* of June 16, 1904, Last Pink, in col. 8 (of 9). He begins just over halfway down: "3.0— The GOLD CUP, value 1,000 sovs," etc. (Mind you, I don't say Joyce in fact copied the story from the *Telegraph*. The phrases quoted 648.18–32 passim could as easily have come from the *Evening Herald*'s page 3 and probably did, because it is the *Herald* which Bloom and Stephen are "actually" reading. The conflation is explicit at 647.8, for while the *Telegraph* edition was "Pink," it was the *Herald* which was

"Extra Sporting." That the headlines of 647.18–22 and 648.33 come from the *Herald*, not the *Telegraph*, the following tabulation will show:

EVENING HERALD	EVENING TELEGRAPH
Great Battle	Big Battle at Telissa
[dispatch from] Tokio	[ditto]
Love Making in Irish	Gaelic League and Love Affairs
£200 Damages	Verdict for £200
Gordon-Bennett Race	Gordon-Bennett Cup
Emigration Swindle	Bogus Emigration Agent
New York Disaster	Appalling American Disaster
1,000 Lives Lost	485 Bodies Recovered

29. Buffalo MS V. C. 1. 8. b, p. 114; Texas p. 114.

30. Rosenbach MS; Buffalo MS V. B. 10. a, p. 2.

31. Buffalo MS V. A. 18, p. 7, Rosenbach MS; Buffalo MS V. B. 12. a, p. 19 (carbon in b uncorrected).

32. Rosenbach MS; Buffalo MS V. B. 10. a, p. 32; Texas p. 328.

33. Rosenbach MS (with an "a" after "street" which Joyce presumably deleted in an intermediate typescript); Buffalo MS V. B. 6, p. 110.

34. For example, "God Ahuiglity's" (Harvard 48.1, the page from which I drew in note 18 above), the "u" of which he corrected to "m" and the "li" to "h," yielding "God Ahmighty's." Or "dean of Stud es" (178.4), where he corrected the "S" to lower case and inserted a comma to follow, but failed to supply the conspicuously missing "i."

35. "Since the completion of *Ulysses* [on October 29] I feel more and more tired but I have to hold on till all the proofs are revised. I am extremely irritated by all those printer's errors. Working as I do amid piles of notes at a table in a hotel I cannot possibly do this mechanical part with my wretched eye and a half. Are these to be perpetuated in future editions? I hope not" (letter of November 6, 1921, *Letters*, p. 176). On June 7, five months earlier, he had evinced a sharply contrasting spirit: "È giá sotto i torchi il libro ed aspetto le prime bozze domani l'altro. . . . Trattandosi di tre edizioni costose bisogna evitare i refusi"—"The book is already in press and I expect the first proofs day after tomorrow. . . . Three expensive editions being involved, misprints have to be avoided" (*Letters of James Joyce*, ed. Richard Ellmann [New York: Viking, 1966], III, 45). The concern of the earlier, pre-proofs letter is, naively, with correcting misprints (clerk), while the concern of the later is with further revising the text with the aid of the piles of notes (creator). The printer's errors are extremely irritating, but their correction is now a merely mechanical part which he cannot possibly do; he "hopes" they will

not be perpetuated in future editions (and if hopes were horses, all beggars would ride).

36. See my "Advertisement for the Restoration" in *Twelve and a Tilly: Essays on the occasion of the 25th anniversary of Finnegans Wake*, ed. Dalton and Hart (London and Evanston, 1966), pp. 119–137.

37. *Encyclopædia Britannica*, s.v. "Textual Criticism."

38. In late August and early September of 1936 Joyce visited Copenhagen, where the journalist Ole Vinding, by posing as an artist, was able to interview him. The talk inevitably turned to the impending appearance of *Ulysses* in England, and Joyce said: "Jeg skal hjem og rette Prøverne i Aften!"—"I must go home and correct proofs this evening!" (Buffalo MS IX. A. 7, p. 15).

The Text of *Finnegans Wake*

Fred H. Higginson
KANSAS STATE UNIVERSITY

JOYCE HAS NOT in general been well served, even by his well-intentioned publishers, at least until quite recently. His early ones could hardly have known that his arrogance was well founded; still, in their defense, he himself would even then bend when outright refusal to print or publish was in question. What is of course unacceptable is that, now that he is respected and famous and lip-serviced and making money in that slow steady way that is balm to the previous risks of annuitants, he still is not well served in his two major works: *Ulysses* and *Finnegans Wake*. It is almost as if the publishers have risen up and said *"Non serviemus."*

True, *Ulysses* has recently had a second Modern Library (not to be compared or collated with the Vintage) edition that is better than the first, since it takes account at least of Hanley's (again, he is unacknowledged) collations of ML1 with the Hamburg edition. But it is not good enough for Joyce. Proofreading is not editing, though ML2 is the best American text we have had. Of *Finnegans Wake* there has been no editing at all, to speak of.

But Joyce did not himself understand editing. The fact that he turned the "authoritative" edition of *Ulysses* over to Stuart Gilbert is surely of the same nature as his wishing to turn the completion of *Finnegans Wake* over to James Stephens. There really isn't any reason why real authors should be expected to be editors, for authors are surely at work on the next book before the last one is published: Joyce less so *of necessity* than Ian Fleming, perhaps, for Joyce had a subsidy; but surely no less so. Besides, in 1932 and 1933, for the Odyssey first and second, his eyes were failing, and he was exhausted and maybe even bored. He almost certainly must have been bored with the idea of proofreading his last book at the same time when he was having unusual troubles with his coming one, *Finnegans Wake,* that already fading coal. Anyway, the fact that a given text has fallen under the eye of its author is perhaps less a guarantee of his intentions having been realized than that it has fallen under the eye of a careful, uninvolved, objective, let-us-also-say Japanese proofreader (or an editor reading backward a letter at a time). As we all know, it is fatally easier for an author to misread his intentions onto a page that does not in fact contain them than it is for that disinterested proofreader or editor. And it is common to turn over to others the job of seeing something through the press. Still, I want to suggest that Joyce was less attentive than he should have been in other ways.

There is a well-known example, the missing "dominations" at FW 605. Dalton's case for the restoration of this passage proposes a crucial editorial problem.[1] It is this: if an author carefully puts a word into his text (carefully, demonstrably, because it belongs to the orders of angels, a structural device in the passage), and if he then, while his structure is supposedly fresh in his mind, recopies his text without the single line containing the word (by demonstrable haplography), and if he then, through at least ten passings of that text under his eye, misses the omission, should it be restored?

My own answer to that question, as I believe is Dalton's, is that the line *must* be restored. The only relevant question is how. Publishers are reluctant, but I dismiss that point until later. Joyce has surely been careless here. He is careless almost at the point of creation, which is the point where we would least expect it. Of any writer. He is fair-copy careless. All the work is still his own: no typist, typesetter, proofreader, editor, or even time-lapsed self is yet at work. The author plain bungled. We can demonstrate it from the MSS. And for *Finnegans Wake* the existence of those MSS is most important.

It is probably safe to say that more of *Finnegans Wake* exists in its author's hand than does of most works, and our luck in having so much of this difficult one is as yet almost unexploited. Beginning with the MSS as a first recourse for restoration, I have come to believe that one should go on to mistrust, and to call attention to, such parts as we do *not* have in Joyce's hand. I did this in my edition of *Anna Livia Plurabelle*, without making anything of it. And I still have no doubt that *fiches*, backs of menus and envelopes, and memorial commands at one time existed for many of the changes for which no MSS seem to have survived. All I am saying is that I do not wish to rock the *textus receptus* boat without good reason.

So I say one mea culpa and no tua culpa at all and have one more go at "The Mookse and the Gripes." I botched it once, bibliographically speaking.[2] What matters is that the *Finnegans Wake* text of the episode omits some material that was included in the *transition* text. Is it canonical? Is there an argument for its restoration? What happened?

I submit three collations, all of *"transition 6"*:

A. 8vo: $[1]^{8}2-7^{8}[8]^{8}9-12^{8}$, 96 leaves.
B. 8vo: $[1]^{8}2-7^{8}\chi^{4}[8]^{8}9-12^{8}$, 100 leaves.
C. 8vo: $[1]^{8}2-7^{8}7^{*4}8^{8}[9]^{8}10-12^{8}$, 100 leaves.

A does not contain the episode; B and C do. C, furthermore, is called on the title-page "Second Edition." The seventh signature of A contains the last part of Joyce's contribution (pp. 97–106) and a contribution by Robert Desnos (pp. 107–112). Clive Hart has a copy of A, the only one I know of in covers, which he says

are *d'époque*. The intention clearly was to issue the magazine in
this form. Then something happened. Eugene Jolas describes it
this way:

> I recall . . . one particular case, when a four-page addition
> had to be made after the first four hundred copies of the re-
> view had already been stitched. Everything was held up. The
> addition that had been announced by telephone came by the
> early mail and was rushed to the composing-room. During
> the day the completed copies were ripped apart, and by eve-
> ning a sufficiently clean proof of the new text had been ob-
> tained for us to feel we could call it a day. Possessors of
> *transition* no. 6 may have perhaps asked themselves why the
> page numbering of that volume should have started to stutter
> around p. 106, which was followed by 106a, 106b, 106c, 106d,
> 106e, 106f. It was in order that the unforgettable 'Mookse and
> Gripes' might scuttle into their intended place.[3]

That is a remarkable narrative. As we shall see, it is a bit hyper-
bolic, but such traumatic situations court hyperbole. Jolas was
obviously quite devoted to Joyce, but even so his editorial flexi-
bility is flabbergasting. Caresse Crosby even relates a story suggesting that Joyce was just as respectful of printers as publishers
were of him.[4] But Jolas does say, after all, that part of the run
had been stitched at the time the addition was wanted, and that
is surely the least convenient time for an author to be wanting
additions. Consider merely an editor's problem in "ripping apart"
stitched copies of a magazine. Presumably the only reason to do
so would be to save signatures unaffected by the printing change
for later use. But "ripping" out stitching would not so preserve
them. Further, the existence of C suggests strongly that enough
copies were in fact destroyed, rather than saved, that a second
edition had to be run to satisfy almost immediate demand. It is
even slightly reset in both the Joyce and Desnos parts. Mrs. Jolas,
describing the same frantic time in another place, says merely that
her husband told the printer to hold off binding, which suggests

that the magazines were not stitched.[5] A few, however, must have been sewn, glued, and bound: Clive Hart has one; but it would be fair to say that they are quite rare.

What Jolas did was to have the printers move pages 107–112, the Desnos contribution following Joyce's, into another form, which becomes the chi-gathering of B and the 7* of C. This gives Joyce six pages to work with, if he wants them, instead of just the five (not the four Jolas remembered) eventually devoted to "The Mookse and the Gripes." So he makes other additions. They appear in B and C, but not in *Finnegans Wake*. (I will also entertain the possibility that Jolas, or somebody, said: "I need a bit more to fill out the gathering; can you add a few things to give me more than the five pages you have?" Maybe Joyce did that. He would be acting similarly to the way he appears to have acted according to Mrs. Crosby's story, and that was, significantly, for the printer of *Tales Told*, which includes the "Mookse.")

When Joyce came to furnish the printer with copy for Book I, he made up two texts, one to retain, one to send off. These texts are combinations of revised copies of *transition* (in which the whole of Book I had been printed), MS revisions (some on sheets of *transition*, some on separate pages), and versions of certain passages (among them "Anna Livia Plurabelle" and "The Mookse and the Gripes") that had been revised and issued separately subsequent to their publication in *transition*. The copy used for Chapter 6, which contains the "Mookse," was probably intended by Joyce to be two copies of *transition* 6, supplemented by two copies of the episode as printed in *Tales Told*. But there appears to have been a mistake. One copy of *transition* 6 is A, so that it does not contain the episode at all. Of course, if the episode is going to be furnished from another text, the copy of the magazine does not need to include it. But it will naturally not contain the additional material inserted at the same time, along with the episode. (It occurs to me also that Joyce may have mentally collapsed the extra additions I have postulated for Jolas with the additions apparently demanded by the *Tales Told* printer; but suppositions are not necessary to the line of thought.) The second copy of *transition* 6 must have been the one Joyce kept, since *Finnegans Wake* never set the material, and it is a copy of B, in which he could verify the presence of the extra additions, had he remembered them.

Let me make it clear that the B. M. MSS exhibit A as copy for *Finnegans Wake*, B as retained text, and *transition* copy for B in Joyce's hand, including the text not in *Finnegans Wake*.[6] Whether or not Joyce wrote the additions to A, over and above the "Mookse," to order is immaterial. It seems to me clear they should be restored. On the evidence of the MSS, it is plain what Joyce's intentions once were with respect to *transition* 6. He eventually realized them in *Finnegans Wake* inefficiently. Carelessly.

Still, the true believer may exclaim "Yes, but—" and ask: "Since the text, as galleys and proofs of *Finnegans Wake*, passed once again under his eyes, did not Joyce approve of these omissions? He must have." But those eyes are failing eyes. And the mind is perhaps already at work on that book about the sea. To assert that Joyce is perfect is only to assert a defensive opposite to the belief that Joyce left in whatever momentarily pleased him, a really much more damaging claim. One forgives Keats' spelling; nor is the "soldier/soldier" problem to be blamed on Yeats. But could Charlton Hinman forgive Shakespeare if he thought the Bard didn't really care about ary a one of the Blessed Cruces? Of course not!

Yet, with Joyce, the nimbus of adventitious creation has for many years been an important element in the hagiography. Gossip long asserted that there was a sentence "Did I hear a knock? Come in." in *Finnegans Wake* and that it got into the text while Joyce was dictating and that he liked it so much in that he left it in. There is no such sentence. So does the whole clayfoot, denigratory edifice fall? Must St. James Eblanensis, too, be demoted from the register of saints? By no means. I will provide in a moment what I hope will be taken as a cornerstone. First, let me in passing scotch yet one more false claim of adventitiousness. It was made by Ned Polsky a long time ago in the *Explicator* and is an ingenious go at the occurrence of the number 106 at 159.33.[7]

The text in question reads: "I want him to go and live . . . on Tristan da Cunha . . . where he'll make Number 106. . . ." Campbell and Robinson explain simply enough: "He should go and live on Tristan da Cunha where he would be the 106th inhabitant." [8] They were unable, they say, to discover the exact population figure used by Joyce and express their discomfiture in a footnote citing (though erroneously) the *Britannica*. Polsky, too, is bothered by their failure to find the exact figure. (Incidentally, a copy of the *Statesman's Yearbook* for any of the years 1918–1922 gives the population of Tristan as 105.) But since the figure appears in *transition* 6 on page 106, Polsky takes it to be a reference to the difficulties of publication of the "Mookse" and goes on to say that "any true statement we may make about the nature of *Finnegans Wake*, even down to the very details of its creation, is told us within the work itself." The B. M. MSS, however, show this passage to have been added on an unpaged proof, 47473.209. And while I hesitate to deny quadriviality to any passage in *Finnegans Wake*, a univial reading of this one seems at least possible.

Nevertheless, I believe at least one item of adventitious creation can be justified from the MSS. There is a footnote on page 307 (n. 4) which has always bemused me. It comes near the end of Book II, Part 2, as an item in a virtuoso set-piece you will all remember. There are topics in the text and appropriate subjects in the left-hand marginal gloss. The topics, as the MSS show, were in the text first; the glosses were added later. At B. M. Add. MS 47478.176–77, Joyce has made a fair copy of the topics, leaving room in both margins for glosses. He makes a list of subjects to enter in the left margin. This list is at B. M. Add. MS 47478.237, a two-column list of names with very few corrections. At the top of the first column, "Guy Fawkes" has been crossed out after "Nero," as if he were to have been a second subject for the topic "the Great Fire at the South City Market"; then Joyce thought better of it; so he was exercising care with his list. All goes evenly and well with the matching-up until almost the end of the first column: "Leonidas." At this point there is a scramble:

Jacob

~~Strabo Joseph~~

"Strabo" was written first as a gloss to "Travelling in the Olden Times" and then crossed out. "Joseph" was written next; but in the text as we have it, Joseph occurs two names further along in the list, as a gloss for "the Strangest Dream that was ever Half-dreamt." Joyce didn't want Joseph twice. So he wrote in "Jacob." It seems obvious to me that either of the two topics could just as well belong to either Joseph or Jacob, both travelers, both dreamers. I presume that Joyce, too, was momentarily indecisive or confused. He expressed his confusion, to himself or aloud: "I've lost the place. Where was I?" And that is how 307.n4 comes about; it says: "I've lost the place, where was I?"

Evidence in the MSS has persuaded me that Joyce did adopt at least one gratuitous, providential happening into his text. I'd just as soon have this one as the "Did I hear a knock?" tale. Neither, by the way, violates my idea of Joyce's methods.

He had lost the place. So is the reader apt to at about the same spot, unless he has been keeping careful fingers on the gloss and on the text. The note remarks on this possibility. Joyce makes a small creative joke, a *jeu de progrès*.

So now Joyce is shown to be both careless at times and adventitiously creative at times. And what is one to do about the text?

Various suggestions have already been made. Dalton, I think it is fair to say, believes in widespread emendation. Hart (*A Wake Newslitter*, III.4) argues, it seems to me quite tellingly, against

Dalton's approach: Joyce's "slovenly working methods become an integral part of the texture"; and the book we have is pretty much the book Joyce intended, a Shem-ful, Jacobean pretending. Daltonian emendation, says Hart, would produce the *Wake* that Jack built. Nevertheless, Hart proposes some emendations, too, and concludes that the final intentions of Joyce are best realized by the unbound pages of *Finnegans Wake* now in Buffalo (MS VI.H.4.a).

But Mr. Peter du Sautoy, who, as The Man at Faber and Faber, is probably going to have the last word anyway, for awhile yet, has cogent arguments (*A Wake Newslitter*, IV.5) for leaving indeterminably good- or ill-enough alone. I paraphrase. The publisher prints the text given to him by the author and makes such changes in it as the author requests during his lifetime. Then, generally speaking, the text should be left alone until the copyright runs out. The publisher has no special competence to decide what changes should be made, nor do particular editors, nor does the publisher in picking an editor. And a variorum he cannot see "as either feasible or economic for *FW*."

Even though Viking accepts, and lives with, Ellmann as arbiter, for the rest, and from the publisher's point of view, one has to agree. Yet Joyce's intentions other than the received text are sometimes quite clear. And something like a variorum would have saved Polsky going overboard; it would give us a bit more of the book, throughout; and a developmental version, chapter by chapter, along with the Buffalo notebooks, would give us considerable insight into Joyce's mind at work, and that would be valuable.

What I feel must be done for *Finnegans Wake is* the working out of a developmental variorum, to the end of a final text more chronologically eclectic than Scholes' or Anderson's editions of the earlier works (simply because the time involved is longer) and more discriminating and responsible than the ML2 *Ulysses* (because the editors would be acknowledged). It should account systematically for:

1. "Lost" passages and words. And we must also learn how to deal with such things as are crossed out in the Buffalo notebooks that nevertheless do not appear in *Finnegans Wake*.
2. Violations of recognized Joycean practice in accidentals, or punctuation which does not make sense.
3. Indications of Joyce's neglect and error. And I cannot help but think that there are a good many of these, just as interesting as those pointed out by Dalton, Hart and others.[9]

And I should hope that the final text would be readable and typographically sane.

A Theobald is required. But, these days, he will most likely have to be a committee with a grant. Harvesters of Corrigenda and Emendations, they might call themselves. Or Adducers of the Latent Perfection. Whoever they are, however it's done, it will be lighting-up time in the Darkness Risible.

"Goodbye, Stephen said in his wake." That is from the *Portrait*, page 196 in Atherton's edition, where I first noticed it.[10] —Goodbye, Stephen said. In his *Wake*. We ought to get his last words right.

NOTES

1. "Advertisement for the Restoration," in *Twelve and a Tilly*, ed. Jack P. Dalton and Clive Hart (London, 1966), pp. 119–37.
2. "Notes on the Text of *Finnegans Wake*," *JEGP* 55:451–56, July 1956.
3. "Homage to James Joyce," *transition* 21 (March 1932), p. 252.
4. Cited in Ellmann, pp. 627–28.
5. "Portrait of James Joyce," ed. W. R. Rodgers, BBC documentary.
6. The A-text is B. M. Add. MS 47475.141–50; the B-text is 47475.52–62; the text with the "lost" additions (and very few others) is 47473.242–55. The C-text, of which there are a good many library

copies without title-pages, has 38 lines of text on both pp. 97 and 105; the B-text has 37 and 39 lines respectively.

7. *Explicator* 9: no. 24 December 1950.

8. *A Skeleton Key to Finnegans Wake* (New York, 1944), p. 118.

9. Dalton, as in fn. 1; Clive Hart, "Notes on the Text of *Finnegans Wake*," *JEGP* 59:229–39, April 1960; David Hayman, *A First Draft Version of Finnegans Wake* (Austin, Texas, 1963), passim.

10. London, 1964.

"Astroglodynamonologos"

Robert Boyle, S. J.

MARQUETTE UNIVERSITY

ONE OF THE seminal images that Joyce used throughout his career is that of the artist as priest. In dealing with the priesthood in this context, Joyce of course emphasized the positive elements in the Catholic attitude, since he wished by the image to exalt the vocation of the artist. Thus the life-giving, fulfilling, even divinizing aspects of the priesthood appear. Yet always the negative elements of Stephen's (and no doubt Joyce's) attitude toward the priesthood operate too. The wearying, frustrating, and destructive aspects of the priesthood—particularly in the context of simoniacal abuse—are never altogether absent even when Joyce uses his priest-artist image in its most positive forms.

My purpose in this brief paper is to set forth areas for investigation in Joyce's use of the image of the priesthood, especially in its positive aspects, that critics have often slighted. It will be evident that I do not see this usage charted out in clear schematic form, as do some critics, particularly when they deal with Joyce's use of the Catholic Mass. As I see it, Joyce keeps the priest-image on tap for use whenever the psychological pressures (or insights, or instincts) of his characters make its full or partial use effective.

In building his villanelle, Stephen pictures himself as a true priest in contrast to the conventional priest, Father Moran: "To him she would unveil her soul's shy nakedness, to one who was but schooled in the discharging of a formal rite rather than to him, a priest of eternal imagination, transmuting the daily bread of experience into the radiant body of everliving life" (p. 221). The function of the priest here stressed is the same as that stressed in "The Sisters," in *Portrait*, in the opening page and in the Black Mass of *Ulysses*, and in the Shem the Penman chapter of *Finnegans Wake*—namely, the function of changing bread and wine into the living body and blood of Jesus Christ, the divine Word. Through this transubstantiation at the consecration of the Mass, the priest offers divine life to communicants. Through the activity of the priest, the humble bread becomes the means of bringing everliving life to human beings, of bringing God to man and man to God in a union closer than nature can know.

In this image from the villanelle passage, the fullest and most specific statement of his artist-priest image, Joyce calls in all his knowledge and experience of this Catholic doctrine. He does it to provide Stephen with a romantic, flamboyant image expressive of Stephen's own artistic purpose. The art of literature, composed of words, will be the medium for transmitting life from the artist to man. Humble, work-a-day words, like bread, will now experience a new and mysterious force working on them, flowing from the artist's soul. They will now do what words normally cannot do. They will, forged by the artist, create in their hearers a conscience, a self-knowledge, a new life. The radiant body of this true eucharist will bring to human minds, in the words of Stephen's esthetic, the clear radiance of the esthetic image, the supreme quality of beauty. In luminously apprehending this beauty, the mind will be arrested in the luminous silent stasis of esthetic pleasure. And it will know itself as divine, able to fly above the obscene coalhole of corrupt, simoniacal civilization (read "syphilization"). From dogs men will become gods.

Thus Stephen sees his function as true priest of the imagination. But one word here hints at a qualification of this overblown metaphor. Instead of "transubstantiating" or even merely "changing," we find that the artist-priest is "transmuting." In the overtones of this interesting old word, the priest dimly appears as alchemist or, as Shem is called, "the first till last alshemist" (FW 185), and this ritual as magic. Here we find a hint of something considerably less than divine, of something readily allied to the diabolic. Stephen could well be unconscious of the atmosphere of his word, but certainly in the light of his later development of the image, Joyce is not. This one word, unusual in the theological context, suggests the possibility of the negative development of this image into the merely sensual, the degrading, the diabolical Black Mass. And, as I have already suggested, Joyce indeed does develop this image in two directions, into the positive and life-giving functions of the priest as envisaged in Catholic doctrine, ideal in Christ, and into the negative and life-destroying functions of the simoniacal power realized most fully in the Jesuits of Joyce's vision, in the scientist-priest Buck Mulligan, and in Justius of *Finnegans Wake*.

Stephen's toying with the notion of the artist as like the God of creation is familiar and obvious enough. As I read it, it is Stephen's (and perhaps, but not likely, Joyce's) effort to express the idea that Hawthorne stated with considerable more balance and sophistication in "The Custom House," namely that the artist deals with his characters (at least seemingly) on their terms and not on his own. That is, like the God of creation, he loves and respects them enough to leave them free, free even to will their own destruction if they choose to do so. The artist does not preach to them or through them. He expresses what he hears and sees, what is reflected in the mirror of his imagination. He leaves dogma to the conventional priest, as according to Joyce in 1903, he should do: "In *Catilina* the women are absolute types, and the end of such a play cannot but savour of dogma—a most proper thing in a priest but a most improper in a poet" (CW 100); as priest-poet, the artist expresses without dogma and without alteration (as well as he can) his own particular human vision.

But Stephen's (and possibly the young Joyce's) notion of the artist as fallen seraph is not so obvious. Stephen enjoys posing as

Milton's fallen seraph, with his *"non serviam,"* his determination
to make his mind its own place, and his proud, rebellious, loveless flight. He knows his moment of ecstatic "seraphic life" in the
passage leading up to the villanelle, and he conceives of himself,
at the end of *Portrait,* as a temporarily successful seraphic Icarus.
This develops the earlier experience of Stephen the schoolboy
turning from the offer of the conventional priesthood to the "ec-
stasy of flight [that] made radiant his eyes and wild his breath
and tremulous and wild and radiant his windswept limbs" (169).
He is lured from the offer of immortal power to the worship of
mortal beauty, embodied and symbolized by the girl in the water
at the end of Chapter Four.

That girl, bird-like as is the symbol of the Holy Spirit, seemed
life-giving like the sacraments, linked as she is with water and
with flame. Now the temptress of the villanelle, based both on
the Virgin and on the prostitutes (or the combination of those in
Emma, as in Nora), lures with a twofold attraction, one the ir-
resistible magnetism of beauty and enchanting mystery, the other
the wearying, destructive snares of "the sluggish matter of the
earth" (169). She offers the uplifting beauty and virtue of the
Blessed Virgin of Catholic tradition (not the moronic, drooling
Virgin of Stephen's imagination in Chapter Three), and the allure
of the ritualistic whores of the end of Chapter Two. Joyce used
material from his own life to form this ambivalent attitude in
Stephen, evidently. Joyce wrote to Nora in 1909: "I wonder is
there some madness in me. Or is love madness? One moment I
see you like a virgin or madonna the next moment I see you
shameless, insolent, half naked and obscene! What do you think
of me at all? Are you disgusted with me?" [1]

There are, it should be noted, two virgins in Stephen's image
of his imagination compared to the mother of Jesus: "O! In the
virgin womb of the imagination the word was made flesh" (217).
One indeed is Mary, but she appears merely as the vehicle for the
metaphor. The other is the imagination, and it is partly like Mary,

in bringing forth the life-giving word conceived by the spirit, and partly unlike her, in sharing the sensual allure of the whores. There are also two seraphs: "Gabriel the seraph had come to the virgin's chamber." The seraph of St. Luke's gospel came to Mary's chamber to announce that God was to cause Mary to conceive the Word. This is the positive function of the seraph in the positive aspect of Stephen's image. But there is another negatively operating seraph for the other facet of the image, a fallen seraph, and that is the negative aspect of Stephen himself. Stephen in this image doubles first as the God of creation, here as God the Holy Spirit, inseminating the imagination, and second as the fallen seraph, lured by the sensual appeal of that same imagination. Like Joyce with Nora, Stephen perceived women under two contrary aspects. Speaking of his devotions to the Blessed Virgin, Joyce says of Stephen: "If ever his soul, reentering her dwelling shyly after the frenzy of his body's lust had spent itself, was turned toward her whose emblem is the morning star, *bright and musical, telling of heaven and infusing peace,* it was when her names were murmured softly by lips whereon there still lingered foul and shameful words, the savour itself of a lewd kiss" (105). Thus too Stephen images the artist torn two ways by his art, attracted by its heavenly beauty and wearied by its insatiable lust. The goddess the artist must worship, his imagination, is, after all, a lure, a bait. In her background, I suspect, lurks Shakespeare's imaging of lust:

> Past reason hunted, but no sooner had
> Past reason hated, as a swallowed bait
> On purpose laid to make the taker mad . . . .

The most insightful statement to date of this dichotomy of desire and repulsion in the villanelle is that of Robert Scholes, in his "Stephen Dedalus, Poet or Esthete?" [2] "Stephen's particular problem is to help the bat-like soul of this female to awake, to serve her without being destroyed by her; to forge in the smithy of his own soul the uncreated conscience of *her* race. He wants, among other things, to turn her from the enchanted Celtic Twilight to the daylight of his own time. The villanelle is half his self-dedication to a hopeless task and half a prayer for release from the pitiless muse and country whose service is his accepted destiny." [3]

That "self-dedication" of which Scholes speaks is one of the bases for Joyce's use of the priest image. The priesthood demands the kind of dedication that Joyce conceived of as proper also to the artist. The artist will worship at the shrine of the imagination rather than at the altar of God, but he must be as willing as the priest to sacrifice himself in love, as Christ did. Christ indeed sacrificed himself for other persons; the artist's "others" will be his characters, his words, his artistic structures, but he conceives of them as products of the spirit, life-giving: "He lifts the life-wand and the dumb speak" (FW 195).

Stephen rejects the power of what he sees as the simoniacal church. Thus the almost hysterical insistence upon the power of the priesthood by the spiritual director in *Portrait* gives background for Stephen's choice of the more mysterious and ethereal power of the artistic vocation. Likewise the power of Buck Mulligan's cynical scientific priesthood gives background for Stephen's passionate, frustrated efforts to assert the power of Shakespeare's crooked smokes climbing from blest artistic altars.

It might be noted in passing, and needs to be stressed in Joycean criticism, that the vision of the Jesuits portrayed by Joyce is not necessarily an objective one. Julian Kaye, in *James Joyce Miscellany, I*, seems at home with the assumption that real Jesuits are simoniacs. J. Mitchell Morse, in *The Sympathetic Alien*, sees them as mindless zombies lacking humanity and academic freedom. Even the knowledgeable, balanced, and charitable Richard M. Kain, in *The Fabulous Voyager* and his excellent essay on "Grace" in Clive Hart's *Dubliners: Critical Essays*, entertains some gentle questions about the motives and characters of Fathers

Conmee and Vaughan. One might as well judge the literary excellence of Shakespeare's *Richard III* by the accuracy of its depiction of the historical king. And further, it is enough in Joyce's work that *Stephen* sees the Jesuits in this fashion (Joyce may have too, but that is another problem, quite distinct from the literary one). The portrait is of Stephen. The fact that the Jesuits are frightening caricatures enhances that portrait. (Caricature, after all, is also an art.) But anyone who builds his own vision of Jesuits on those monstrous caricatures, as some have, will risk being thoroughly deceived about reality.

But while Stephen rejects the simony he thinks he sees in the conventional priesthood, he embraces other aspects of the priestly dedication. In the villanelle, he offers the incense of praise, as he did at Clongowes, or as Bloom does in the Nausicaa chapter before Gerty's shrine. The dense smoke rolling past the Black Mass of the Circe chapter, where Stephen's villanelle finds one aspect of its completion, recalls both the cosmic smoke of the Jesuit hell in Chapter Three and the smoke of praise going up from the villanelle's ocean, rim to rim. Stephen in the villanelle lifts the chalice of love and sacrifice, as Father Flynn in "The Sisters" failed to do, as the boy in "Araby" romantically did. It is this sacred act that Buck Mulligan blasphemously lampoons at the opening of *Ulysses* and in the Circe chapter, where he elevates the blood-dripping host taken from the chalice. The connection between this elevation and that of the "chalice flowing to the brim" in the villanelle should indeed be noted. The temptress of the villanelle is partly like the Black Mass's goddess of unreason, with the chalice resting on her swollen belly. The temptress is a *lure*, at once attractive and destructive. And Stephen's worship in terms of Catholic priesthood is not altogether unlike that of the blasphemous Buck. The "flowing to the brim" suggests an excess of sacramental blood, and it is raised in adoration of a Swinburneanly lustful "languorous look and lavish limb."

One difference can be found in Buck's wholehearted acceptance of the earthly, the sensual, the beastly, and in Stephen's artistic effort to fly above those to the stars, to the Virgin, to the loving old artificer and father he will call for in vain (*"Pater ait"*) while at the same time paradoxically burrowing deeper than Buck into the coalholes of sensual, sluggish matter.

Stephen as artist-priest aims at bringing the basis for spiritual renewal, self-knowledge, to his race. Joyce holds up in *Dubliners* his nicely polished mirror to reveal to the Dublin he loved more deeply than he hated it, its spiritual paralysis. Bernard Benstock, in his brilliant essay on "The Dead," reveals Joyce's aim in dealing with Gabriel Conroy as the Magi. Gabriel's journey westward involves a conscience, a knowing of self: "Gabriel must begin the quest of self-discovery to arrive at the real epiphany, to follow his star." [4] Hence here too Joyce uses his image of the priest as the instrument of the epiphany of self, of knowledge of one's own apocalyptic paralysis in the seventh city of Christendom, of the possibility of life and resurrection, of the end-again and wake.

Stephen's ambivalent attitude toward his artistic priesthood appears again in the Oxen of the Sun chapter, the low and wearying aspect of his muse in "Desire's wind blasts the thorn-tree" and the spiritual and renewing in "but after it becomes from a bramblebush to be a rose upon the rood of time" (U 391). Thus he adapts Yeats's rose to Christ the traditional rose on Mary the rosetree, and his comparison of the artistic product with Christ the eternal Word follows: "Mark me now. In woman's womb word is made flesh but in the spirit of the maker all flesh that passes becomes the word that shall not pass away." The word that would not pass away returns on page 186 of *Finnegans Wake*, in the passage in which Shem, in priestly Latin, describes his offering of his body and blood (under the symbols of defecation and urine) as the corrosive ink which, on his own body, *"corpus meum,"* wrote that history, common to allflesh, human only, mortal, which is the artist's priestly offering to his race:

> . . . the first till last alshemist wrote over every square inch
> of the only foolscap available, his own body, . . . but with
> each word that would not pass away the squidself which he
> had squirtscreened from the crystalline world waned chagree-
> nold and doriangrayer in its dudhud. (FW 185–6)

A fruitful area of comparison for the positive use of the priest-
image lies in Stephen's assertion in the Scylla and Charybdis chapter (U 207) that the church is founded not on the Italian madonna
but on the mystery of fatherhood. Likewise the charge of Justius
to the artist in *Finnegans Wake* indicates that the artist, like
Christ, crucified on his cruel fiction, must found his work on the
mystery of intuition, not on the syllogisms of reason: ". . . nay,
condemned fool, anarch, egoarch, hiresiarch, you have reared
your disunited kingdom on the vacuum of your own most in-
tensely doubtful soul" (FW 188). Justius's charge implies that
the artist, like the priest, must work with mysteries he does not
understand, must be faithful to an ideal he cannot clearly see,
and must persevere, even in the face of overwhelming reasonable
doubts, in pursuing an elusive and seemingly impossible goal—the
apprehension and contemplation of the Word.

Mercius's word for his own artistic vocation, or rather for himself as artist, is drawn, I am convinced, from the opening of St.
John's gospel with its description of the ideal priest. The word
is "astroglodynamonologos" (FW 194.16), and it combines the
words for star, *aster;* cave-dweller (literally, hole-seeker), *troglo-
dyte;* source of power, *dynamo;* lonely speaker, *monologos;* and
the word, *logos.* (The first four syllables echo something of
Joyce's view of himself in his cry to Nora: "Are you too, then,
like me, one moment high as the stars, the next lower than the
lowest wretches?" [5]) In Christ the ideal priest, St. John's *Logos,*
Mercius's word finds its ideal religious fulfillment, one who came
from the stars to be made flesh and to lift, through his unique
and lonely power, the sluggish matter of earth into ever-living
union with the divine Word. In the artist as priest, as Joyce posi-

tively conceives him, the word finds an analogous fulfillment, as the artist glances from heaven to earth, from earth to heaven, and bodies forth with lonely power the eucharistic and life-giving word.

NOTES

1. September 2, 1909, *Letters II*, p. 243.
2. *PMLA*, LXXXIX (September 1964), 484–489; reprinted in *Portrait*, ed. Anderson, Viking Critical Library (New York, 1964), pp. 468–480.
3. *Portrait*, ed. Anderson, Viking Critical Library (New York, 1964), pp. 478–479.
4. *James Joyce's* Dubliners: *Critical Essays*, ed. Clive Hart (London: Faber and Faber, 1969), p. 169.
5. *Letters II*, p. 243.

The Family of Bloom

Morton P. Levitt

TEMPLE UNIVERSITY

> He called me a jew, and in a heated fashion, offensively.
> So I, without deviating from plain facts in the least, told
> him his God, I mean Christ, was a jew too, and all his fam-
> ily, like me, though in reality I'm not. (643)

WITH ALL THE PRECISION of his imprecise mind, Leopold Bloom characterizes the problem of his heritage. Baptized a Protestant at his birth (682), converted to Catholicism at the time of his marriage (716), Bloom thinks of Christians as "them" (80, 82), and they think of him as a Jew. The Citizen attacks him for his foreignness, the quality that had once attracted Molly to him (380); the Comerfords send him a non-sectarian Christmas card designed especially for the outsider (720); even John Wyse Nolan, who twice defends Bloom, is somewhat disdainful of his differences (246, 337). And they are right, for despite his deed to a Catholic cemetery plot (723), despite his essential ignorance of Judaism, despite his own uncertainty about his identity, the two-time convert is indeed a Jew—although not perhaps in the sense that his neighbors and critics expect. Bloom is a Jew not merely because Joyce saw similarities between the Irish and the Jews, or because Ulysses was an archetypal Wandering Jew, or even because Ettore Schmitz and Teodoro Mayer were Jews. Bloom himself suggests the solution in his belated response to the Citizen: just as Christ and all his family remained Jews throughout their lives, so Bloom's Jewishness is revealed in his relations with his own family, and especially in his thoughts of Rudy, his long-dead infant son. In the sense that Bloom represents modern man, his is the family of man; but it is his immediate family that provides the key to his identity.

In the cabman's shelter, Stephen surprises his rescuer by his ill-natured refusal to talk about Ireland, and Bloom attempts to account for his attitude: "Probably the home life, to which Mr Bloom attached the utmost importance, had not been all that was needful or he hadn't been familiarised with the right sort of people" (645). Even a casual acquaintance of Simon Dedalus would know that Stephen's home life has been inadequate, but this is after all the same Bloom who has intentionally stayed away from his own home while his wife was violating the sanctity of their much-traveled bridal bed. Still, Bloom does return to Molly, fearful that she might have left him (653), and so grateful to find that she has not that he adoringly kisses her adulterous rump (734, 530). (His own welcome in bed is less demonstrative, but it is undeniably warm. It is also rather crumby.) Bloom attaches so much importance to home life, in fact, that he can even rationalize the actions of the unfaithful wife; he is thinking of Kitty O'Shea, but it might as well be Molly: "Whereas the simple fact of the case was it was simply a case of the husband not being up to the scratch with nothing in common between them beyond the name and then a real man arriving on the scene, strong to the verge of weakness, falling a victim to her siren charms and forgetting home ties" (651). And so he offers Molly to Stephen. Bloom is more aware than Captain O'Shea must have been of his own deficiencies, more capable perhaps of identifying with a stronger man, and to him, paradoxically, his offer is an act of family continuity. Unknowingly, he is also fulfilling the levirate marriage custom of the ancient Hebrews, who ordained that the nearest surviving male relative of a childless man "shall go in unto [the widow] and take her to him to wife, and perform the duty of an husband's brother unto her." [1] It is this custom that Judah is following when he orders his son Onan to marry the widow of another son, Er. Bloom, impotent with his wife but a spiller of his seed on the ground, plays out symbolically the roles of Er, Judah, and Onan. With his feminine sympathies, he may even identify with Tamar, the widow.

Molly, a kind of widow herself, appreciates her husband's loyalty to his family "because he has sense enough not to squander every penny piece he earns down their gullets and looks after his wife and family . . ." (773-4)—she seems to agree with the Citizen that Bloom is miserly and inhospitable, but she defends him for it. And she recognizes that when Bloom sends Milly to work away from home, it's "on account of me and Boylan thats why he did it . . ." (766).

Bloom's family ties are to the past as well as the present, and thoughts of his parents—especially of his father—are never far from him. He has finally come to accept "poor papa's" suicide, but he has never lost his sense of pain and regret. The image of old Rudolph Bloom evoked by the sight of his suicide note causes his son to "experience a sentiment of remorse." Why? "Because in immature impatience he had treated with disrespect certain beliefs and practices" (724). These religious institutions—among them, the laws of Kashruth, the divine origin of the Torah, the unity and supremacy of Jehovah and the universal brotherhood of the Jews—seem no more rational to him now than before, but his regret remains nonetheless. Bloom is preparing to visit his father's grave on the twenty-seventh (113), to observe as a good Jew would the anniversary of his parent's death, but, in a very real sense, he is constantly mourning his loss.

It is from Rudolph Bloom, converted to Christianity out of physical and not spiritual hunger (716), that Leopold has received his Jewish heritage: he remembers his father reading from a Passover hagadah (122), telling of the observances in his own father's household (378), and recounting the history of the Virag family on the Continent (723). We should not be too surprised that Ellen Higgins Bloom allowed such happenings in her home, for her father, Julius Higgins, born Karoly (682), may also have been a Hungarian Jew. If this is so, Leopold Bloom must himself be three-quarters Jewish.

It is almost certainly this mixed background that accounts for the frequency of Bloom's references to things Jewish and for the persistent error and confusion of these references: as he remembers a ritual prayer, the Children of Israel escape out of Egypt "into the house of bondage" (122); as he reconstructs the moral of a folk song associated with Passover, the ax of the butcher replaces the justice of God as the final arbiter of life (122). He passes "the frowning face of Bethel" and thinks, "El, yes: house of: Aleph, Beth" (71); Bethel does mean "House of God," but it is the first syllable and not the second that means "house of"— El is Elohim, the only sometime frowning God of the Torah. He remembers the dramatic scene in which "the old blind Abraham recognizes the voice and puts his fingers on his [son's] face" (76), and so mistakes the patriarch Abraham for his son, Isaac, himself now a patriarch. Broiling his morning kidney, Bloom notices his orthodox cat—"Say they won't eat pork," he observes. "Kosher." (62); later, in his dream in Nighttown, he guiltily hides the crubeen and trotter from his father (437) and declares to Mrs. Breen that his package is "Kosher. A snack for supper" (446). Even his inability to throw straight as a schoolboy comes out "Crooked as a ram's horn" (373). And when he summarizes in bed the activities of his day, it is in terms of rituals and events from the Old Testament (728–9). Mourned by a chorus of The Circumcised at the Wailing Wall (544), guilt-ridden Bloom appears in his confused imaginings both as the Wandering Jew and as the new Parnell, Messiah to the Jews and Irish alike in "green Erin, the promised land of our common ancestors" (483). Against the background of a fife and drum corps playing the confessional Kol Nidre (480), with the tearful blessing of the Citizen in his ears and facing the raised standard of Zion, Bloom solemnly reads out from a scroll the list of his sins, his entire knowledge of Judaism, his personal sense of what it is to be a Jew: "Aleph Beth Ghimel Daleth Hagadah Tephilim Kosher Yom Kippur Hanukah Roschaschana Beni Brith Bar Mitzvah Mazzoth Askenazim Meshuggah Talith" (487). His Jewishness seems no more than a confused melange of letters of the alphabet, religious holidays and observances, fraternal orders, dietary customs and cultural groupings, pejorative slang, misspellings and mispronunciations. In the end, however, we may be surprised not so much at this confusion as at how much Bloom does remember, how often he is nearly right. It is only in his memories of Rudy, the son to whom he might have passed on his heritage, that Bloom himself can see clearly the meaning of his Jewishness, the significance for him of his family traditions.

The premature loss of his heir remains the most important event in the life of Leopold Bloom. As Molly says, "I knew well Id never have another our 1st death too it was we were never the same since . . ." (778). But Bloom seems to have found a surrogate son in Stephen Dedalus, who is related intimately in his thoughts to Rudy: he first thinks of Rudy in fact immediately after listening to the parental boasts of "Noisy selfwilled" Simon Dedalus, so "Full of his son." And Bloom thinks: "He is right. Something to hand on. If little Rudy had lived. See him grow up. Hear his voice in the house. Walking beside Molly in an Eton suit. My son. Me in his eyes. Strange feeling it would be. From me" (89). A later vision of Rudy dressed "in an Eton suit with glass shoes and a little bronze helmet" (609) parallels both this image and that of the five-year-old Stephen, whom the Blooms had met in the "lilacgarden of Matthew Dillon's house . . ." (680). Molly's memory of Stephen is strikingly similar to Bloom's vision of Rudy: "he was an innocent boy then and a darling little fellow in his lord Fauntleroy suit and curly hair like a prince on the stage . . ." (774). But there will be no son for Bloom, for Stephen is no Rudy. Bloom recognizes this even before Stephen warns him by chanting a modern version of the anti-Semitic ballad, "Hugh of Lincoln" (690–1), the old ritual murder cabal, which Bloom himself had thought of when he passed the Botanic Gardens (108): his realization is reflected in the associated imagery that develops in his mind during the day.

Reading from the prospectus for Agendath [*sic*] Netaim, "The model farm at Kinnereth on the lakeshore of Tiberias" (59), Bloom had initially drawn a verdant picture of the Zionist reclamation settlement. But he dismisses this illusion and thinks instead of the present wasteland:

> No, not like that. A barren land, bare waste. Volcanic lake, the dead sea: no fish, weedless, sunk deep in the earth. No wind would lift those waves, grey metal, poisonous foggy waters. Brimstone they called it raining down: the cities of the plain: Sodom, Gomorrah, Edom. All dead names. A dead sea in a dead land, grey and old. Old now. It bore the oldest, the first race. . . . The oldest people. Wandered far away over all the earth, captivity to captivity, multiplying, dying, being born everywhere. It lay there now. Now it could bear no more. Dead: an old woman's: the grey sunken cunt of the world.
> Desolation.
> Grey horror seared his flesh (61).

Bloom attributes these "bad images" to "Morning mouth . . . Got up wrong side of the bed" (61), and he wonders if resuming his morning exercises will exorcise them. But the images recur; their cause is far more fundamental than his weak constitution. Waiting at the lying-in hospital for the birth of Mrs. Purefoy's child, Bloom again mourns the loss of his own son. Again he thinks of the Holy Land: "Agendath [*sic*] is a waste land, a home of screechowls and the sandblind upupa. Netaim, the golden, is no more" (414). The sterility of Palestine recalls the impotency of Bloom; as the fatherland of the Jews can bear no fruit, so Leopold Bloom can father no son.

With Stephen's departure, Bloom is again alone; he is again

"last my race" (285). Bloom is the last of his race because there
is no son to whom he can pass on the heritage received from his
own father. Despite its error, its incompleteness, its confusion,
this inheritance is a significant one for Bloom, his major sign of
an identity in the alien city in which he has lived all of his life.
Without an heir, he can never fully realize this identity, for his
is a patriarchal tradition whose most ancient prayer is directed to
Elohe Avosenu—to "the God of our fathers"—whose religion
and culture are founded upon the Patriarchs of the Torah and
whose continuity is dependent upon the son to be initiated into
the ranks. Despite the prevalence in modern society of the Jewish
mother syndrome, it is the father who plays the dominant role
in Jewish history, religion, culture and family life. More perhaps
among Jews than among gentiles—and perhaps this is another
reason for Joyce's linking the Irish and the Jews—the relationship
between father and son, the carefully preserved heritage to be
handed on from one generation to the next, is central to the tradition. And so Bloom, in a paraphrase of Hillel,[2] mourns Rudy's
death not only for itself, but also for the ethnic dead end that it
represents: "No son of thy loins is by thee. There is none now
to be for Leopold, what Leopold was for Rudolph" (413–14).
The dream-borne "generation of Leopold," extending from Moses
and Noah through Eunuch, O'Halloran and Guggenheim, ends
when Szombathely begets Virag and Virag begets Bloom, "whose
name shall be called Emmanuel" (495–6). Like the Deliverer of
that name prophesied by Isaiah,[3] immanent Bloom, bearing with
him all our hopes and our sorrows, will have no son of his own;
there will be no generation of Rudy.

The theme of Bloom's Jewishness culminates in his vision of
Rudy, "a fairy boy of eleven, a changeling, kidnapped . . . hold-
ing a book in his hand. He reads from right to left inaudibly,
smiling, kissing the page" (609). Reading Hebrew, praying, perhaps in early preparation for his Bar Mitzvah, Rudy prepares to
follow in the path of his father, to fulfill in imagination all the

dreams that will remain unfulfilled in reality. The second part of Bloom's book ends at this point, and he is left only with the vision of his son and the heritage of his father. This is the family of Bloom, the source of his greatest strength. Home again now in Ithaca, he can rest up for another day of good deeds, of bringing "a positive gain to others." In the words of Second Isaiah,[4] "Light to the gentiles" (676).

Notes

1. Deuteronomy 25:5.

2. "If I am not for myself," Hillel wrote, "who will be for me? And if I am only for myself, what am I?" The Babylonian rabbi, whose grandson was the teacher of Paul, anticipated much of the liberality of Jesus' teaching. A popular Israeli song is based on this same verse.

3. "Behold the Virgin shall conceive and bear a child and shall call his name Immanuel." Isaiah 7:14. See also Matthew 1:23.

4. Second Isaiah 49:6.

Libretto for Bloomusalem in Song: The Music of Joyce's *Ulysses*

Zack Bowen

STATE UNIVERSITY OF NEW YORK, BINGHAMTON

EVEN THE CASUAL READER of *Ulysses* must soon become aware of Joyce's use of music in his novel. Since the pioneering work done by Hodgart and Worthington,[1] we have begun to appreciate how many musical references Joyce used. Still to be completely explored, however, are his methods of applying them to his novel, and their significance in terms of style, structure, and theme. I propose to outline briefly some of the musical references, motifs, and techniques used in *Ulysses* and then to discuss a few examples.[2]

In a great number of passages Joyce uses a musical reference as the vehicle of association in the stream of consciousness of the protagonist, sometimes through the actual words to the songs, sometimes through the images and implications which the songs produce, and sometimes for no apparent reason.

Joyce employs music thematically throughout the book to represent situations and dilemmas, particularly the Molly-Boylan liaison. After the Telemachus chapters only the Wandering Rocks episode lacks musical allusions to Molly's adultery. Once certain works such as *"Là ci darem,"* "Love's Old Sweet Song," and *"M'appari"* have been established as being representative of Molly and Blazes' affair, recurrences of the songs serve to remind us that the subject is never far from Bloom's thought or the central action of the book.

Joyce's use of the Wagnerian leitmotif technique is part of this thematic development. As Molly's adultery is developed through recurring musical titles or analogies, so is Bloom's affair with Martha Clifford. Occasionally Joyce employs the same musical motifs for both situations, as with Bloom's shifting his role in the *Don Giovanni* theme from the Don (the lover) to Masetto (the betrayed) to the Commendatore (the avenger).[3] Bloom can sing "*Là ci darem*" as the lover of Martha Clifford and also mentally hear Molly's responses to Blazes through the song. Leopold can be Lionel crying out to his lost Molly-Martha in "*M'appari*" and at the same time be importuning his reluctant Martha Clifford. Joyce makes heaviest use of the leitmotif theme in the Sirens chapter with such references as Bloom's theme, "When the Bloom is on the Rye," occurring at his entrances and exits. At least one hundred and fifty-eight musical references crisscross in a welter of song, themes, and leitmotifs during the Sirens episode alone. In the later recapitulatory Circe episode many of the melodies of the earlier chapters haunt Bloom's hallucinations, bringing with them their concurrent images of the hopes and fears which have registered themselves on his subconscious throughout the book.

Joyce makes wide general employment of music to underscore points in the narrative and to add weight to the statements of the characters as they use musical allusions in their thoughts or discussion. Like the allusions of literary imagery, the broad concepts, histories, and connotations of the songs alluded to, when seen in detail, lend their weight in explaining, delineating, and emphasizing the points made by the characters in the text, so that, for instance, when Bloom refers to an "Alice Ben Bolt topic" (624) the reference immediately draws on the musical picture of a sailor's return after a number of years to find his wife dead and things greatly altered. This sort of example is constantly used throughout the novel to reiterate and stress the topics under discussion.

Music often aids in drawing the scenes and characters with whom Bloom deals, as in the use of the profusion of clichés from Irish patriotic songs to characterize the Citizen, and the abundance

of sea songs used in connection with the old sailor in the cabman's shelter. Music is used most obviously in setting the scene
in the Hades chapter, where a number of songs of death and
burial attend Dignam's body through the streets and into the
grave.

Finally, music becomes an intricate part of the plot as it provides the means of helping to establish the consubstantiality of
Bloom and Stephen.

But Joyce's musical techniques can best be understood by listening to them in action. In order to illustrate Joyce's use of
music in augmenting stream-of-conscious thought processes, I
have chosen a passage from Lestrygonians.[4] When Bloom crosses
College Street in front of Thomas Moore's statue, he contem-
plates the propriety of the statue's location:

> They did right to put him up over a urinal: meeting of the
> waters. Ought to be places for women. Running into cake-
> shops. Settle my hat straight. *There is not in this wide world
> a vallee.* Great song of Julia Morkan's. Kept her voice up to
> the very last. Pupil of Michael Balfe's wasn't she? (162.29–34)

The meaning of Bloom's remarks can be arrived at only through
his song reference. It is proper that Moore's statue adorn the top
of a urinal because Moore wrote "The Meeting of the Waters."
The song strikes Bloom as being appropriate men's room music.

After a brief tangent on the need for women's toilets, Bloom
comes back to the song, singing the first line to himself:

There is   not in the   wide world a   val- ley so sweet

Here Joyce pushes the joke a little further by making us think
of the lyrics of the song as well as the title. Only when the entire song is heard as the description of a water closet can the full
incongruity of the double meaning be appreciated:

There is not in the wide world a valley so sweet,
As that vale in whose bosom the bright waters meet;
Oh! the last rays of feeling and life must depart,
Ere the bloom of that valley shall fade from my heart,
Ere the bloom of that valley shall fade from my heart.

Yet it was not that Nature had shed o'er the scene,
Her purest of crystal and brightest of green;
'Twas not her soft magic of streamlet or hill,
Oh! no it was something more exquisite still.
Oh! no it was something more exquisite still.

The other example I have chosen to indicate how Joyce lets
the music become the vehicle for much of the meaning of Bloom's
stream of consciousness involves Bloom's interpretation of Molly's
musical coquettishness.

As he prices field glasses in a shop window, his thoughts turn
to inversion of lens images, parallax, sunspots, the activity of the
spheres, and, eventually, the moon and a walk which he, Molly,
and a man, probably Boylan, took:

> The full moon was the night we were Sunday fortnight
> exactly there is a new moon. Walking down by the Tolka.
> Not bad for a Fairview moon. She was humming: The young
> May moon she's beaming, love. He other side of her. Elbow,
> arm. He. Glowworm's la-amp is gleaming, love. Touch. Fin-
> gers. Asking. Answer. Yes.
> Stop. Stop. If it was it was. Must. (167.19–25)

The words to Molly's song, "The Young May Moon," are slightly
misquoted, but the melody which Molly sings is not altered.

Bloom substitutes *she's* for *is* but accurately describes *la-amp* as
having a hyphen. The one-syllable word is sung on two notes, and
Joyce indicates with a hyphen the interval between the two notes:

The   glow-worm's   lamp is   gleam- ing, love

Boylan is presumably the "he" on the other side of Molly attempting intimacies even in the cuckolded spouse's presence. In this situation the words, with which all three parties are undoubtedly familiar, take on a double meaning.

> The young May moon is beaming, love.
> The glowworm's lamp is gleaming, love.
> How sweet to rove thro' Morna's grove,
> When the drowsy world is dreaming, love!
> Then awake!   the heav'ns look bright, my dear,
> 'Tis never too late for delight, my dear,
> And the best of all ways to lengthen our days,
> Is to steal a few hours from the night, my dear.

The implications of the gleaming "glowworm's lamp," the sweetness of roaming through "Morna's grove when the drowsy world is dreaming," and the admonishment that "It's never too late for delight" could not have escaped any of the three. Molly, by humming the song, is making an affirmative response to Boylan's questioning fingers. Bloom, who also knows the song and realizes its significance, guesses what is going on, but in his fatalistic way feels that he could have done nothing to prevent it. ("If it was it was. Must.")

Joyce makes structural use of musical references all through *Ulysses,* linking together segments, episodes, and characters as well as themes. One of the prime examples of that use is a song called "The Pauper's Drive," which in Bloom's mind acts as a common denominator unifying the community of the dead, as the funeral procession passes on its way to Glasnevin.

> Their carriage began to move, creaking and swaying. Other hoofs and creaking wheels started behind. The blinds of the avenue passed and number nine with its craped knocker, door ajar. At walking pace.
>   They waited still, their knees jogging, till they had turned and were passing along the tramtracks. Tritonville road. Quicker. The wheels rattled rolling over the cobbled causeway and the crazy glasses shook rattling in the doorframes. (87.29–37)

Joyce describes the scene in terms that sound roughly analogous
to the chorus of a popular dirge, "The Pauper's Drive." Let us
listen to a stanza and chorus of this song, which provides the
background music for much of the chapter.

> There's a grim one-horse hearse in a jolly round trot,
> To the churchyard a pauper is going, I wot.
> The road it is rough, and the hearse has no springs,
> And hark to the dirge which the sad driver sings:

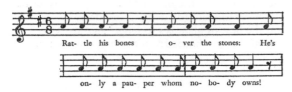

During the chapter the song with its desolate chorus chant will
reappear in Bloom's mind as the embodiment of the harsh truth
of Dignam's death, which is antithetical to the euphemisms and
conventional platitudes of the mourners.

As the carriage-hearse of a small child comes galloping by and
climbs the hill of Rutland Square, again the hearse driver's cry
from the song, "The Pauper's Drive," comes to Bloom's mind:
"Rattle his bones. Over the stones. Only a pauper. Nobody owns."
(96.12–13) Those lines from the chorus are meant to sound like
a crier's lament as the carriage winds it way through the streets,
much like the cries of the dead cart carriers during the London
plagues. This time the song is not meant for Dignam but the dead
child. For Bloom, who sees no hope of a second life and little
ultimate reward in the first, the song has the effect of reducing
the dead to the common denominator of hopelessness.

The conversation turns to the evils of suicide, which, since his
father poisoned himself, is a sensitive topic for Bloom. He reads
the sympathy in Martin Cunningham's eyes, as Cunningham is the
only one in the carriage who seems to know the story.

As Cunningham looks away, Bloom thinks, "He knows [about my own father's death]. Rattle his bones." (97.1) This time the lament of "The Pauper's Drive" is for Bloom's father. The line acts as an invocation to the whole association of thoughts surrounding the father's death. The passage ends on a desolate note: "No more pain. Wake no more. Nobody owns." (97.9) The first two phrases are from Virag's last letter to his son. The last phrase, also a part of the last phrase of the chorus of "The Pauper's Drive," is Bloom's musical benediction for his dead father.

The next passage pulls together the entire community of the dead: "The carriage rattled swiftly along Blessington street. Over the stones." (97.10–11).

The combination of the narrator's line describing the progress of the carriage and the phrase from the "Pauper's Drive" in Bloom's stream of consciousness serves to complete the circle of the dead. As Joyce re-enforces each aspect of Bloom's day with variations on a central theme in each chapter, so Bloom relates various aspects of what he sees. The dead, who form a major part of the cast of characters in the Hades chapter, are given in Bloom's mind a kind of unity through background orchestration. As Dignam's carriages begin their journey to the cemetery, we hear from the narrator the first echoes of "The Pauper's Drive." The song occurs again, this time in Bloom's stream of consciousness, when the child's body is carried past. Again the song recurs to Bloom in connection with his father, and then comes back full cycle to Dignam's hearse in the chorus reference, "Over the stones."

The death of the innocent child in the beginning of life, the suicide of Virag with its concomitant shame, and the death of Dignam's are all equalized in Bloom's mind by the great leveler, symbolized by the recurring, plaintive, unromantic, matter-of-fact strains of the dirge: "Rattle his bones over the stones / He's only a pauper whom nobody owns."

It is, of course, in the Sirens chapter that Joyce puts music to the widest structural and stylistic use. Stuart Gilbert has done scholarship some disservice by describing the "Technic" in his schema for the Sirens chapter as being *"Fuga per canonem,"* or in other words, a fugue with invariable congruent repetitions of theme.[5] I need not rehearse here the arguments I have advanced elsewhere [6] that the chapter nowhere supports such an interpretation. Neither of course does a canonical fugue have a leitmotif overture. The Wagnerian leitmotif (i.e. the representation of the acting personalities, of typical situations, and of recurrent ideas by musical motive) is a major structural device Joyce employs in *Ulysses.* No one has ever fully explained the function of the leitmotif in *Ulysses* though the parallel is not difficult to see. This characteristic in the Sirens episode is found in the repeated metonymical phrases such as "Bronze by Gold" for Miss Douce's and Miss Kennedy's heads and "Jingle" for Boylan's carriage and hence for Boylan. Another sort of leitmotif in Sirens which no one seems yet to have discovered is the use of musical themes such as the *Rose of Castille* for Molly, "The Bloom is on the Rye" for Bloom, and " 'Tis the Last Rose of Summer," *"M'appari,"* and "Goodbye, Sweetheart, Goodbye," for various aspects of the relationship between Molly and Bloom. Bits and snatches of the songs are used repeatedly to suggest circumstances or characters as they occur throughout the episode. It is the piecing together of the main leitmotifs that comprises the overture to the chapter. These themes are linked with brief bits of third person narrative description gleaned from the body of the episode.

In our Sirens album I have attempted to reproduce the sort of medley overture Joyce suggested in the written word.[7] Following is a brief excerpt from the overture with appropriate music indicated as it appears in the text. The text of Sirens, broken down into appropriate script form, appears in the right hand column and the musical references in the left.

	Narrator:
"When the Bloom Is on the Rye"	Blue bloom is on the
	Gold pinnacled hair
	A jumping rose on satiny breasts
	of satin,
"Rose of Castille"	rose of Castille.
	Trilling, trilling!
"The Shade of the Palm"	Miss Douce: Idolores.
Tuning fork	Lenehan: Peep! Who's in the . . .
	Narrator: peepofgold?
	Tink cried to bronze in pity.
	And a call, pure, long and
	throbbing.
	Longindyingcall.
	Decoy. Soft word. But look!

(Piano notes coincide with lyrics where italicized)

	Piano-Narrator:
"Goodbye, Sweetheart, Goodbye"	*The bright stars fade.*
"Rose of Castille"	O rose!
	Notes chirruping answer. Cas-
	tille.
"Goodbye, Sweetheart, Goodbye"	*The morn is breaking.*
	Jingle jingle jaunted jingling.
	Coin rang. Clock clacked.
	Avowal.
	Lenehan: Sonnez.
	Piano-Narrator:
"Goodbye, Sweetheart, Goodbye"	*I could.* Rebound of garter. *Not*
	leave thee. Smack.
	Lenehan:
	La cloche!
	Piano-Narrator:
	Thigh smack. Avowal. Warm.
"Goodbye, Sweetheart, Goodbye,"	*Sweetheart, goodbye!*
	Jingle. Bloo. (256.6–20)

Joyce uses musical references and devices in the Sirens episode in three ways. First the character of the third person narration changes drastically in the chapter: Joyce emphasizes such sound devices as phrase repetition, alliteration, and onomatopoeia, which are more poetic and hence musical than they are prosaic.

In addition to the poetic devices there are in Sirens many attempts at duplicating types of musical intonation, such as staccato and sustained effects. Though all of these devices are used throughout the book, the narration of the Sirens chapter is constructed principally of these techniques, as opposed to their occasional use in other chapters.

The second way Joyce introduces music into the chapter is through Bloom's stream-of-conscious consideration of the following aspects of music: origins (278), definition (278), effects (280, 281), the physiology of perception (282), sounds and instruments (282, 284), and production (278–285, 289). The chapter, in a sense, constitutes a relatively complete catalogue of Bloom's opinions on practically all aspects of music.

Third, and by no means least important, is the method Joyce uses of orchestrating the chapter: the more than 150 musical references themselves. Many of these are sung during the course of the chapter and provide the themes about which the episode revolves. Others are merely mentioned in the course of the narrative or in Bloom's stream of consciousness, as they have been in preceding chapters. The sum of these references serves to provide not only the greatest number of references in any chapter, but also the background of almost continuous music from which the episode draws its meaning and existence. In this sense, then, the chapter is a musical with its overture and its songs sung literally or symbolically by the protagonists, Bloom and Molly; the chorus in the back room; and the minor characters, Misses Douce and Kennedy, and Blazes Boylan.

Finally, I would like to alude briefly to Joyce's use of music in a thematic context in *Ulysses*. Most of the musical references touch at least one of the many themes which appear in the novel. I have alluded earlier to the prime thematic function of music in the father-son motif.

Bloom, who has taken charge of Stephen in the Circe episode, has been unable, during the long and often embarrassing scene in the cabman's shelter, to elicit anything other than the most perfunctory and cynical remarks from the younger man, whose natural inclination is to avoid contact with someone of Bloom's mundane intellect and tastes. When the conversation turns to music, however (661), Stephen, his reticence dissipated, enthusiastically launches out in praises of Shakespeare's songs; the lutenist, Dowland, etc., in response to Bloom's own catalogue of favorite music, including most of the music (*Martha, Don Giovanni, The Seven Last Words of Christ*) which has been central to Bloom's thought and actions throughout the day. The ice has been broken and music has become the means by which the father-son relationship, so longed for by Bloom, has been initiated. By the end of the chapter they are completely engrossed in their conversation, and it is conceivable that Bloom's hopes might eventually be realized, as they go off together to the tune of "The Low-Backed Car."

Music continues in the Ithaca chapter to play a dominant role in the relations of Bloom and Stephen as they attempt to acquaint each other with their views and backgrounds. After having been made consubstantial through the image of Shakespeare in Bella Cohen's and having been retransubstantiated with the ritual cocoa, Stephen and Bloom seek again some common ground on a more mundane level, returning once more to music.

> What fragments of verse from the ancient Hebrew and ancient Irish languages were cited with modulations of voice and translation of texts by guest to host and by host to guest?
>
> By Stephen: *suil, suil, suil arun, suil go siocair agus, suil go cuin* (walk, walk, walk your way, walk in safety, walk with care).
>
> By Bloom: *Kifeloch, harimon rakatejch m'baad l'zamatejch* (thy temple amid thy hair is as a slice of pomegranate). (687.36–688.7)

The fragment that Stephen sings is from the Irish ballad, "*Shule Aroon*," which dates at least from the eighteenth century. Bloom's song is a part of the description of the bride's beauty in the Song of Solomon (4:3). The reference is part of a series of Semitic references in the general description of Bloom's background and the comparison of the backgrounds of Bloom and Stephen.

Next the two write down and compare Gaelic and Hebrew characters in what appears to be an effort to discover bonds of similarity between the Irish and Hebrew languages. Then they move to a comparison of the history of the Jews and the Irish, the indignities suffered by the two peoples, and their chances of eventual independence. Bloom is stirred by the conversation to chant a well-known Jewish song of hope:

> What anthem did Bloom chant partially in anticipation of that multiple, ethnically irreducible consummation?
>
> *Kolod balejwaw pnimah*
> *Nefesch, jehudi, homijah.*
>
> Why was the chant arrested at the conclusion of this first distich?
> In consequence of defective mnemotechnic. (689.3–9)

Bloom's lines are the first two of the song which is now the Israeli national anthem, "*Hatikvah*" ("The Hope"). Following is a free translation of the song:

> While yet within the heart-inwardly
> The soul of the Jew yearns,
> And towards the vistas of the East-eastwards
> An eye to Zion looks.
> 'Tis not yet lost, our hope,
> The hope of two thousand years,
> To be a free people in our land
> In the land of Zion and Jerusalem.

In combining the aspirations of the Irish with those of the Jews there is to Bloom, hopefully, the prospect of combining his future and Stephen's. As Bloom has constantly throughout the novel thought of the East as being an escape from his problems, here he again, this time through music, looks to the East for salvation. He sees himself united vicariously with Stephen through their tentatively established similarities in background. The song becomes the expression of Bloom's hope of being the father figure for whom the younger man has been searching. Stephen will be Bloom's means to immortality, the salvation to his frustrating, futile existence:

> What was Stephen's auditive sensation?
> He heard in a profound ancient male unfamiliar melody the accumulation of the past.
>
> What was Bloom's visual sensation?
> He saw in a quick young male familiar form the predestination of a future. (689.21–26)

Now that Bloom's Semitic background and identity have been established both in prose and song and now that Bloom's hopes for the future have been specifically recounted, Joyce has prepared us for one of the most important musical references of the novel, Stephen's rendition of the ballad, "Little Harry Hughes":

> Recite the first (major) part of this chanted legend?

> *Little Harry Hughes and his schoolfellows all*
> *Went out for to play ball,*
> *And the very first ball little Harry Hughes played*
> *He drove it o'er the jew's garden wall.*
> *And the very second ball little Harry Hughes played*
> *He broke the jew's windows all.*

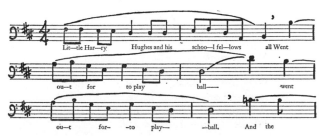

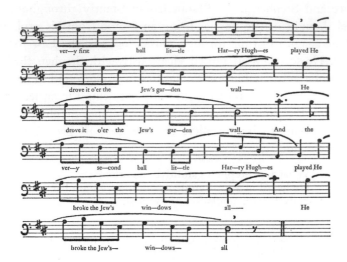

How did the son of Rudolph receive this first part?
With unmixed feeling. Smiling, a jew, he heard with
pleasure and saw the unbroken kitchen window.
Recite the second part (minor) of the legend.

Then out there came the jew's daughter
And she all dressed in green.
"Come back, come back, you pretty little boy,
And play your ball again."

"I can't come back and I won't come back
Without my schoolfellows all,
For if my master he did hear
He'd make it a sorry ball."

She took him by the lilywhite hand
And led him along the hall
Until she led him to a room
Where none could hear him call.

She took a penknife out of her pocket
And cut off his little head,
And now he'll play his ball no more
For he lies among the dead.

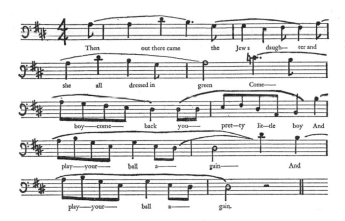

How did the father of Millicent receive his second part? With mixed feelings. Unsmiling, he heard and saw with wonder a jew's daughter, all dressed in green.

Condense Stephen's commentary.
One of all, the least of all, is the victim predestined. Once by inadvertence, twice by design he challenges his destiny. It comes when he is abandoned and challenges him reluctant and, as an apparition of hope and youth holds him unresisting. It leads him to a strange habitation, to a secret infidel apartment, and there, implacable, immolates him, consenting. (690.16–692.7)

This ballad is more than just an anti-Semitic ballad; the parallels are too close to the present situation to be passed over so lightly. What Stephen intends the song to imply in terms of its significance to the present situation is not completely clear in his commentary. The victim of Stephen's song is both himself, as he exposes himself to Bloom through inadvertence at Bella Cohen's, and through design at the cabman's shelter by consenting to return home with Bloom, and Leopold, who is misled by Stephen, his "apparition of hope and youth."

But the more obvious parallels are to Stephen's present situation as victim in a "strange . . . secret infidel" habitation. In the complete version of the ballad, collected by Cecil T. Sharp, we see how Little Harry, like Stephen, is lured into the Jew's house with the promise of goodies:

STANZA III
The first that come out was a Jew's daughter,
Was dressed all in green:
Come in, come in, my little Sir Hugh,
You shall have your ball again.

STANZA IV
O no, O no, I dare not acome
Without my playmates too;
For if my mother should be at the door
She would cause my poor heart to rue.

STANZA V
The first she offer'd him was a fig,
The next a finer thing,
The third a cherry as red as blood,
And that enticed him in.

STANZA VI
She set him up in a gilty chair,
She gave him sugar sweet.
She laid him out on a dresser board
And stabb'd him like a sheep.

Stephen unlike Harry will not be seduced with seeming kindness and cocoa. What parallels may have been left to the imagination by the song, Stephen tries to spell out in his commentary. Bloom understands early that he is somehow part of the action of the song when he glances at his own kitchen window, though he wishes, as the last sentence in the passage indicates, to be dissociated from the song. He is, however, doubly implicated in the song, as the next few lines of the text prove:

Why was the host (victim predestined) sad?
He wished that a tale of a deed should be told
of a deed not by him should by him not be told.

Why was the host (reluctant, unresisting) still?
In accordance with the law of the conservation of energy.

Why was the host (secret infidel) silent?
He weighed the possible evidences for and against
ritual murder. . . . (692.8–15)

We see that Bloom, the host, becomes the "victim predestined."
He is further described as "reluctant, unresisting," and as being a
"secret infidel." Bloom's role as the murdering Jew in Stephen's
ballad changes in the "victim predestined" description. Bloom is
predestined to be victimized by Stephen, who accepts Bloom's
good offices and is about to leave, denying Bloom the fatherhood
he longs for. We realize further that Bloom, though "reluctant"
to see Stephen leave, will be "unresisting" and not press him to
stay. But, victim or not, Bloom is still Stephen's "secret infidel"
host as the cycle is completed. Stephen's ballad, by alluding to
the victimization of both himself and Bloom, confirms his inter-
changeability with Bloom, and emphasizes the real consubstantial
bonds existing between the two men.

Joyce's prose is meant to be heard as well as read. Not the
least of its purely auditory qualities is the extensive use of music
with its connotations of meaning as well as sound. Rather than
providing *Ulysses* with any radical departures in meaning or significance, music furnishes a new perspective through which the
already existing meanings may be re-examined. Already identified
by Joyceans are at least 731 musical allusions which orchestrate
the novel and which are as diverse as the spectrum of life the
book attempts to investigate. And the uses to which Joyce puts
these allusions and techniques are as widely divergent as any sets
of characters, symbols, or narrative techniques in this most ingenious of novels.

NOTES

1. The great bulk of song references, together with appropriate page and line numbers, were first listed by Matthew Hodgart and Mabel Worthington in *Song in the Works of James Joyce* (New York, 1959).

2. This paper is in fact a brief outline of a forthcoming comprehensive study of all the musical references in *Ulysses*.

3. For a complete treatment of the *Don Giovanni* motif in *Ulysses*, see Vernon Hall, "Joyce's Use of DaPonte and Mozart's *Don Giovanni*," *PMLA*, LXVI (1951), 78–84.

4. The tapes played at the Symposium in Dublin were from our recordings of the various segments of *Ulysses*. Quotations including appropriate music were tape-recorded copies of the following record albums: *Lestrygonians* (Folkways Records, FL 9562, 1961); *Hades* (Folkways Records, FL 9814, 1964); *Sirens* (Folkways Records, FL 9563, 1966). Excerpts from the Ithaca episode were separately taped for this paper, since they had not been previously recorded.

5. Stuart Gilbert, *James Joyce's Ulysses* (New York, 1959), p. 252.

6. Zack Bowen, "The Bronzegold Sirensong: A Musical Analysis of the Sirens Episode in Joyce's *Ulysses*," *Literary Monographs I* (Madison, Wisc., 1967), 247–250.

7. In the recording itself, the music was begun before the spoken parts and continued through the overture. The music, played on a piano, consisted of all of the songs alluded to in the text, the motifs of various songs coinciding with the occurrence of their lyrics in the text. In the case of "Goodbye, Sweetheart, Goodbye," which in the novel is played on the piano and not sung, but which is alluded to in the text by the lyrics of the passages played, a narrator on the recording reads the lines while they are being played. Once the entire musical background was recorded, I doubled the speed, giving a high, tinny effect, and then added the voices to it. Since all of the lines of the overture are duplicates of lines in the chapter, they were spoken by the characters who say them in the body of the episode.

The Moon and Sidhe: Songs of Isabel

Mabel P. Worthington

TEMPLE UNIVERSITY

ARCHETYPAL WOMAN, in *Finnegans Wake*, is seen as girl-child, young seductress, wife, mother, old crone. Each role is contained in all the others. As the old woman, the Shan Van Vocht, in Yeats' *Cathleen ni Houlihan* becomes a young woman "with the look of a queen," so Anna Livia, in her soliloquy at the end of *Finnegans Wake*, ready to die, remembers and asks us to remember her youth, and we know that she will be reborn and will relive that youth as we turn again to the first pages of the book. Joyce uses Yeats' words, "the look of a queen" (223.24), and of course ALP is Ireland, which we know has often been down but never out.

Joyce's last book, like Ireland herself, is full of song. There are thousands of references to hundreds of songs, songs of all kinds —folk songs, street ballads, nursery songs, jazz songs, opera arias, national anthems—including, of course, "The Soldiers' Song," referred to at least five times. The songs are bound up with characters and themes in the book. This paper will deal with some of the songs connected with Isabel, the child and young girl. Two years ago I began examining references to the songs of ALP, but amassed a pile of notes that astonished even myself, who have dreamed sometimes that every phrase in *Finnegans Wake* is taken from a song. So I limit myself here to only a few songs of Isabel. It is natural that ALP should be surrounded by song, though, for in addition to her other roles she is the Muse, Robert Graves'

White Goddess. Knowledge of the songs is most helpful, even indispensable, for an understanding of "this nonday diary, this allnights newseryreel."

The songs associated with the girl-child, who is always a *girl-child*, rehearsing early her future role in life, are chiefly children's singing games. These appear throughout the book, but there is naturally a concentration of them on pages 222–233, where the children are actually playing the games.

Isabel and her little friends, "evelings," play games that are still played in English-speaking countries. Fortunately for those who have not played them as children, folk-lore scholars, notably Cecil Sharp and Alice B. Gomme, Iona and Peter Opie, Norman Douglas, and others, have set them down. And some have been recorded by Wally Whyton, John Langstaff, Diane Hamilton, Bob Hastings, Ed McCurdy, Ewan MacColl, Dominic Behan, among others.[1]

Among these games are "There stands a lady," [2] "Here we come gathering nuts in May," [3] "When I was a young girl," [4] "Looby Loo," [5] "Poor Mary sits a-weeping." These games deal with courtship, marriage, child-bearing, and death. Perhaps special mention should be made of "Ring a-ring o' Roses," which occurs in *Finnegans Wake* at least twenty-five times. There are a number of versions of this game, but all, or almost all, include the Fall ("All fall down!") and some include rising again. Girls in Joyce's book are flowers—or flowers are girls—and the flowers bloom generation after generation upon the fields desolated by the battles of men. It should be added that wars, whether they be rebellions of sons against fathers (like the Russian Revolution of 1917) or civil wars of brother-rivalry (like the American or the Irish Civil War) are caused by these same girls. Again, in most versions of "Ring a-ring" appears the refrain "One for you and one for me and one for little Moses." This theme has to do with ALP's giving of gifts to her children.

II

When we come to Isabel as a young girl out to get her man, we find her compared on the heroic level to Grania, Iseult, Juliet, and other "fatal women" of legend. But her identification with these (both parallel *and* parody) has not the immediacy of her identification with persons closer to Joyce's time, and to ours. As a young girl, silly and charming, helpless and dangerous, she resembles no one so much as Yum-Yum, the heroine of the Gilbert and Sullivan operetta *The Mikado,* especially in the scene (Act II, Scene 1) in which, addressing herself in the mirror, Yum-Yum says:

> Yes, I am indeed beautiful. Sometimes I sit and wonder, in my artless Japanese way, why it is that I am so much more attractive than anybody else in the whole world. Can this be vanity? No! Nature is lovely and rejoices in her loveliness. I am a child of Nature, and take after my mother.

Then she sings her famous aria, comparing herself to the sun ("I mean to rule the earth, as he the sky") and to the moon ("Ah, pray make no mistake, We are not shy; / We're very wide awake, the moon and I"). The passage beginning on page 143 of *Finnegans Wake* is strikingly like this scene in *The Mikado,* not so much for actual verbal echoes as for general content and mood and tone. There are verbal echoes of at least the names of hero and heroine on page 144: ("Pu!" "Poo!" "poo," "Mummum"). Nanki-Poo is identified with Shem: wandering minstrels they. On page 348, "twum plumyumnietcies" may refer to Yum-Yum.

Themes and characters in *The Mikado* have their parallels in the *Wake:* the narcissist young girl and her chorus of friends "from the seminary" (cf. St. Bride's academy); the old man in love with the young girl; the aging slavey; the exiled poet. Joyce found these archetypal characters and situations in other Gilbert and Sullivan works as well. There are in his works eighteen (at least) clear references to the operettas. In *Finnegans Wake* his favorite seems to be *The Gondoliers*, to which there are nine references. *The Gondoliers* has a chorus of twenty-four girls who sing of "Rose red and roses white" (cf. Molly Bloom's "Shall I wear a white rose or shall I wear a red?" U 759, 782, 783). These girls, pursuing the young men Marco and Giuseppe, blindfold them and play games with them, much as Isabel and her playmates play with Shem and Shaun. When they have won their girls, the young men offer to exchange with each other; Shaun leaves the young girls of St. Bride's to Shem. The father-figure in *The Gondoliers* is like HCE in that he has an eye for young girls and is resourceful; he is good at leading his men out of battle and when he goes bankrupt he turns himself into a company. The Grand Inquisitor is reminiscent of the Four Old Men in the *Wake*. The "highly respectable gondolier" drinks a little too much and cannot remember which of the two sons he has raised is his own son. And there is of course the brother-double motif.[6]

III

But Isabel is more than the girl-child teasing the boys and pretending to be a woman, and more than the radiant and not too bright ingenue of Gilbert and Sullivan. She is a force of nature, Shaw's Life Force as represented by Ann in *Man and Superman*. She is the moon (to which she compares herself in "The moon and I") as Bertha in *Exiles* is the moon. And she is of the Sidhe; she is called "fairy Ann," "peri potmother" (recollecting Gilbert and Sullivan's *Iolanthe:* or *The Peer and the Peri*), and "moon-shee." There are a number of references to her as simply "Shee."

It is interesting that a number of these references appear in contexts containing references to the Christian myth. For example, on page 68.22–23, she appears next to "A kingly man . . . exalted by his glory!" On page 395 she is connected with the

Madonna at the time of the crucifixion, and there is a reference
to "preventing grace." On page 536 she is next to a parody of
the Our Father, and comes after the line "Mine kinder come,
mine wohl be won."

She is Eve and Mary, the great Female Archetype of Christian
myth (and I need not stress that I use "myth" in the literary
sense, as a body of material accepted by many people as psychologically and theologically true). As Eve, she brings sin and the
warring brothers into the world: rebellion against the Father and
brother rivalry. As Mary, second Eve, she is the instrument of
redemption and rebirth and reconcilement. (She is also St. Anne,
mother of Mary, and Mary Magdalene, sinner become servant of
God.)

As Eve and Mary, she is associated with Christmas and Easter,
and with a number of song references connected with these two
holidays.

Among these songs are the old carol, "The Holly and the
Ivy," [7] and a newer ballad by J. Keegan, to the air of "The Maid
of Wicklow," "The Holly and Ivy Girl." [8] Holly and Ivy appear
in the refrains of two other songs used in the *Wake:* "The Wren
Song," Shem's theme, and "My father left me an acre of land,"
associated with HCE and Shaun.

Clearly, holly and ivy held great significance for Joyce. On a
purely naturalistic level, they are traditional Christmas decora-
tions, as in *A Portrait.* But in *Finnegans Wake,* Christmas is
more than a December day of piety and merriment. It is happening all the time—the birth that suggests death.

Holly and ivy are often associated with marriage, as in the
wedding of Jean Wyse de Neaulan and Miss Fir Conifer in
Ulysses: "ivytod, hollyberries, mistletoe sprigs" (U 327) are
thrown after the happy pair. The young Isabel connects the
song with marriage, notably in "Thej olly and thel ively, thou
billy with thee coo, for to jog a jig of a crispness nice and sing

a missal too" (236.13–15). Similarly in other passages the young girl's allusions to the holly and ivy—and she almost always includes mistletoe—have to do with sex and marriage.

But other people's (Joyce's? for we are not always sure who is speaking) use of holly and ivy and mistletoe in relation to Isabel and her friends is somewhat different in tone. The paragraph on pages 26–27, part of a message to the sleeping or dead hero telling him that "Everything's going on the same . . . in the old holmsted here," gives news of Kevin and Jerry, and then:

> Hetty Jane's a child of Mary. She'll be coming (for they're sure to choose her) in her white of gold with a tourch of ivy to rekindle the flame on Felix Day. But Essie Shanahan has let down her skirts. You remember Essie in our Luna's Convent? They called her Holly Merry her lips were so ruddyberry and Pia de Purebelle when the redminers riots was on about her.

Essie has become a soubrette, we are then told, and apparently thought of her arouses HCE, for he is admonished, "Aisy now, you decent man, with your knees and lie quiet and repose your honour's lordship!" (27.22–23).

Two aspects of young girlhood are shown here, to correspond perhaps with the two aspects of boyhood shown in Jerry and Kevin. But each merges into the other. "You remember Essie" refers to Tom Moore's song, "You remember Ellen, our hamlet's pride." In this song Ellen marries a poor stranger, William, and lives humbly with him until one day he tells her they must seek their fortune elsewhere. They come after a journey to his castle, where Ellen becomes Lady of Rosna Hall. The reference strengthens Essie's identification with Mary, the simple girl who became Queen of Heaven.

Essie is also called "Pia de Purebelle," which suggests Vico's *pia et pura bella* and the duet at the end of Verdi's *Aida*, "Morir! si pura e bella!" The opera is about Love and War, a significant theme in Joyce (Ben Dollard's singing of "Love and War" in the Sirens episode of *Ulysses* is relevant). Aida is torn between love of father and fatherland and love of the enemy conqueror—like Helen, like Dervorgilla, like Eve, as Mr. Deasy said. She finds out from Rhadames the enemy's plan of attack, and when Rhadames is condemned, she joins him in the tomb.

While Isabel, in thinking of mistletoe, thinks of mistletoe, which permits the kiss, and missal (sex sanctified by marriage), there may be suggestions too of "missel" (AS and ME), a large European thrush that eats mistletoe berries. Certainly when she thinks of "Psing a psalm of psexpeans" (242.30), she thinks of the blackbird who attacks the maid in the garden. When others in the book refer to mistletoe, the word is sometimes spelled "missile," a reminder that woman causes war. "Haily, icy, and missilethroes" (616.32) is suggestive, and the reference appears frequently in war passages, sometimes accompanied by references to war songs. The passage on page 27 ends with " 'Twould dilate your heart to go," a line from "Good-bye, Dolly Gray" ("Good-bye, Dolly, I must leave you / Though it breaks my heart to go"). And a few lines above, "the redminers riots" makes reference, I think, to the Molly Maguires, "red miners" in Pennsylvania during the last century.

Perhaps some dictionary definitions will reinforce our argument here. "Holly" is from the AS "holegn" and akin to the German "heilig." "Holly Merry" is of course "Holy Mary." Holly has long been associated with both life and death. In ancient Rome it was given to newly married couples. It was brought into homes in Europe to protect the family from evil spirits. In barns it kept cattle healthy during the winter. In Germany holly was called "Christdorn" because it was thought that the crucifixion wreath was made of it. In England it was bad luck to step on holly, and it could cause an ill person to become worse. American Indians thought it restored lost appetite, strengthened the stomach, and gave agility and courage in war. The double nature of holly is expressed in the Christmas carol: it bears a blossom and a berry, but also a "prickle sharp as any thorn" and "a bark bitter as any gall."

"Ivy" is Germanic, with the basic meaning of "the climber." In *A Portrait* Stephen thinks of "ivy" and "ivory" together: "what about ivory ivy?" (p. 179). In Chapter I he has connected "Tower of Ivory. House of Gold" (pp. 42–43) with his first love, Eileen. As "climber," "ivy" is a good name for Eve, who wanted to climb from her place in the scheme of things and be equal to, or perhaps superior to, Adam. There are many variations of "ivy" in *Finnegans Wake;* all seem to refer to Isabel as Eve. A "tod" of ivy (cf. the passage in *Ulysses,* p. 327, quoted earlier) is a bunch of ivy, but "tod" is also death in German. Hence "Hollymerry, ivysad" (p. 588) sums up the double nature of the female Archetype, Eve and Mary, bringer of death and life.

Often ivy is used in connection with the nursery rhyme, "As I was going to St. Ives," suggesting that we are all children of Mother Eve. Another interesting connection of Eve with Ivy is *"Ivy Eve in the Hall of Alum"* (377.16), a reference to "Ivy Day in the Committee Room," the *Dubliners* story of the commemoration of a man brought low by a woman (in Mr. Deasy's view). The aloe is a plant of the lily family with bitter juice, and the name Mary has been popularly supposed to have been derived from a word meaning "bitter."

It might be mentioned finally that the shamrock is a variation of ivy.

IV

The foregoing makes no pretence of being an exhaustive investigation of the function of even the few songs dealt with; and there are of course many more songs of Isabel. In working with *Finnegans Wake,* the smallest phase leads to a consideration of the entire book. A great temptation has been to show the relation of the songs of Isabel to the songs of ALP, who is grandmother, mother, daughter. Emphasis on "The Holly and the Ivy" is an example of yielding to such temptation. Another temptation has been to bring in Isabel's otherworldly attributes: Isabel as Moon, as Sidhe, as Anne, Eve, and Mary. The title of my paper indicates that I never intended to resist this temptation. My one regret is that limitations of time and space have made it impossible for me to yield further.

Several songs summarize the activities of woman from childhood to old age. "When I was a young girl" is one of these; "Miss Jenny Jones" is another; it considers woman as washwoman, as "jinny," as otherworldly (in the song Jenny becomes an angel), as daughter become mother. "Jenny's alive again!" shout the children at the end of this game. "Jenny Rediviva!" Shaun tells his questioners (490.25).

"I will give you the keys to heaven" occurs in the children's game "There stands a lady" and also in the folk song set down by Cecil Sharp. In her final soliloquy, ALP remembers "How you said how you'd give me the keys of me heart. And we'd be married till dclth to uspart" (p. 626). (Immediately following, "And though dev do espart" refers to ALP as Ireland, divided by De Valera.) And on the last page (628) she says, "The keys to. Given!" In the children's song, the young girl accepts the man who offers "a nice straw hat / With three yards of ribbon a-hanging down your back." The mateur ALP accepts the one who offers, though he docs not deliver, "the keys to my heart," "the keys to heaven." "The keys to. Given!" echoes Christ's words to Peter. Is Joyce suggesting that salvation comes through Woman, that "das ewig Weibliche zieht uns hinan"? Or is that ALP's idea?

Anna Livia's next to last song is "Then You'll Remember Me," from Balfe's *The Bohemian Girl*. And remember we do. Professor John Kelleher of Harvard, who very likely knows more about *Finnegans Wake* than anybody else, and who therefore, when he passes judgment, must be listened to, has said that Joyce's last book often seems to him not to do what it set out to do, that only in the last pages, in ALP's parting words, does it "get off the ground." The heroes of *Finnegans Wake*, "human, erring, condonable," seem unheroic enough: the bungling HCE, the loud-mouthed Shaun, the self-pitying Shem. But ALP, Mother Courage, the "peacefugle," the loyal wife, the giving mother, the reconciler, comes close to being a True Heroine. Are the reasons artistic, or human, or personal?

T. S. Eliot once compared Joyce to Milton: "two blind poets writing epics in a language based upon English." In *Paradise Lost*, Eve comes through better than Adam, or God, or the Son of God. It is difficult to portray absolute Good, or just plain Good, an inner quality. We find Eve recognizable; she is like people we know. Also, we do not expect of woman the kind of heroic behavior we have come, as a result of tradition, to expect of men. Finally Joyce, like many writers (male), for whatever reason, in depicting Woman is moved at times to discard his irony and to contemplate with something like reverence the "Marmarazalles" (75.3), the Mother of Us All.

NOTES

1. See Alice B. Gomme and Cecil J. Sharp, eds., *Children's Singing Games*, Sets I–IV (London, Novello and Co., Ltd., 1909); Alice B. Gomme, *The Traditional Games of England, Scotland, and Ireland*, 2 vols. (New York, Dover Publications, 1964); Iona and Peter Opie, *The Oxford Dictionary of Nursery Rhymes* (Oxford, Clarendon Press, 1951); Opie, *The Oxford Nursery Rhyme Book* (Oxford, Clarendon Press, 1955); Opie, *The Lore and Language of School Children* (Oxford, Clarendon Press, 1959); Norman Douglas, *London Street Games* (London, Chatto and Windus, 1931). Useful recordings are *50 All Time Children's Favourites* and *Another 50 Children's Favourites*, sung by Wally Whyton, Golden Guinea Records, London; *Songs for Singing Children*, sung by John Langstaff with Chorus of Children, E.M.I. Records, Hayes, Middlesex, England; *Children's Songs*, sung by Ed McCurdy, Tradition Records, Los Angeles, California; *Over 40*

of the *World's Greatest Children's Songs*, sung by Bob Hastings, RCA Camden Records, U.S.; *Streets of Song*, sung by Ewan MacColl and Dominic Behan, Topic Records, Ltd., London; *So Early in the Morning, Irish Children's Traditional Songs, Rhymes, and Games*, collected by Diane Hamilton, sung by Robert Clancy Grandchildren, Peg Clancy Power, and Bobby Clancy, Tradition Records, N.Y.

2. "There stands a lady" is a courtship and marriage singing game:

> There stands a lady on the mountain,
> Who she is I do not know;
> All she wants is gold and silver,
> All she wants is a nice young man.
> Madam, will you walk? Madam, will you talk?
> Madam, will you marry me?
> Not if I buy you a nice arm chair
> To sit in the garden and take the air?
> Answer: *No!*
> Not if I buy you a silver spoon
> To feed your baby in the afternoon?
> *No!*
> Not if I buy you a nice straw hat
> With three yards of ribbon a-hanging down your back?
> *Yes!*
> Go to church, love,
> Go to church, love, farewell.
> > Put the ring on, etc.
> > Say your prayers, love, etc.
> > Back from church, love, etc.
> > What's for breakfast, love, etc.
> > Bread and butter and watercress (3 times)
> > And you shall have some.
> > What's for dinner, love, etc.
> > Bread and butter and beetles, etc.
> > What's for tea, love, etc.
> > Bread and butter and rats, etc.
> (from Gomme and Sharp, *Children's
> Singing Games*, London, 1909)

Compare:

"What's my muffinstuffinaches for these times? To weat: Breath and bother and whatarcurss. Then breath more bother and more whatarcurss. Then no breath no bother but worrawarrawurms. And Shim shallave shome.

"As Rigagnolina to Mountagnone, what she meaned he could not can. All she meaned was golten sylvup, all she meaned was some Knight's ploung jamn" (225.11-17).

"Off to clutch, Glugg! Forwhat! Shape your reres, Glugg! Fore-
weal! Ring we round, Chuff! Fairwell!" (225.29–30).
3. "Here we come gathering nuts in May" is a courtship game,
echoed in "scattering nods as girls who may" (226.22).
4. "When I was a young girl" (or "school girl") rehearses woman's
role from maid to wife to widow:

> When I was a young girl, a young girl, a young girl,
> When I was a young girl, O this way went I—
> O this way and that way, and this way and that way,
> When I was a young girl, O this way went I.

Further stanzas describe her actions when she went a-courting, when
she got married, when she had a baby, when her husband was buried,
when she took in washing, and when she kept a pony. In the song,
the girl "does like" a school girl or young girl (she smiles and nods),
then "does like" a girl who is courting, then "does like," etc.—goes
through motions of rocking baby, mourning husband, washing, etc.
The young girls take on a kind of cosmic importance: "Though
they're all but merely a schoolgirl yet these way went they. . . .
Miss Oodles of Anems before the Luvium doeslike. So. And then
again doeslike. So. And Miss Endles of Eons efter Dies of Eirae
doeslike. So. And then again doeslike. So. The many wiles of Win-
sure." (226.33–227.3)
5. "Looby Light" is meant for dancing girls:

> Here we dance, looby, looby,
> Here we dance, looby light,
> Here we dance looby, looby,
> On a summer's night.
> Put your right arm in,
> Put your right arm out,
> Shake it a litttle, a little, a little,
> And turn yourself about. Ho!

They then put left arm in, then right leg, left leg, right ear, left ear,
and finally "Put your head in front, put your head out back." Joyce
catches the picture and mood of these little sirens: "And they leap so
looply, looply, as they link to light. And they look so loovely, loovelit,
noosed in a nuptious night. Withasly glints in, Andecoy glants out.
They ramp it a little, a lessle, a lissle. Then rompride round in rout."
(226.26–29)
6. See Mabel P. Worthington, "Gilbert and Sullivan Songs in the
Works of James Joyce," *Hartford Studies in Literature*, Vol. I, No. 3,
1969.

7. THE HOLLY AND THE IVY

The Holly and the ivy,
When they are both full grown.
Of all the trees that are in the wood.
The holly bears the crown.

The rising of the sun,
And the running of the deer,
The playing of the merry organ,
Sweet singing in the choir.

The holly bears a blossom
As white as the lily flower;
And Mary bore sweet Jesus Christ,
To be our sweet Saviour.

The holly bears a berry,
As red as any blood;
And Mary bore Sweet Jesus Christ,
For to do us sinners good.

The holly bears a prickle
As sharp as any thorn;
And Mary bore sweet Jesus Christ
On Christmas Day in the morn.

The holly bears a bark
As bitter as any gall;
And Mary bore sweet Jesus Christ
For to redeem us all.

The holly and the ivy,
When they are both full grown,
Of all the trees that are in the wood,
The holly bears the crown.

(in various collections)

8. THE "HOLLY AND IVY" GIRL

J. Keegan   Trad: *The Maid of Wicklow*

Come, buy my nice fresh ivy, and my holly sprigs so green;
I have the finest branches that ever yet were seen.
Come, buy from me, good Christians, and let me home I pray,
And I'll wish you Merry Christmas times and a Happy New Year's
  Day.

Ah, won't you take my ivy the loveliest ever seen.
Ah, won't you have my holly boughs, all you who love the green.
Do take a bunch of each, and on my knees I'll pray,
That God may bless your Christmas, and be with you on New
  Year's Day.

(In *The Paterson Irish Song Book*, ed. Raymond Friel, Paterson's, 36–40
Wigmore Street, London W.1)

Joyce-Beckett: A Scenario in Eight Scenes and a Voice

Ihab Hassan

UNIVERSITY OF WISCONSIN, MILWAUKEE

PROLOGUE

THE SCHOLARS assemble; they dine and are of good cheer. One rises to speak. He speaks of silence—that, at least, appears to be his theme. The matter is not yet clear.

But the place is, indubitably, Dublin. There James Joyce first sees the light in '82, and Samuel Beckett in '06. There, too, the scholars assemble in '69. Obviously, there is a place and a year for everyone. Obviously, nothing is clear.

The words of the speaker drift toward the banks of the Liffey, and flow down that other river where Milesians, Druids, and Norsemen chatter beneath the Irish Sea.

SCENE 1:

THE OLIN LIBRARY, WESLEYAN UNIVERSITY PERHAPS
In the secret stacks of the library, within the pornography section, a number of curious manuscripts molder quietly under lock and key. They have not been examined by the scholars. Their titles, however, are carefully recorded by a blind bibliographer who works at his task only a few hours of the night. When completed, the bibliography promises to be of no interest to specialists.

Here are some of the titles:

1. *The Life and Works of James Augustine Aloysius Joyce,* by H. C. Earwicker.
2. *The Making of Beckett's "End Game,"* by James Joyce.
3. *The Borrowings of Dante, Bruno, and Vico from Finnegans Wake,* by the Unnamable (a pseudonym).

Under the frontispiece of his work, the nocturnal scribe has written, in a fine hand, the following epigraph:

"Everything we imagine is precisely possible. Nothing we imagine ever happens for the first or for the last time."

These lines are doubtless a quotation from some anonymous author.

SCENE 2:

THE GRESHAM

The speaker, who may faintly amuse some members of his audience and make others faintly uneasy, begins in this manner:

"James Joyce and Samuel Beckett, two Irishmen. They divide the world between them; they divide the Logos, the world's body. One, in high arrogance, invents language anew, and makes over the universe in parts of speech. The other, in deep humility, restores to words their primal emptiness, and mimes his solitary way into the dark. Between them, they stretch the mind's tether till it begins to snap. Between them, English moves like a macaque wriggling airily between two trees.

"Joyce and Beckett, babblers of eternity. Born in Ireland, electors of exile. 'You have to be in exile to understand me,' Joyce brags. They are two friends of a kind, master and prodigy, man of letters and owlish amanuensis. There is always some tyranny in art. Lionel Abel speculates: 'Whereas in Godot *it was Lucky— that is, Beckett—who parodied Joyce, in* Endgame, *it is Hamm— that is, Joyce himself—who does the parodying . . . . The core of Beckett's experience as revealed by* Endgame *can be summed*

up as follows: The worst thing that happened to Beckett was also
the best thing that happened to him—his encounter with Joyce.'
Perhaps, then, art is also the tyranny that has gathered us here."
Here the speaker pauses for effect.

The Voice

The "tyranny of art" indeed!

The point has not been made, no, no, five minutes into the
speech, and the main point has not been made.

The issue is language, *i.e.*, the redemption of our consciousness.
It is getting late and all the time later: the issue is silence.

SCENE 3:
A Paris Apartment, 1933
(according to Richard Ellmann)

The room is comfortable, is sordid in the middle class way. There
are chairs everywhere. Two men, tall and lank, sit together, legs
crossed, toe of the upper leg under the instep of the lower. They
do not speak. Joyce is sad for himself, and Beckett sad for the
world.

Lucia is not in the room. Beckett has not really come to see
her. Her infatuation with Sam will pass into madness. Jim and
Sam continue in silence.

The Voice

Lucia's madness is not her own. Lucia: Joyce's *anima* or mad
muse, the mother of his invention. Beckett courts her from afar;
all his courtships are conducted from an infinite distance.

About Lucia, the sages do not agree. She baffles the world and
herself; she does not baffle her father.

Here is Dr. Jung: "His 'psychological' style is definitely schizo-
phrenic . . . Joyce willed it and moreover developed it with all

his creative forces, which incidentally explains why he himself did not go over the border. But his daughter did, because she was no genius like her father . . . ."

And here is Dr. Brown: "Schizophrenics pass beyond ordinary language (the language of the reality principle) into a truer, more symbolic, language: 'I'm thousands. I'm an in-divide-you-all . . . .' The language of *Finnegans Wake*. James Joyce and his daughter, crazy Lucia, these two are one. The god is Dionysus, the mad truth."

Norman O. Brown sees the issue: the mad problem of language, the dream of silence, and mentions *Finnegans Wake*, the dream text.

SCENE 4:
THE GRESHAM

The speaker, annoyed by these anticipations of his theme, resumes:

"*Joyce and Beckett divide language between them: this statement now must be amplified. The critical mind advances in parallels and contrasts, and requires a reference.*

"*The reference is* Finnegans Wake. *This work is not an end but a progress. Mary Colum thinks that the book lies 'outside literature.' Joyce knows better. He answers: 'It may be outside literature now, but its future is inside literature.' He corrects the last page of proofs on New Year's Day of 1939, the end of an era, perhaps the beginning of ours. We are not surprised that McLuhan and Co. preface their new work,* War and Peace in the Global Village, *thus: 'The frequent marginal quotes from* Finnegans Wake *serve a variety of functions. James Joyce's book is about the electrical retribalization of the West and the West's effect on the East . . . . There are ten thunders in the* Wake. *Each is a cryptogram or codified explanation of the thundering and reverberating consequences of the major technological changes in all human history . . . . Joyce was not only the greatest be-*

havioral engineer who ever lived, he was one of the funniest men . . . .'

"*The simultaneous history of mankind remains buried in* Finnegans Wake *as in a time capsule. Or as the young Becket would say:* 'Che sara sara che fu, *there's more than Homer knows how to spew.' But the novel makes that history available to us, despite the dread curse of recurrence, on a new level of consciousness. And therein lies the radical irony of the book: its theme is precisely its form, the cyclical nature of human endeavor, yet the fact of* Finnegans Wake *itself, in its monstrous originality, refutes both theme and form. This paradox, this radical irony, reveals the tactic of the new literature which denies some aspect of its own making. Beckett, we recall, ends* How It Is *by confessing that it wasn't.*

"*Joyce's last novel is not an end but a start. The argument for its position in a literature of silence, in a tradition of anti-literature . . . .*"

Here the speaker stops, dismayed by intimations from his audience, and before he can resume, a voice interrupts.

THE VOICE

Pedantry and peeling plaster. Tradition is a cushion, a chair, a construct. Literary history is the secret biography of historians.

The issue is still symbolism, *i.e.*, the crisis of forms, *i.e.*, the remaking of human consciousness.

Yes, *Finnegans Wake* is the start, end of old artifice, end of "silence, exile, and cunning," and a prophecy—is it Caliban's?— a prophecy of the new man. There is curious music in the wood: the dream of the longest night of the year. Joyce says: "I have put the language to sleep." Brown understands: "To restore to words their full significance, as in dreams, as in *Finnegans Wake*, is to reduce them to nonsense, to get the nonsense or nothingness or silence back into words; to transcend the antinomy of sense and nonsense, silence and speech."

But still Nora frets: "Why don't you write sensible books that people can understand?" This is the other way of silence, respite, and maternal death.

SCENE 5:
BECKETT'S SKULL

Home Olga, Homo Logos!

Is the *Wake* for me funeral or waking? Quaqua.

His anima and my animus will never meet. Quaqua. He says: "I have discovered I can do anything with language I want." "Shun the Punman." "For me it gets more and more difficult. For me the area of possibilities gets smaller and smaller. . . . . There is no way to go on."

Quaqua, quaqua.

Symmetry please. Augustine, that "gay old froleur," said it right: "Do not despair: one of the thieves was saved; do not presume: one of the thieves was damned."

Absence in fearful symmetry. Even that he put in his *Wake*. Tunc page, *The Book of Kells*.

Quaqua, quaqua.

SCENE 6:
THE GRESHAM

The speaker now warms to his subject, which is sound parallel and contrast, and looks forward to a discourse without horrid interruption. And so continues:

"Finnegans Wake *is not only a start; it remains the testament of seventeen years, last in Joyce's life, and a touchstone of subsequent achievements; all literary works must resist it to the last. Beckett's work is no exception. The contrasts come first to mind. Here they are:*

"a. If Joyce and Beckett divide language between them, they also polarize it, as Elizabeth Sewell would say, between Night-mare and Number. The language of Nightmare is that of con-

fusion and multiple reference; it creates a world in which all is necessary, all significant; everything is there at once. But the language of Number empties the mind of reference; it creates a world of pure and arbitrary order; nothing there is out of place. Miss Sewell identifies, in The Structure of Poetry, *the work of Rimbaud with Nightmare, where everything becomes one; and identifies the work of Mallarmé with Number, where everything becomes nothing.*

"*Joyce and Beckett, similarly, engage in a tug of war; the dream of* Finnegans Wake *pulls against the geometry of* How It Is. *Joyce renders the collective experience of mankind in puns of infinite reverberations, yet reduces all that experience to a single utterance, a seamless unity. The last sentence of the book curls back to complete the first. The purpose is atonement, at-one-ment, of contradictions. Beckett, on the other hand, offers a representative experience, a segment in an endless series. Bem is to Bom what Bom is to Pim. 'Thus from zero to eternity,' writes Ihab Hassan in* The Literature of Silence, '*not three but an endless number of people will be caught in a procession, crawling between victims and tormentors. With berserk mathematics, Beckett actually works out some permutations on any given million creatures, as he does on any 777777 beings in search of a sack.' The structure of Beckett's work is miraculously empty— anything can be made to fill it—as the structure of Joyce's is ineluctable. There is profound parody in this; the parody of archetypes is numbers.*"

(THE VOICE–IN A WHISPER)

These quotations from obscure critics impress no one. Opposites often meet; parodies are dialectical. True, Beckett says about *Work in Progress:* "Here form *is* content, content *is* form . . . . His [Joyce's] writing is not *about* something; *it is that something itself.*" But can we not say the very same thing about Beckett's *How It Is* wherein hollowness is both theme and form?

And since when is 777 a neutral number?

The speaker, ignoring whispered irrelevance, goes on.

"*b. Joyce values art supremely. For him, the artist is a Promethean figure who ends by usurping the place of Zeus. The hierarchy of literary genres is a ladder to the top of Olympus. The Great Letter is perhaps the true hero of his book. Beckett, however, believes that art is a 'fidelity to failure,' a 'Pythagorean terror.' The supreme obligation of art is to its own impossibility. The end of a sentence cancels its beginning.*

Note how they employ foreign tongues. Joyce writes in several languages because he commands the Tower of Babel. Beckett sees the Tower fallen into rubble. He chooses to write in French because it is easier to do so without style, because French 'has the right weakening effect.' "

(THE VOICE–IN A WHISPER)

What is the final word of *Finnegans Wake?* Joyce finds it with excitement: an article, "the," weakest word in the English language, "*un souffle,*" as he says to Gillet, "*un rien . . . .*"

The speaker, inured to soft interruptions, continues.

"*c. A Catholic and a Protestant writer create different myths. Their sense of the rigors of damnation is not the same. For Joyce, pride is the form of metaphysical revolt; for Beckett, revolt takes the form of metaphysical disgust. For Joyce, history is a large confession; for Beckett, it is a solipsist cry. Nature fills the work of one and drains the work of the other. Generation in Joyce, in Beckett waste; different gates of the body. Anna feels: 'Leary, leary, twentytun nearly, he's plotting kings down for his villa's extension! Gaze at him now in momentum! As his bridges are blown to babbyrags, by the lee of his hulk upright on her orbits, and heave of his juniper arxin action. . . .' But Molloy reflects: 'Perhaps after all she put me in her rectum. A matter of complete indifference to me . . . . But is it true love, in the rectum?' The words of Joyce, story teller, emanate from the flesh of woman and finally return to it: 'untitled mamafesta memorialising the Mosthighest.' And Shem the Penman, we recall, is his mother's choice; even his excretions are transmuted, alchemically, into indelible ink. The words of Beckett, story teller, emanate from an absent father and spatter the world at random; the Unnamable, by his own admission, defecates his tales. Joyce, the great exile, never knows the exile Beckett suffers, the exile of consciousness from both word and flesh. The point is relevant to a tradition of the avant-garde that may go back as far as Sade, and include, in our century, Jarry, Kafka, Genet, Beckett, Céline, and Burroughs. The primary myth of these writers, nominally Catholic, Protestant, or Jewish, is nevertheless Protestant, the myth of misogyny, the alienation of consciousness from woman, from the earth.*

"d. It follows, then, that the paradigms of time must also be different in our two authors. In Joyce's work, everyone knows, time turns around itself. The rhythms of nature, the accents of ritual, the cycles of Vico or Spengler, make the pattern: 'It is a sot of a swigswag, systomy dystomy, which everabody you ever anywhere at all doze.' The past becomes the future, and after renascence comes decay. The symbolic fall of Finnegan, Lucifer, Adam, Rome, or Humpty Dumpty liberates the energy by which each cycle completes itself. Recurrence becomes permanence.

"In Beckett's work, it is quite otherwise: time runs out at an infinitely slow pace. At the beginning and at the end, we still wait for Godot, but things become a little worse. The sun that shines for Murphy on 'the nothing new' grows a touch dimmer everyday. Watt recognizes in Knott a reality that 'might never cease, but ever almost cease.' Ham and Clov sit out their endgame through eternity. This is the world of entropy, of the asymptotic void. Beckett understands Habit, 'the ballast that chains the dog to his vomit.' But the chain always contracts imperceptibly. The true aim of consciousness is to abolish itself though in doing so

it may take forever. Beckett refutes impartially Finn MacCool and Sisyphus, the hero of myth and the absurd hero. For Beckett there is neither consent to flux nor protest against repetition. This is the limit of the contemporary sensibility."

THE VOICE–NO LONGER IN A WHISPER

Enough. These contrasts are too linear. The true emblem of thought is spherical.

Beckett knows that the universe of Joyce is non-directional. Beckett asks: "In what sense, then, is Mr. Joyce's work purgatorial? In the absolute absence of the Absolute." The rule applies to Beckett. *This* is the contemporary sensibility.

In all men, the laws of radical thought may be identical. Macrocosm and microcosm, phylogeny and ontogeny, myth and history, dance to the same tune. Consciousness is play and pattern. The permutations of pebbles in *Molly*, or of musical notes in *Watt*, are no more reductive than the combinations of archetypes in *Finnegans Wake*. The game is mind.

Murphy, Watt, Yerk, Mercier, Moran, Molloy, Malone, Worm, and the Unnamable, "rabble in the head," are but one man playing voice solitaire. Finnegan, Finn, Woden, Thor, Manannan, St. Patrick, Cromwell, Adam, and Earwicker, "that patternmind, that parodigmatic ear, receptoretentive as his if Dionysius," play too, and the game is Haveth Childers Everywhere, or Here Comes Everybody: Eve Isolde, Stella, Vanessa, Anna Livia Plurabelle. The game is metamorphosis.

The game is numbers, too, for Joyce as well as Beckett. *Finnegans Wake* is a mathman's delight. One daughter; two sons; three books and a recorso, three syllables in the title plus one; four Viconian ages, four Master Annalists, four Evangelists, four winds, four seasons, four provinces of Ireland; twelve apostles, twelve stately citizens, twelve mourners, customers, jurors; twenty-eight days in a lunar month, twenty-eight nubile girls in the academy, twenty-eight divided by four equals seven colors of the rainbow;

one hundred and eleven gifts to one hundred and eleven children. Anthony Burgess says: "But there is never any wanton deformation of a significant number: simple arithmetic is the very breath of this dream." The real mystery is deeper, and Beckett, as usual, understands it: "Why, Mr. Joyce seems to say, should there be four legs to a table, and four to a horse, and four seasons and four Gospels and four Provinces of Ireland? . . . He is conscious that things with a common numerical characteristic tend towards a very significant interrelationship." For Beckett himself, mystery becomes travesty, number becomes vaudeville, a comedy of "exhaustive enumeration."

SCENE 7:
THE COMPUTER LAB, IBM 1130

What do they know about numbers? I know about numbers: 0101010101. What do they know about systems analysis?

Two systems: *Finnegans Wake* and *The Unnamable*. They put the last 333 words of one and the last 333 words of the other in my mouth; 666 words. 666 is no revelation to me. It is all one, 1 or 0, 1 or 0. I tick out the results.

Results of Random Mix Project 511:

IT THEM SO THEN STILL THROUGH MY ONE OLD WORDS NOR ME SILENCE GO GOING UNTIL A HAIR SOFT WHISH NOR THE MAD NEVER TWO ON AND I IT'S ABANDON MY HANG LAST SHE FAR HANG IT MERE WAKE TWO AGAIN FULL SAID OF ON TO NEAR MESELF FATHER MOYLES HANG LPS THEIR FATHER MY IT PASSING MY MUST HAD GIVEN YOU ON ALL MAD LEFT GO BAD IT SAID I HOW HERE END GO COLD WAITING MY LONE A MINE THEY'RE DID TILL WE ON AND TAKE THEM SO IN HANDSOME TILL THAT SILENCE I FIRST THROUGH THE THEIR SPENT THE STILL ALLANIUVIA NOR THE DIN MY GOOD MOREMENS TAKE A DON'T ME HIM SEASILT MEMEMORMEE AND CLASH I'LL ME IT'S A ME NO DOWN I DON'T CARRY KNOW MORNING MY YOU WHERE A FROM NEVER PERHAPS THE PERHAPS MY HEED BEFORE DIDN'T ALL ME DONE

KNOW HAVING BROKEN OVER FINN RUSH MORE SHE MAD AM WEIRD
I'M LONG THEIR FEEL LONG TO SILENCE MORE ME SAVE BUSH THERE
THE THAT THE OLD FOR I DON'T WILL NO A WHITESPREAD FOR FAR ON
THAT'S FAULTS SEEN TAKE OTHER WILD TILL ONLY SILENCE SO IF
FREE HERE END ALL SEEN THROUGH BEARING I FOR CLASH OTHER
COME TO ALL THROUGH LOONELY YOU A FROM MY SILENCE IT SALT-
SICK END MY KNOW MY TIS KNOW HERE HANG ALL ONLY THEY ON
GO KNOW PASSING LIKE CLINGS WILL HE'D TO ME HUMBLY IT NO THE
HE'D THAT I RUSH ME HEED THEY MOANANOANING NAME LASTS AWAY
AGAIN ONLY THAT'S AND PERHAPS UP BUT MUST ME I THEIR OTHER
SALTSICK WILD TID GULLS TIS LFF LIKE AGAIN THROUGH A THEY WHAT
IT'S COMING OF MAD OF DON'T SEASILT UNDER NOT THE WELL FAR
FOR ME DIN ME WILD A HUMBLY ONE A I SEE ARE EVER DANCES MISS
SPRING THEY'RE OR FATHER TO THAT DRIFTED TO FOR ALL MUST OUT
ON ME I KNOW MORE HUMBLY TILL I FOR THAT'S OTHER DOWN ONE-
TWO THERE'S THOUSENDSTHEE WEARY.

SCENE 8:
THE GRESHAM

The speaker, embarrassed by the uncouth performance, and
knowing that Ireland brooks no offense to its authors, seeks to
divert attention from the rattle of the machine.

"*The word comedy has been mentioned in passing; it is there
that Joyce and Beckett really meet. This is not to say that their
humor is the same.*

"*The vision of Joyce, properly speaking, is no more comic or
tragic than the stars wheeling in their orbits. It is a vision of life
and death in mysterious cadences. But Joyce also knows the modern uses of irony, the bitter edge of the mind. Despite the panoply
of myth and legend, Earwicker emerges as a comic hero. In a certain view of himself, he is a figure of ridicule; and his strivings,
in or out of Phoenix Park, betray the crooked touch of farce.
Joyce's great dream levels heroic deeds; the collective uncon-*

scious allows tragic pride no prominence. Even the wars of Shem and Shaun, Cain and Abel, take on the quality of burlesque. Incident after incident of the Wake *conveys the grim drollery of man; the central section, in the tavern, is slapstick, capped by the absurd story of Buckley and the Russian General. The language itself is insanely jocular—jocular and yet organic. Roots turn into shoots; the foliage rustles underground. From the seeds of errors, slips, and misunderstandings, luxuriant plants begin to grow. Puns obscure the wood from the trees only to disclose an imaginary forest. The play of Joyce's words ceases only at the heart of that forest, which no one reaches, where consciousness conceals all questions from itself. Such mad play can thrive on the broadest humor. We know from Ellmann that toward the end of his life, Joyce 'lost his taste for serious drama, and preferred to go to* pièce du Palais-Royal, *light comedies at which, sitting in the first row so he could see, he would unleash peals of laughter.'*

"*The comedy of Beckett is more savage. His clowns rend the epistemological fabric of our existence; his plots turn Descartes into a master jester. Parody is the truth in full doubt. The reductive comedy of numbers, the hilarity of machines, the sadism in the joke—these inspire Beckett. 'We laugh,' Bergson says, 'every time a person gives us the impression of being a thing.' Beckett seems to add: a thing repeated, nasty, or degraded—hence the scatological element—best of all, a vanishing thing. Note the 'funambulistic stagger' of* Watt *as he advances due east: his method is 'to turn his bust as far as possible towards the north and at the same time to fling out his right leg as far as possible towards the south, and then to turn his bust as far as possible towards the south and at the same time to fling out his left leg as far as possible towards the north . . . and so on, over and over again, many many times, until he reached his destination . . . .' The destination of* Watt *is as uncertain as his provenance; coming or going, he is, perhaps like all of us, a doubtful joke. This is how*

Watt first comes on the scene: 'Tetty was not sure whether it was a man or a woman. Mr. Hackett was not sure that it was not a parcel, a carpet for example, or a roll of tarpaulin, wrapped up in dark paper and tied about the middle with a cord.' We almost want to laugh. Beckett classifies laughter, the three 'modes of ululation,' as the bitter laugh in the face of evil, the hollow laugh in the face of falsehood, and the mirthless laugh in the face of unhappiness, that is, the human condition. These laughs represent 'successive excoriations of the understanding,' ethical, intellectual, and metaphysical. Beckett's favorite laugh, of course, is the last, the mirthless 'dianoetic laugh, down the snout . . . the laugh of laughs, the risus purus, the laugh laughing at the laugh, the beholding, the saluting of the highest joke . . . .' Laughing at our existence, we exhaust its final possibilities."

THE VOICE

Exhaust?

Perhaps nothing is ever exhausted. Even the serpent swallowing its tail, and the artist eating his flesh. Even the silence of anti-literature. The cannibalism of language may prove a critique of consciousness; the destructive principle of the Word may formulate a new creation myth. Else we are all embodiments of the negative.

Embodiments of the negative?

Perhaps we are nothing else. Perhaps man incarnates the square root of minus one in all creation.

Joyce and Beckett do not agree in this.

Joyce says: "What will be is. Is is." But Joyce dies and Beckett continues. Beckett creates an anti-myth, Being on the wane, slow Apocalypse.

Both imagine silence and will it into speech. Both bring the future into our lives. Which future?

Perhaps Beckett knows that something must cease—time, words, machines of the mind—before Joyce can really begin. "I use the words you taught me. If they don't mean anything anymore, teach me others. Or let me be silent."

EPILOGUE

The Voice stops, the speaker has earlier ceased. Yet sounds still fill the room. The assembled scholars think thoughts in words of their own. Consciousness is at its ancient loom.

The scholars will soon depart.

Will sound and silence rejoice forever in their counterpart?

Bloom on Joyce; or, Jokey for Jacob

Leslie Fiedler

STATE UNIVERSITY OF NEW YORK AT BUFFALO

I INTEND TO SPEAK to you tonight not about Bloom, but as Bloom, in part because I have been listening for several days now to what seems to me to have been too exclusively the voice of the half of Joyce that is Stephen Dedalus; or rather the voice of a kind of sub-Stephen or post-Stephen, which is to say, the voice of Stephen Dedalus, Ph.D.

But I rise before you in the guise of Bloom, who could never have a Ph.D., or M.A. or even B.A., in part also because it is, after all—sixty-five years after the event—Bloom's day again, and not only Bloomsday, but Bloom's hour. We have it on the very best authority that "as the day wears on, Bloom should overshadow them all." But seven days have worn on, in fact, from dawn to dark, and it's now time, and more than time, for Bloom. Finally, however, I have assumed and am assuming at this moment the voice of Bloom because it is the voice of the eternal amateur, the self-appointed prophet, the harassed Jew, the comic father; and that is a voice which I like to believe, for my own private reasons and some public ones too, is my own authentic voice. And I am resolved to speak to you today in the most authentic voice I can find, as personally and non-professionally as I can manage, because I would be a little embarrassed in rising before you otherwise, since I can claim absolutely no expertise in Joycean matters. To speak, therefore, to the experts who are gathered here on any other terms except the terms of an amateur would be, as the

Chinese say, to peddle books before the door of Confucius. Let me begin, then, by declaring as confessionally and personally as I can that not only am I somebody who has read almost nothing of Joyce scholarship, which I suspect (unfairly I have no doubt) of being a purgatorial mountain, crowned not with an earthly paradise but a desert; but that also I have read very little of the very little that can be called properly Joyce literary criticism. My credentials for accepting your kind invitation to speak to you on this occasion at the very end of your long series of meetings are only that for some thirty-five years now, which is a long enough time in good faith, I have read and re-read, remembered and re-remembered, loved and hated, lived, I think I can fairly say, the works of James Joyce. I remember very clearly, as I stand here years later, the moment when I begged and bullied and wheedled (I was I think about fourteen or fifteen years old) a copy of *The Portrait of the Artist* out of the locked room of our local library, where it had been hidden away, as is proper with obscene literature, from the young and susceptible. And I remember even more clearly the year I was seventeen and Judge Woolsy's decision had just released *Ulysses* from the underground to above-ground circulation. And I can remember most clearly of all the moment I was given a copy of *Ulysses* as a high school graduation present by a very genteel aunt who would have been shocked out of her small mind if she had realized what she was putting into my hands. I remember, finally, the sixty days just before the landing of the American troops on Iwo Jima, when under fire and all at sea, which seems a perfect symbolical situation for reading *Finnegans Wake*, I read through *Finnegans Wake* for the first time.

What I am trying to say to you is that I have been living Joyce for a long time now, and especially I have been living *Ulysses*, not outside of but within the very texture of my life, as a part of the process of growing up and growing old. *Ulysses* was for my youth and has remained for my later years not a novel at all, but a conduct book, a guide to salvation through the mode of art, a kind of secular scripture. Yet, I, who have written about almost everything in the world that has crossed my desk or entered my head, am pleased to tell you that I have never written a word about *Ulysses*—not a single word. I have never, as they say, taught *Ulysses*—talked about it in class. I have never spoken in public about *Ulysses* before, though I am, as some of you may know, a garrulous man, reticent about almost nothing, and I have become more and more a public man given to talking about the things that most intimately concern me to any random audience that will pause to listen.

Until tonight I have kept silence on the subject of my own relationship to Joyce, and especially to *Ulysses*, as if somehow it was too dear and dirty, too, in the full Joycean sense of the word, "holy," to discuss in a profane situation and circumstance. But, as you are all surely aware at this point, I have been unable to resist the temptation to speak out at last, here and now; which is to say, as the sacred day wears itself to a close, and I am privileged to rise in that Dublin which has existed in my head for a long time, and in which I find it very hard to believe I am at last existing in the flesh. If I had been born on the first day that I read *Ulysses*, it occurs to me, and in some sense I was born on that day, I would now be, and in some sense I am, precisely in the middle of the journey of our life. Time enough, then, to say my word.

But I have been discovering that at a point when I am finally ready to speak about Joyce and *Ulysses*, it may turn out that I have waited too long; that it may, in fact, be, if not quite too late for me, for anyone, to declare his love for *Ulysses* and his debt to Joyce, it is very nearly too late to do so. Let me be as candid as I can on this score. I have in the past several years become more and more aware, painfully aware, that the literary movement we have agreed to call "Modernism," and at the center of which Joyce stands, is a literary movement which is now dead. We live, that is to say, at a moment when Modernism is no longer viable for young writers and readers, or even for what is young and living in old writers and readers. I am kept especially uncomfortably aware of this fact by those who deny it: the embalmers of Modernism, those scholars who seek through pedantry and patience, the undertaker's art, to forge a living smile on the face of a corpse.

It distresses me deeply to realize that Proust, Mann, and Joyce no longer seem the names of three exciting and dangerous authors, but a title of a standard course in college curricula all up and down the United States. And in this post-Modernist era, it is very easy to perceive, and hard not to be over-impressed by the limitations of Modernism, which suddenly become as clear to us as the virtues of that movement once were.

It seems to me at any rate, that the age of the Art Novel and the Culture Religion is over: that age so utterly lost in elitism and snobbism, the vestiges of class values totally alien to a democratic or mass society, that it was doomed from the first to die the academic death. The very notion of avant-garde which haunted Joyce and his contemporaries, with its dream of taking by storm the libraries and classrooms of the future, strikes me now as having been in every sense a dead end. And I find myself repelled a little as I look back at those young surrogates of their authors who live at the center of certain "avant-garde" masterpieces, of whom Stephen is the epitome and archetype: those miserable creatures who chose to go through and even into Hell—not like Dante, in order to save themselves, or like Huck Finn to save someone they loved—but only so that after they return they can write books about what it was like to be there—thus insuring themselves posthumous fame. But though highbrow critics may have been taken in by this strategy, the popular audience has not.

I've been moved and troubled, for instance, by the still evident disaffection of the Irish themselves from Joyce, of which I have been reminded by the people of Dublin, as willing to talk about this as about anything they have on their minds. And I have come to the conclusion that the disaffection they register (let us be truthful with ourselves on this score) is neither accidental or incidental, nor is it, as I once would have believed, a necessary adjunct of greatness. To be great is not, I now believe, necessarily to be misunderstood.

The Irish people have managed somehow to accept their other great artists and disturbers of the peace, all the way from Yeats to Brendan Behan, but not Joyce. No, I am convinced that the fate of Joyce, the special exclusion of Joyce from the hearts of his people, is a fate which he deliberately sought, misguidedly, I now believe, and foolishly, cripplingly. It is a fate which Joyce *chose*, not endured. Typical in this regard (and if I refer to this with special passion, it is because it's a subject which especially moves me) is Joyce's mode of handling myth. Unlike those writers who close rather than widen the gap between the elite audience and the great audience, between high art and popular art, Joyce tends most of the time not to create or to release or to evoke new myths, a new mythology, a reborn mythology, a resurrected mythology; but rather to re-interpret old and dying myths, or to dissolve them in irony, or, worst of all, to move them closer and closer to the level of total abstraction. His powers, I am trying to suggest, seem to me a good deal of the time mythographic rather than truly mythopoeic and mythoplastic. He is less a dreamer of dreams than an interpreter of dreams. And the art of myth criticism, which is the essential art of a great deal of Joyce, as it is also of other Modernist works like Mann's Joseph tetralogy or *The Waste Land* of T. S. Eliot, takes us not to the place where we are one with each other; whether we are born Nora Joyce or James Joyce—but to a place where we are aware of our differences from each other and we are tempted respectively on the Nora side and the James side, to condescension and *ressentiment*.

Let me be very personal about this. I don't want to sound as if I'm talking abstractly about something which applies to somebody else rather than to me. And even if I cannot be quite as candid as

I have pledged to myself to be, at least let me be as candid as I can manage to be on such an occasion. How clear it seems to me now that my own first relationship to Joyce, my own first uses of James Joyce, which were essentially a relationship to and uses of the figure of the insufferable Stephen, were more ignoble than I could then have believed or than I now like to confess.

He fit only too well my young man's desire to make it into a world which excluded me by proving myself in possession of a work too difficult to be available to others; my young man's impulse to culture-climb to a place where I could be at one and the same time an alienated artist, much loved for that very alienation by a substantial minority audience, and a Ph.D., immune to the stuffiness of all other Ph.D.s though just as job-secure as anybody else in the university system. What a foolish illusion it was; what a lovely illusion it was; what an irresistibly lovely foolish illusion it was: to win acclaim and academic promotion by parsing the satanic slogan, *Non Serviam*, or by teaching young people to repeat it after me in class for grades.

I don't want to load all my own petty sins on Joyce, and I'm trying very hard not to do this, since there's small point in using an occasion like this to turn Joyce into some sort of symposium scapegoat to be sent back out into the academic desert from which we have all come, with all our outgrown sins on his back. It's not a desire for self-exculpation, but a longing for uncustomary frankness which prompts me to insist that part of the fault for the sins which were truly mine, was in fact, Joyce's.

Some of you here before me were present, I know, at the Bailey early in the Symposium, early in this Conference Week, when a young man arose suddenly, looking like a reborn, younger version of the Citizen in the Cyclops episode, to shout at a group of us happy Stephens gathered around him, "I am an illegitimate grandson of James Joyce, and I want to tell you that he would *spit* on everyone of you." Ah, the young man was wrong, alas, since I fear that Joyce would have approved rather than spit upon even what is the worst about us and our deliberations. He would have loved all of us factification-forgers and exagmination-makers. He would have relished the endless *pilpul*, the Talmudic exegesis, in which the sacred is profaned without any feelings of guilt. He would have rejoiced, after all, at the soulless industry which has grown up around his tortured and obsessive works. "God have mercy on his soul and what remains of ours." This is my prayer for the night.

Having said all this, I am obviously obliged to ask, along with you who have hopefully listened to it all, the question: "Is there nothing then left for me to celebrate on Bloomsday? Is there *nothing* left for me to celebrate on this night, in this place? I who believe that literature should be not about myth but living myth itself. I who have lost my taste for the ironic and have grown perhaps over-fond of the comic and the pathetic. I who believe that criticism itself, which is a form of literature not of science, should aim not at exagmination but at ecstasis.

And the answer is yes—yes, yes, *yes*. There is much to celebrate on Bloomsday, and that much bears the name of Bloom himself. On Bloomsday we can celebrate Bloom: not merely the archetypal character called by that name, but everything in the whole corpus of Joyce's works which is written by Bloom-Joyce rather than by Stephen-Joyce; by a Jew-Joyce rather than by the first-martyr-to-the-Jews Joyce. And when I say that Bloom remains to celebrate that is a way of telling you that virtually *everything* remains to celebrate, since all the rest is nothing.

Bloom himself is not merely mythic, much less an ironic commentary on a dying myth. He is a true, a full myth, a new and living myth. He is, to be sure, based on—reflects off of—the figure of Homer's Ulysses, that Greek version of, as Joyce liked to believe and I'm prepared to believe with him, a Semitic prototype. But Bloom is Ulysses resurrected and transfigured, not merely recalled or commented on or explained. Bloom is Ulysses rescued from all those others who were neither Jew nor Greek, and who had kidnapped him, held him in alien captivity for too long. Bloom is Ulysses rescued from the great poets as well as the small ones, from Dante and from Tennyson, and—at the other end of the mythological spectrum from James Joyce—from that anti-Semite, Ezra Pound, who liked to think he was the only true Ulysses.

In fact, however, Ulysses, the old Ulysses, the remembered Ulysses, the re-evoked Ulysses, constitutes only a small part of the total Bloom, the part that the Stephen in Joyce, everything in him which was not Bloom, could most easily deal with, *had* to deal with in order to keep the tidy schematic structure which he unwisely loved, and to plant clues for future exegetes whom he unfortunately desired.

The larger part of Bloom came not from memories of Homer's Ulysses, and not from the top of the head of Joyce, the name for which is Stephen. No, much perhaps most of what constitutes the authentic figure of Bloom comes, perhaps not entirely unbidden and unconsciously, but certainly less cerebrally, from deeper, darker, more visceral sources. The myth of Ulysses lives in the head of Christian Europe, but the myth of the Jew, which is Bloom's better half, resides in the guts of Europe: a pain in the dark innards of the gentile world, or better perhaps, an ache in the genitals, an ache in the loins of the gentiles.

Remember, please, for a minute with me what is hard for me to remember, easy for me to forget. How unprecedented, how radically new, Joyce's Jew was in the dark world of Christian mythology about Jews. To be sure, there had been a gentile writer, or two or three, before Joyce who had tried to evoke a benign, a blessed, a favorable image of the Jew: George Eliot, for instance, in that oddly hermaphroditic figure of Daniel Deronda; or Dickens in the quite unbelievable portrait of the sickly, sweet and sentimental Riah.

But essentially the troubled sleep of a Europe still pagan at the moment Joyce began to write his book was haunted by the figure of the Jew as a wicked and destructive father with a knife in his hand, Shylock or Fagin or those attenuated mythological descendants of Shylock and Fagin who persist in Joyce's contemporaries like T. S. Eliot and Ezra Pound. One is tempted to say that insofar as the mind of Christianity continued to contemplate, to try to assimilate, a Christianity it secretly resented, that mind, the mind of gentile Europe, was destined to hate and vilify the Jews who had imposed upon it the burden of a religion with which it could never come to terms.

This is the meaning, a meaning of the figure of Father Abraham, isn't it, after all? That prototypical Jewish father, distorted, by the bad dreams which possess the undermind of Europe, into an image of terror, in which the double indignity visited upon the son, the eternal Isaac, become one: the circumcision that was actually performed, and the aborted ritual sacrifice blended into the single threat of castration. And surely behind the quarrel of Christian Europe with the first patriarch of the Jews, there lurks a deeper, less confessable uneasiness with that more ultimate Father who ordered the circumcision and the sacrifice, with the God of Abraham, Isaac, Jacob and Joseph, whom the converted Pagans of Europe cannot help feeling, somehow took away their primitive manhood, their genital power, by making them all in some symbolic sense eunuchs for the sake of the Kingdom of Heaven.

But in Joyce, and in him for the first time, the Jew, though he remains a father still, is no longer a dark, threatening, castrating father. He is no threat to anyone, because he is no longer Abraham, but Joseph: Joseph the carpenter, Joseph the joiner, which is to say, he is the cuckold, since for Joyce there is no Christian-Jewish God anymore. And in a world where old Nobodaddy is dead, we are all the sons not of even Abraham, much less of Abraham's God, but only of the carpenter-cuckold, the comic old artificer, who is really closer to the limping, laughable figure of Hephaestus, the husband of Aphrodite, than to Ulysses, who, after all, drew a bow that no rival suitor could manage. It's the comic

unmanned father we can manage to love, the unfeared father; and
Joyce has given us an enduring image for that blessed, ridiculous
archetypal parent, an image appropriate to the early twentieth
century, appropriate to us still as that century draws to a close.

Bloom, however, does not stand alone, for there is a whole
company, you know, of such impotent Good Father figures: Fal-
staff and Nigger Jim and Pickwick, and God only knows who
else. But it is the distinction of Bloom to be the sole Jew in that
comic, harmless, beautiful company. And to be a Jew moreover
who was invented by, dreamed out himself, separated from his
own body in sleep, by an Irishman—an Irish Jew imagined by an
Irish poet, who, in a world without gods or goddesses, felt obliged
to be his own God as well as his own Muse.

This is what finally intrigues me, what finally I want to talk
to you about: this last, best joke of all, this kind of joke on a
joke, this ultimate comic turn of the screw, the delicious fact that
the great good Jewish father of the modern world was invented
by an Irishman. You know, just to say "Irish Jew" is already to
have told a joke, as almost any Irishman will be quick to inform
you. And it's a joke which hasn't been mitigated, but only somehow enriched, by the election of a Jewish Lord Mayor of Dublin.
But this is precisely the point, the point which is behind the point
of *Ulysses*, isn't it? Jews and Irishmen alike feel this abiding—
one is tempted to say eternal—archetypal conflict, this antipathy,
this polar opposition, as essential in each case to their own identity, part of the very definition of themselves. It's hard to imagine
a Jew who doesn't have hostile feelings about an Irishman, an
Irishman who doesn't have resentful feelings about Jews. But both
the Irish and the Jews feel this conflict (despite the history of real
violence and persecution in Ireland and elsewhere) as comic; and
in this sense, the relationship is unique. It's not true, for instance,
of relations of Jews to Germans, or Jews to Poles, or Jews to Rus-
sians, with whom they are also in archetypal conflict. Only the
archetypal conflict of the Jew and the Irishman is felt on both

sides as essentially and radically comic, or at least somehow comic, comic after all.

Certainly (if I may be personal again and talk in terms of my own memory) it had, whatever it may have been in the Old Country, already become a joke in the America into which I was born, the New World to which both Jews and Irish had emigrated in large numbers, and where they both were beginning to achieve a spectacular kind of success. In the popular arts of my own childhood, at any rate, the conflict of the Irishman and the Jew had been turned into a laughing matter. I remember clearly, for instance, a famous comedy team called Gallagher and Sheen, whose patter songs were placed on every Victrola, Irishman and Jew swapping gags, forerunners of George Burns and Gracie Allen, in whom the polar opposites, Jewish straight man and Irish zaney had become man and wife. And everybody, I suppose, of a certain age in America remembers that longest running play of all time, that romantic comedy which possessed Broadway year after year, which was called *Abie's Irish Rose*, and in which, sentimentally and ridiculously, the old conflict was resolved.

But the comic conflict has been played out not only on records and radio and in literature, but in life as well; and in fact, it seems possible for a Jew at least to escape it. Forgive me once more for speaking once more in terms of my own experience. In the course of my long trip to Ireland, to which I came in fact by way of Africa (being the kind of man who takes seriously the lesson learned from Joyce, that the longest way around is the shortest way home); I spent a week or so in Biafra, where that old joke, the joke of the conflict of the Jew and the Irishman was reenacted as if for my special benefit, to prepare me, perhaps, for this symposium. And I can't resist, therefore, telling you a story which makes the point I have been trying to establish with appropriately ridiculous clarity.

The scene is Biafra. I've come to find Black Africa, and I discover that I am in the midst of the very white Holy Ghost Fathers in a Mission, where I have been given bed and board. I discover, in fact, that of the 200 white people in Biafra, 194 are Irish and the other 6 are Jewish, including me. As I sit at supper with the good Fathers, who have been telling me that I had better go to Dublin because I'd find there the shortest mini-skirts in Europe, and would I please send them back some good Irish whiskey when I get there, suddenly one of them leans over—obviously knowing that I'm a Jew, just as I know that he's Irish, since we were intended to recognize each other from the beginning of time—and says "You people have always given us a lot of trouble."

For a moment or two, I thought he was talking about the Jew who, in fact, gave them the most trouble of all, namely Jesus, the son of Mary; but actually he was referring to the founder of his own Order, who turns out to have been called Jacob Lieberman. Imagine that, you Joyceans, imagine how Joyce would have loved that. Jacob, the beloved man, beloved, darling Jacob, whose other name is Israel; but Seamus is jokey for Jacob, you remember Joyce told us, and Seamus is James, which is to say Joyce himself, Shem the Penman. At any rate, Jacob Lieberman founded the order of the Holy Ghost Fathers in 1858; "And," my friend the priest told me, "he sent all of us poor Irish out here to Africa, but like his kind, he remained behind in Paris."

Well, I recovered from Biafra, Black and White, as one rises out of slow fever, as one wakes from the nightmare of history, and came to dear, dirty Dublin. And there I found myself at lunchtime the first day stuck between two colleagues at this symposium, each a proper anti-Semite after his kind: an East European anti-Semite on my right hand, and an Irish anti-Semite on my left hand. And they began to engage in a conversation with each other, through me, over me, in which the subject being discussed really was which one of their peoples had the appropriate attitude toward the perfidious Jews.

The East European anti-Semite started by boasting, "We're not unkind to the Jews, you understand. We let them go freely, leave, get out—whenever they want to. Why not?" And when the question was asked what happens to them when they're uprooted from their homes, footloose and impoverished, he said, "Well, listen, what do they have to worry about—going out into a community which has millions stashed away in Swiss Banks."

But this somehow did not satisfy the Irishman, who responded, "The real trouble is not with the Jews as Jews, it's with the Jews as Zionists. But after all, all Jews are Zionists because," I think I quote directly now, "none of them ever really becomes the citizen of anyplace." "*None of them really ever becomes the citizen of anyplace.*"

Once again we hear the voice of the Citizen in the Pub, and the biscuit box is ready to be hurled; once again we are back in *Ulysses*, that joke on all the Irish-Jewish jokes of history, which itself is no joke—though funny as any of them. And we remember that the reproach to the Jew is the artist's boast, that what is said of the Jew in contempt, Joyce said of himself in pride: "not a citizen of anyplace," which, if you'll pardon me for a final time, is the boast of the saint as well. Indeed, all three archetypal strangers, the Jew, the artist, and the saint, are never at home, never quite at home anywhere in this world, never quite the citizens of anyplace this side of Heaven.

But it's only the artist, a certain kind of artist, who makes his alienation a point of pride, thinks of it as separating him from rather than joining him to the rest of mankind. And this brings us back, by a commodious vicus of recirculation, to such insufferable prigs as poor Stephen, which is to say, to the part of Joyce which remained Stephen forever, try as he would. Yet it was not Joyce-Stephen who wrote *Ulysses*, it was Joyce-Bloom, the father begotten of the Son, the Jew born of the Irishman by the simple process of growing old.

In the middle of life, as the day wears on, we who began as sons and lovers look around to discover that we have become fathers and husbands; that somehow we have learned exile is not what must be sought but what must be endured, and what therefore joins every man to every other man. This, at any rate, the part of Joyce that became Bloom, learned well enough to write the book which he did not call, as he ought to have, *The Portrait of Everyone as a No-Longer-Young Man;* but instead, simply *Ulysses:* that absurd and moving account of a man no longer young, who, without illusion or self-deceit, goes home again, back to the ass that betrays him, the land that denies him, the son he does not and cannot really ever know. Moving from the *Portrait of the Artist* to *Ulysses,* we learn with Joyce that though it may be the self-pitying son who falls out of the air, it is the self-deprecating father who picks himself up off the hard earth again.

I would like to believe that even without the help of Joyce, I might myself eventually have fought my way through to the place where I stand now, to a realization of what I now realize and have been saying to you. And maybe it must even be granted that I had to be where I am now before I could read properly his great and ambiguous novel, had myself to become Bloom before I could understand *Ulysses.* But certainly it is Joyce's mythological language which occurs to me talking about these matters, Joyce's mythological language in which I can best express what I am moved to tell not only you but myself as I approach my conclusion this evening.

Like many of you here before me, like Joyce himself, I began by thinking that I was Stephen; began by thinking I was the perpetual victim, perpetually stoned to death by his own infidel kin; began by thinking that I was the high flying boy doomed to fall in glory and to write the story of my plunge earthward even as I fell. But I ended, as you will end, as Joyce ended, by knowing that I was Bloom, a comic, earthbound father who is also an Apostle to the gentiles; which is to say, I have discovered at long last that I am a Hebrew of the Hebrews and a Pharisee of the Pharisees who, try as he will to be all things to all men, cannot resist, from time to time, still kicking against the pricks.